GREENER PASTURES

Greener Pastures

MARNIE REED CROWELL

ILLUSTRATED BY THE AUTHOR

FUNK & WAGNALLS   **NEW YORK**

Photo credits: frontispiece, Marnie Reed Crowell; "Autumn Woods," Timothy Blair Gage; "Winter Snowshoes," Kenneth Leland Crowell; "Spring Maple Sap Buckets," Marnie Reed Crowell; "Summer Ferns," Timothy Blair Gage; jacket slide, "Sunset with Cows," Kenneth Leland Crowell

Designed by Ingrid Beckman

Manufactured in the United States of America

ISBN 0–308–10080–8

1 2 3 4 5 6 7 8 9 10

Library of Congress Cataloging in Publication Data

Crowell, Marnie Reed.
    Greener pastures.

        1. Farm life—New York (State)   I. Title.
S521.5.N7C76   917.47   73-7551
ISBN 0–308–10080–8

CONTENTS

DRAWINGS

PIERREPONT AS IT WAS AND IS

I knew when not a tree was cut
   Upon the Pierrepont hills;
When not a sheep or a cow was seen
   By all her rippling rills:
When bears and wolves and panthers prowled
   Through all her shady glens;
And I could hear their distant howls,
   And chased them to their dens.

When Indians, in their light canoes,
   Came gliding up our streams
To hunt the deer or chase the moose,
   But yesterday it seems.
But I have seen her forests fall;
   The Redman pass away,
And flocks and herds feed by them all,
   While mansions line the way.

Now splendid orchards grace our farms,
   And gardens fill'd with flowers;
And waving fields of grain add charms
   To this fine town of ours.
Houses of learning where the youth
   Improve the golden hours,
And trained to virtue and to truth,
   Grow up like native flowers. . . .

—Oringe Smith Crary,
"The Pierrepont Poet,"
1803–1889

GREENER PASTURES

AUGUST

STEVEN CRARY paid fifty dollars to have a picture of this house included in the *History of St. Lawrence County, New York,* back in 1878. The house had been built some fifty years earlier by his father, Nathan, an emigrant from Vermont to this nearly unbroken wilderness. Most of his fellow colonizers of the Pierrepont land grant (pronounced "Pierpoint" by those who live here) were also Vermonters. Like so many of his new neighbors, Nathan had served in the Revolutionary War and gone "West" to settle the new lands opened up after the conflict. He had been a drummer boy; it seems that a lot of family trees around here have Revolutionary drummer boys in them.

This is our house now for a while. The farm is locally known as the Rood place because the people who lived here before us were of that name. When we are gone it will be known as the Crowell place in that curious North Country way of acknowledging tenancy but one.

We chose this farm because it looks like Vermont, where we spent the first years of our marriage. We are nouveaux rurals, realizing a dream that many share, trying our hand at country living. From the roof of this house we could see the St. Lawrence River to the west and the Adirondack Mountains to the east. On some days a bank of haze shimmers above the valley where the river lies. Occasionally the haze seems suspiciously "industrial" in color. The aluminum plants and all that is Cornwall, Ontario, after all, line the river banks off in the distance, but no one around here ever mentions the haze; it is tacitly acknowledged that one of the rewards for living in the Arctic of New York State is that the air, though cold, is surely clean.

Through a notch in the trees, we can see the blue spire of the chapel of St. Lawrence University, where my husband, Ken, teaches in the biology department, and the small town of Canton, which twinkles glamorously citylike at night, where our sons, David and Tom, go to school.

From the other side of the roof, to the east, we see a row of prosperous farms and the little white church in the village of Pierrepont Center. Beyond the town one has the feeling that the bear would surely have but one more blue hill to go over to see an Adirondack mountain on the other side. Yonder lies the "Blue Line," that legislated boundary of the "forever wild" Adirondack Park.

Only a few miles down the road is Sunday Rock, a charmingly named megalith of pink sandstone standing some ten feet high by the side of the road, which for local people is the real boundary marker for the Adirondacks. It has been called Sunday Rock for so many years that no one quite remembers how it got its name. The old-timers say there used to be a logging camp beyond the rock, where the men worked seven days a week. On the other side of Sunday Rock there were no Sabbaths, and no laws either. The rock is also a monument to a victory over the highway-builders— or at least a draw. Twice when dynamiters threatened the rock with destruction, time and money were mustered to move it out of the way—a matter of feet—and to equip it with a turnout from the busy road and a bronze plaque.

Today the air is warm and clear. The line of maples tunneling over the road stands heavy in the August heat. Because the house sits on a ridge I can see the horizon almost all the way around me, and the wind is usually at work keeping away mosquitoes and blackflies, or whisking golden maple leaves from the front yard, or piling snow in not always convenient places.

Although a heavy dew beaded the cobwebs spread on the lawn and twinkled brightly on the red seed heads of the ripe grasses in our little orchard, it has long since dried off without benefit of breeze. The faraway drone of farm machinery and the enveloping songs of the ground crickets and grasshoppers seem to be the only vibrations in the still, warm air.

Truly hot days are rare in the North Country, so we are all seizing the day by taking a swim in our pond. The pond sits down the hill from the barn in full view of the kitchen window. Cattails stand at one end of it, and the white, lacy blossoms of tall meadow rue share the wet margin with the bright orange trumpets of the jewelweed, which the hummingbirds so love.

A lone pink pasture rose blooms in the mist of meadowsweet bushes by the gate at the front of the pond. The single file of fox tracks has worn a groove through the grasses behind the pond, and winds on underneath the electric fence, around the back half of the dike, down the bank, and off across the meadow.

In the water the boys are splashing, as the ducks are too. Biggy is the drake, the largest. He is supposed to be a Rouen duck ("Ruin" in local parlance). His markings are a wild mallard's, but he is so heavy he can't fly. Biggy is supposed to be a meat duck; he doesn't think so, and the children don't either. He usually looks quite gorgeous with his brown tweed body, dapperly curled white tail feathers, and shining dark-green head. At the moment he is molting, and his head is a moth-eaten brown. His ladyloves— Brownie, Blackie, and Semi, who is marked equally with brown and white—still presumably find him attractive. With much wing flapping, Biggy hurls himself underwater, makes a short distance as a submarine, and pops up to the surface again like a cork. He then sails over to Brownie and bobs his head. She bobs once and swims on without a backward glance. He speeds up, puffs out his breast feathers, and pumps his head vigorously up and down. Brownie stops. Biggy bobs again close by her side. I think we are going to get a birds-and-bees lesson today. But no, he merely stands up in the water, flapping his wings in a shower of glistening droplets, showing off his elegant teal-blue wing patches barred at the edges with white and black. We are all enchanted. So is he. He swims off across the pond, bobbing to himself from time to time.

Blackie and Semi dabble at the far edge of the pond. They completely upend themselves, so that only their tails are above the water. Their heads can dimly be seen underwater, working over the floor of the pond for comestibles, and their orange feet paddle steadily at their Plimsoll mark in an effort to maintain the position.

The boys quit the pond and resume work on a most sophisticated castle, which spans the entire breadth of the narrow beach of sand that we have imported. Sun-blond, tanned, and blue-eyed like his brother but three years younger, Tom, at six, through determination—and a heavier build—has closed the age gap in most respects. Often archenemies, David and Tom are also the best of friends. They are a complementary pair, Tom as effervescent and immediate as his older brother is dreamy and distant.

David moves with the grace of a great blue heron. Setting down a bucket of water for the castle moat, he hitches up his bathing suit automatically as he straightens. He has the hips of a snake. Such fanatics for authenticity are these busy brothers! How is it they remember every detail of bailey, keep, and castle crenellation but never where they left their shoes?

Tom agilely sidesteps a bee that has landed on the battlefield in front of the castle gate. On these hot days our bees often stop by for water to take back to evaporate in the hives—air conditioning. The hives stand along the stone wall that runs parallel to the road, towers of square white boxes stacked in the shade of an apple tree, a butternut tree, and a grape-draped elm.

Our bees are of good disposition and usually give offense to no one. You are far more likely to come to grief by spreading your towel over a thistle at the border of the beach. A few of the thistles still show their flowers in Scottish lavender, but most have exploded into thistledown, to the joy of the goldfinches. These dainty finches curl themselves around the bigger balls of fluff for a few busy moments, then take off twittering to themselves in a jagged scissor flight. They have been waiting all summer long for the thistledown with which they line their nests. Most other birds have reared their young, and some have even started south again, but this little "wild canary" is just beginning to raise a family.

Brownie has by this time disappeared into the grass to one of her secret nests around the pond edge. Blackie and Semi have settled themselves on the bank for a nap while Biggy stands by preening himself. A white down feather floats out into the pond.

I have the water to myself. The softest water I have ever felt flows warmly over my limbs except for a spot of cold water here and there over one of the springs that feed the pond. I swim toward some back swimmers—little diving beetles—which make spirals on the pond surface. They disappear in a quick deep slant. I am the white feather, and I float on my back and enjoy the reflection of the weathered barn, silvery in the water; the small green stable surrounded by golden glow, that old-fashioned dahlia-like flower that is blooming right now at nearly every old farm across New England; the old chicken coop; the garage with grape vines arbored across its wall; and farther up the hill, our house, white, with hollyhocks in red and every shade of pink, bright and tall against its silhouette.

A line of clouds skims by. Nearly always our weather comes through on the same path, the clouds following a steady track across what, to my eyes, are uncharted skies. They always come over the hill from town (for such is Canton called out here), pass over the barn and pine tree and house, and march off over Pierrepont to the Adirondacks. The sky is a clear medium blue, the clouds are mere flattened wisps of white—not like the puffy cumulus clouds of the western skies. This is what is called a North Country sky, so distinctly our own that it is what many North Country natives who have been transplanted to the urban scene miss most.

Tom knows where Brownie is hiding, so we all stalk off to see if she will show us where she puts her eggs. We have worn a path through the tall grass around the middle of the dike that surrounds the pond on the three downhill sides. On one side of us blooms the last buttercup of summer. Black-eyed Susans are beginning to outnumber the daisies. Grasshoppers clatter through the grass ahead of us. We cut down to the water's edge again and again. We find a hollow, some feathers, but no eggs.

At the back end of the pond a siphon tube runs down to a watering trough, from the side of which two dark-eyed, golden-brown Jersey heifers look up at us. They have beautiful eyelashes. The heifers have trampled all the grass away to bare mud around the trough and worn a brown path across the meadow to it. Six more heifers, black-and-white Holsteins, are walking single file up the path to see what's going on. A whole pasture to walk through and they have to go in a line, always on the same path. And they are so curious. One of the Jerseys nudges the other and lowers her square, whiskered muzzle for a drink. A strand of barbed wire keeps them out of the pond. The fence is electrified. They learn that right away, and they can tell when the current is turned off. Courtland Ostrander, the neighbor who owns these lovely creatures and rents our pastures for them, told us that once this summer the watering trough had gone dry. He took the siphon shutcock apart to see what was holding back the water. He gave a mighty suck on the pipe and was rewarded with a fat polliwog for his trouble!

Iridescent-blue tree swallows sit twittering on the fence behind us. They swoop right above our heads and out over the pond to get a drink on the wing or pick an insect from the air. They regroup on the fence or the power lines to twitter-chatter together amiably.

Leaving the pond to the tree swallows, we make our way up the hill in a towel-flapping parade to get ourselves some sandwiches. Near the top of the hill the leader halts and raises an arm for silence. Is the phone ringing? Is it our ring? We share an eight-party line; our ring is one long, one short. I think it might be ours, and I break into a run, trying to balance hurry with caution so as not to come pounding down on a hidden thistle in my bare feet. I thump up the back steps, *hot* in the noonday sun, rout the flies resting on the screen door, and jerk the phone off the hook. I stand panting, saying hello to the dial tone.

We slap together some sandwiches, line them up on a tray with lemonade, iced tea, and garden-sweet crisp canoes of cucumber. I go out into the dazzling brightness of the garden by the steps to pick some mint for the tea.

When I return with my green bouquet, and my eyes have adjusted to the cave gloom of the kitchen, I note that the floor looks and feels like that of a locker room in a swim club. The pipes in the ceiling have begun to sweat. This farmhouse kitchen has interesting plumbing. Since the kitchen is in the ell on the back of the main house it does not have a full cellar under it. Because the sink pipes would freeze in the winter in the crawlspace, some ingenious soul hit upon the solution of running the pipes up through the dining room floor to the ceiling, through the wall, across the kitchen ceiling and down the wall to the sink. The pipes are a set of three: one for the drinking water from the well and the other two for the hot and cold washing water from the cellar cistern that collects rain water from the roofs. The pipes make a convenient hanging place for a yard-long caramel curl of flypaper, but on hot days they do sometimes drip a line of condensation across the floor.

To dry the floor I open the door by the stove and let the breezes blow in from the screened porch that fronts the dining room. The maple door frame is mitered on a slant to accommodate the downward slope of the porch. The door is similarly altered from the customary rectangle. Beneath the pane of glass, the outside of the door sports a charming garland of leaves and blossoms carved in high relief. This dates back to Uncle Ryland's renovations, I am sure.

I recall the afternoon Frank Crary, a dapper gentleman eighty-two years old at the time, paid us an unexpected call with his family scrapbook under his arm. He showed us a picture of the house as it was in 1860. The lofty maples out in front and the pine at the side were then mere saplings, scarcely taller than a man. The large wing on the house and a huge complex of horse barns that are no longer here gave it an air of strangeness to my eyes.

"I've never been in this house before," Mr. Crary told us, looking around the room with a twinkle of satisfaction. "Steven Crary left this place to my Uncle Ryland. Ryland borrowed money from his older half brothers to buy good breeding horses. He was high society with his fancy trotters. Uncle Ryle cut quite a wide swath, I tell you." The old man chuckled. "Anyways, he was a wild spender and he finally went bankrupt. After that my side of the family was none too friendly with him. Uncle Ryle was 'off limits.' "

The clouds came rumbling over our roofs when I set the table on the porch for supper. As I bring the dishes back to the kitchen, a flash of lightning splits the glowering sky. Rain pelts the leaves. The phoebe disappears into the cellar doorway under the porch. Thunder smashes over my head. I hurry into the sun-room and unplug the television and the antenna rotor. Last summer they were zapped and ruined. Rain rivulets course down the long Victorian window panes. (Uncle Ryland had replaced all but the one nine-over-six pane left in the ell attic.)

Another flash of lightning throws the apple tree into dark relief. I consider unplugging the refrigerator as well.

The heifers are standing together in the shelter of the maple trees. The house has been here on this hill for more than a hundred years. The storms always charge through on the same path; there's no reason why lightning should hit today.

I jump as another thunderclap threatens to bring down the ceiling over my head. For my kitchen, I need a stool with glass feet, like the ones lookouts in the fire towers have. Maybe I'd rather be out in the barn with everyone else, feeding the chickens. Now Tom comes running in from the barn, across the yard, laughing through the rain drops, wearing a metal pail pulled over his head. He thinks the rain sounds ringing in his ears are a wonderful joke, and lightning is always somewhere else.

In a few minutes Ken comes in from the barn to tell me that it had hardly been the haven of security I had imagined. At the height of the storm Ken was surprised by a loud *bzzt* and flash from the far end of the barn, which reminded him that a few days ago the heifers had broken the fence by the barn and he had hastily fixed it by looping the wire through the iron handle on the barn door—without using one of the white porcelain insulators that are lying around the barn in such generous quantities. Now he realized the possible consequences of his carelessness. A fire in the country is usually a disaster, a barn fire the most uncontrollable of all. Should he unhook the wire? If the lightning was really a hazard he was risking electrocution; if the storm passed by, there was no immediate need to touch the wire at all. Nonetheless he had compulsively unhooked it, vowing not to tell me.

The storm rumbles off, over to Potsdam. The air is cool and sweet. The phoebe preens its feathers in the little butternut tree. The phone is dead. The Ostranders drive up in their red-and-white pickup truck to see if the electric fence has been knocked out by the lightning. It has. While Courtland and his son and partner, Alan, make repairs, little red-haired Cheryl, third generation, hops down from the truck to play with the boys.

Despite her china-doll looks, Cheryl is perfectly at home slogging about after her father in her own little pair of rubber boots just like his. She is equally at home perched beside her grandfather on his tractor or shouldering her way through their sheep with a bucket of grain.

The lightning split a big tree over at Crary Mills, Cheryl tells us. She has always looked out for our education. That first spring, when her father and grandfather brought a dozen heifers over to summer on our pastures, she turned on David, who had just made

some remark about the cows: "Them ain't cows, they're heifers."
I'm sure David doesn't remember that there was ever a time he
did not know *that*. He and Cheryl and Tom have spent many an
hour playing up on the roof of our old hen house overlooking
the meadow. The pastoral scene before them they take completely
for granted.

There is just enough evening left to give us the perfect arc
of a rainbow glowing against the dark sky above the lush green
meadows. Our heifers, the Ostrander cows from the pasture on the
other side of the Pierrepont road, and the Latimer cows from down
below have gathered at their common corner—a cow convention.
The gentle donging of the bell around the lead cow's neck floats
up to us. Tranquillity.

* * *

The telephone repairman was here this afternoon. The phone
has been ringing all evening for Mary Moran of the fourth and last
farm down our road. When our line gets knocked out by lightning
and the phone man comes to fix it, our numbers get reversed.
Why I'll never know, but it happens every time.

I give new callers our number and tell them to dial it to get
Mary. The old familiars recognize my voice and say, "Oh, not
again, sorry to bother you," and hang up and dial our number.
I'm always surprised when it *is* for me and I laugh through the
story of how Mary had to convince my friends to dial *her* number. Of course, tomorrow, after they get the line straightened out,
we have to go through it all in reverse. Then you do dial Mary's
number to talk to Mary.

The workings of a rural party line are indeed mysterious. We
do not hear the ring of all eight parties on the line—only our
ring and one other. Listening in on other conversations is considered fair game. First you hear a little click, and then perhaps
only soft breathing, unless you say something really funny. On a
long-distance call the volume drains away to practically nothing
as one party after another picks up to listen in.

The hour when the breakfast dishes around the countryside are
done, but the man of the house is still out washing up after milking, is the busiest phone hour of the day. It sometimes takes the
patience of a saint to wait your turn to place a call. Some of the
poor sinners on this line just haven't got it. As you try to conclude

a conversation after that first warning click, you may be interrupted again, if you are not quick enough, by the sound of a loudly whistled tune, or of whiskers being rasped against a phone mouthpiece.

* * *

In the heat of August the tones of green across the hillside once so fresh and sparkling are dark, dusty on the edges, and almost stale looking.

An invisible cicada buzzes in the maples, louder, louder, earning one of its common names, "old scissors-grinder." Along the roadside bumblebees move slowly, almost ponderously, from one red clover blossom to another. The sandiest stretches of roadside still belong to the stove-pipe jointed horsetails, but the moist, fertile ditches are great pink expanses of bouncing Bet, edged with sweet clover and complemented by patches of yellow St. John'swort and occasional blooms of delft-blue chicory. In our neighbor's field the whole hilltop is spread with Queen Anne's lace.

I am learning to read the patchwork of the fields: the smooth level green of a field recently cut in a second haying; another striped with rows of gold—cut hay that will be baled and carted away by tomorrow; a pasture that has been too lightly grazed with thistles and burdock creeping in to take over; and another that is being grazed too heavily—the young stock have cropped off all the grass to the ground, and as there are still some months of grazing ahead, they will soon have to be moved to another field.

The townsman won't see this, of course, but all my neighbors do and keep pretty good track of how tall each other's corn is, how many cuttings of hay so-and-so will probably get this year. And the farmers will feel more deeply than picnickers ever could the vagaries of August showers. Will it rain when they are trying to get the hay in? Will it rain enough so the crops will put on another spurt of growth and reach fruition?

How important the forces that ripen crops in this land, with only barely enough growing days from frost to frost, must have been to the first holders of this land, the Mohawks. They are known to have raised some fifteen varieties of corn, eight kinds of pumpkins and squashes, and at least sixty varieties of beans! All these foods could be dried to provide sustenance over the long winters. With characteristic reverence the Indians called the squash and bean and corn the Three Sisters, Our Life Sustainers. These humble crops formed the backbone of a mighty nation.

All this I ponder as I sit in our lower garden, on a cushion of weeds, picking yet another crop of bush beans. In white man's modern-day terms our garden is not conventional, but in a longer view, I suspect it is very conventional.

We have in the upper garden planted the three sisters together as the Iroquois did, the corn to grow tall for the beans to climb on, and the squash to run along the ground and crowd out the weeds. This is a scientifically sound method: the corn alone would exhaust the soil after repeated plantings, but the beans harbor in nodules on their roots special bacteria that "fix" nitrogen into the forms in which it can be used as nutrient, thus constantly renewing the soil. How often we learn something by stopping to figure out why the old way worked!

Another method we use is also believed to be ancient, judging by the gardening practices of relatively untouched populations of Indians in Mexico today. We plant a little here, a little over there, and all of it hides in the weeds from the hungry hordes of pests that might take it as an invitation to invade if we had planted it in more tempting amounts. Of course you can't let the weeds get too close. When the weeds are tiny you can pull them out, but as they get bigger it is easier just to stamp them back into their own place, or sit on them as I do now. So far this scheme has worked entirely to my satisfaction except that it means I cannot talk about my garden with my town friends. They take great pride in laying out neat rows of well-tended crops, preferably where they can be admired by the casual (or competitive) passerby.

I am sure weeding beats whatever my town friends might well feel otherwise compelled to do, so it is probably better that they do not know that they don't have to weed.

I'm not sure of the status of what I call a kitchen garden among our farm friends. Ironically, quite a few have very little in the way of a garden. Either all hands are required to do the major farm work (and much more than a few tomatoes is needed to pay the taxes and keep everybody in clothes) or it is much more profitable for the wife to hold a second job than tend a kitchen garden. Most seem to have simplified their gardens and have weed-and-mulch schemes that are no better looking than mine.

Pierrepont makes no pretense whatever of being a paradise of self-sustaining homesteaders not tied to the modern world and its markets.

*   *   *

I take two bags from the broom closet, fold my French knife carefully in one of the them, and the family is off to pick kale. I don't have to use my fancy, gift-from-Paris knife to cut the kale. In fact I probably shouldn't, but I like to. To me it is the same as when I learned to crack an egg into the frying pan with one hand.

As we go down the back steps I note that camomile has filled a third of the bed between the walk and the pretty pink sandstone of the house foundation, and mint fills the rest of the bed at the feet of the hollyhocks. I think I will encourage them to keep the whole bed; they cope with the weeds better than I do. Their fragrance is such good company when I sit in the sun on the back steps preparing our food. The back steps are my summer kitchen.

Some of the burgundy-red dahlias are in bloom in the depression in front of the barn. They make a handsome picture with their dark foliage and elegant blooms against the silver-gray barn boards. Ignore the yellow tin sign tacked to the old well-house door, proclaiming that we use De Laval milkers. As David used to say when he was younger, "Tell me a story about a farm that still has its cows."

The barn is very large, much bigger than the house. Its ridge is crowned with lightning rods and a galloping horse weather vane with a few holes in it. The glass is gone from the top windows on the end; traffic in and out is brisk in barn swallows. The barn is cut into the hill as is the local custom. On the downhill side, the cows would have their door to the stanchions and stalls of the lower floor. On the uphill side one can drive a team and hay wagon or a tractor into the storage rooms of the second floor.

Our small assemblage of livestock is confined to the lower floor. At least we try to keep the chickens down there. The bantams love to steal away up to the hay and hide their eggs. For them it is a short flight from the door of the hayloft down to the hen yard. Tom tried it one day. Belle, our beagle, once sent a cat out that way too, in more of a leap than it had bargained for.

Both Tom and cat lived to tell the tale, but both will probably choose more conventional exits in the future.

The second floor of the barn is in many ways more interesting than the first. Here and there are chutes and sliding trap doors for sending feed and bedding down to the animals below. There are haylofts at several levels. Come winter, the open floor space will be filled with an extra Ostrander tractor, the Huntley haybine, which looks like a medieval torture machine but bales hay; and looming over that will be their tall elevator for conveying hay bales up to high haylofts. In some places you will scarcely be able to pass your hand between machine and wall. These are not men to let a good barn stand idle.

One end of the barn is divided into small rooms and halls. One room we call the oat room. The Couglers, our neighbors with the feed store, brought their huge truck up to the barn door, and with a mighty spiral-ribbed hose they blew the room full to the top with oats—thirteen tons of them! Apparently the oat market is no better than the stock market, since there are still several feet of oats in the room. If you find a knothole quietly, you can probably watch a mouse taking a profit in the oat market.

Outside, beyond the barn, we pass the ruins of a silo. David was also the first to point out that we had bought a barn that didn't have a silo. Just beyond the ruins is the sunflower garden. These are Russian Mammoths, dark platters of seeds fringed with yellow ribbons of petals, smiling at the sun from six-foot-high stalks. A red-tailed hawk swings over the butternut tree and sails off over the pastures toward Pierrepont.

The hills are dotted with spacious white farmhouses with fancy carved Victorian gingerbread trim, and a few old red-brick homes. The old-timers built large houses in an exuberant, confident style. Although this is a prosperous area, some of the homes have seen better days, and some of the rustic charm of silvered gray siding and quaint outbuildings is merely poverty in disguise. Up on the hill overlooking the little village is the lone venture in contemporary architecture in the area—an expensive glass creation, hidden away in the trees, perched up on a granite cliff overlooking the countryside.

Court Ostrander is cutting our hay. These hayfields are worse than whiskers—you have to keep them mowed or they grow back to bushes. This field is divided by a stone wall, along which are the beehives, wild grapevines, and a few basswood trees. Basswood-blossom honey is supposed to make the champagne of honeys. I hope our bees know that. The back stone wall with its row of elms, basswoods, and ash trees marks our boundary line with Latimer's farm. We have planted a line of conifers along all the hedgerows that border our fields, pines where the land is well drained, spruces where it is wet. By providing winter shelter, the trees enhance the value of the hedgerows for wildlife.

Here on the height of land is our upper garden. The sunny sky fits around it like a tea cup inverted on its saucer. This is the top of the world and you can see that it is round, and it is good. Alan Ostrander drives by waving enthusiastically from his red and white tractor. He's going to cut some corn in the next field. He pulls an amazing rig that cuts the whole corn stalk, grinds it, ears and all, and spits the green chunks of fodder into the following wagon.

Kale harvesting is more primitive. Just me, my knife, and the kale. But what a knife! It's perfectly balanced, with a beautifully curved black handle that fits my hand well, and a fine triangular blade of steel. It cuts, surgically sweet, into the tender emerald stalks of kale. No one in the family had ever tasted kale when we ordered the first seeds. The catalogue said hardy dwarf Siberian kale. We figured if kale is good for Siberia, kale is good for Canton. Fortunately it does taste good to Crowells. Our kale plants stand about three feet high and three feet wide, rosettes of curly margined silver-blue-green leaves. Cutting only the smallest tender center leaves, I am soon engulfed by the kale smell and the kale crunch of crisp stalks. In no time we have two big shopping bags packed full.

As we thread our way through the weeds over to the squash patch, three, eight, ten chukkars, small brown Hungarian partridge, explode from the grass at our feet, whistle-wing away, and drop into the meadow on the other side of the road. The squash are doing well. We pick a handful of small, yellow summer squash for Ken to carry. By mistake I step on the stalk of a zucchini plant, which pops with a watery, hollow sound. Ken teases me about how awful he thinks zucchini are. We find lots of them, two or three small ones of the best eating size on every plant, many more tiny fingers of squash to come, and two huge ones that look more like watermelons. Ken protests when I load him up with these. When I think of the wrinkled, travel-weary things that command such an exorbitant price in the winter market, I cannot waste these. We'll have them for lunch and the yellow squash for dinner. Too bad I can't figure out how to freeze them. Last year we froze bags and bags of squash. We had bags and bags of tasteless rubber haunting us every time we opened the freezer door.

But kale I can freeze with a light heart. I fill the kitchen sink with water, empty in our bags of kale, and put Tom to work picking off the green caterpillars. I put the old dark-blue, white-flecked enamel canner on the stove with water for blanching, and David and I set up the assembly line. Three minutes in the boiling water and the kale leaves, brighter green than ever, are strained and spread on a special yellow bath towel—my own innovation. I toss the leaves dry and cool, and pack them into freezer bags. I squash the bag into what Ken calls cow pies—flat and round, and air free—seal the bag, and toss it into the other sink of cold well water to cool.

Next batch. "Tom, you missed a caterpillar."

"He'll just add protein," says David. I consider serving it to him.

The towel slowly turns chartreuse.

Steam clouds the window.

Winter seems a long way off.

One of the nicest things about kale is that it comes up in the spring even before the grass is green. New spring kale has a different taste from that of its summer-grown sister. More than just spring-welcome, it is an epicurean marvel. I planted one row of kale by the stable, hoping it would benefit from the warmth and shelter and put forth its tender leaves especially early. I reckoned without Rameses II.

Rameses II is our sheep. He is a young Suffolk ram and our second try at raising our own lamb. We bought Rameses from Alan Ostrander. Al is more than just a sheep raiser, he is a sheep fancier. He and his wife Rita have joined fellow sheep fanatics on sheep-watching trips around this country, and even once, a whirlwind trip to England. That transatlantic flight touched down at seven A.M. and they all hopped on a bus and took right off to watch English sheep. Alan's farm, just down the road from his father's, is a storybook sight in spring. The neat red buildings nestle in front of rolling green meadows dotted with sheep and gamboling lambs. Suffolks are a very attractive breed. Their gentle black faces peer out from thick coats of curly gray wool. Their slender legs are also black. You can't talk sheep very long with Alan without wanting some of your own.

When we decided our farm (and freezer) would be incomplete without our own Suffolk, Alan was happy to oblige. Since Rameses II had lost his lambish charm and was well into his gangly youth stage when we got him, we figured we could eat him without too much remorse. Whatever lingering regrets we might have would be erased as the signs of his impending ramhood became increasingly apparent. It's easy to think of the ram that just butted you as "Ram Chop." With Alan ready to offer advice and assistance, we plunged confidently into sheep raising.

Rameses II has lately been having scours, or loose-bowel trouble. Sheep manure normally comes deposited in a dry, shiny brown-black, neatly accordion-pleated form. If it does not, you have a sick sheep. Sheep are very good at picking up various internal parasites that make them sick, and then they must be "drenched." So Alan told us. And he would take care of Rameses for us. That he did, departed, and shortly thereafter Ken came home from work. A few minutes later he emerged from the barn with a puzzled look on his face. "I thought you said Alan drenched the sheep this afternoon."

"He did."

"Rameses doesn't look it."

"Well, he did." And then it hit me that Ken was expecting a ram dripping with medicine. I tried not to sound too superior as I explained that Alan had administered the medication not with a shower but with a gadget that looked like a cross between a hypodermic needle and a squirt gun. I couldn't sound too superior about drenching—I'm not exactly sure which end of Rameses got the medicine.

However, the medicine worked and in no time our listless ram was back at his old tricks. To say a fence is dog high and sheep tight is quite a claim. A sheep fence is a class of fence unto itself. It is woven of stout wire in squares, not at all like the thin twisted hexagons of chicken wire. Woven sheep fence needs to be strong for obvious reasons, but it is not very flexible. This means that if the ground undulates around the edge of your sheep yard, you have problems. Ours did and we did. You could not see any discontinuities in the bottom line where the fence meets the grass, but Rameses II always knew where they were. He would go over to the appropriate spot, kneel down, folding his knees forward in that curious angle peculiar to his kind, and lean his way under. I'd look out in the yard and there he'd be.

I have decided that farm animals can be divided roughly into two types: the kind you push or get behind and move with the appropriate amount of waving and yelling, and the kind you get in front of and coax or pull. Rameses II belonged to category II. I'd run into the barn, grab up a scoop of grain from his feed bag, and run out to Rameses. Sometimes he'd walk, sometimes he'd run toward me. I would then lead him through the barn door, through the barn, through the part of the milk house where we store the equipment, and into the shed section of the milk house, which was his home. I'd hook the door, then run back through the barn and out to his yard to try to find and stake down the offending fence section more securely before he came out his door. When I was fairly satisfied with the state of the fence I'd go back to the house. Next time when I looked out he might be in the kale again, or just standing in the raspberry canes, bleating. He loves raspberry leaves almost as much as he loves kale. Fence he can push his way out of, but raspberry canes, never!

* * *

Pails clanking at our belts, sounding like a herd of cows, we tramp down the hill to go blackberrying. The hill is an amphitheater in the late afternoon sun, and the crickets and grasshoppers are performing. We try to locate the musicmaker responsible for the long rasping phrases, but he stops abruptly as he feels our footfall. Another kind is singing in synchrony—the hill fairly rings.

The singers might better be termed fiddlers, as most produce their sounds by rubbing together a file and scraper arrangement on their wings or legs. Each performer—this is a male orchestra—produces his own note of nearly unvaried pitch. Because the tempo of the phrases varies with temperature, and the rhythm within the passages is too rapid for the human ear to distinguish, and the critter may have more than one song in his repertoire, I have not been able to identify all the forty or so common species of crickets, grasshoppers, katydids, and cicadas! For me it is enough that I have learned that the different tones I hear mean there are different kinds of insects singing in the pasture.

Above us float rose-tinted thunderheads, not meaning business tonight. From the hedgerow ahead of us a robin calls "quirt, quirt" ever so softly. We climb through the tangle of nightshade, the berries of which sparkle like rubies, past dark-blue dogwood berries—the few that haven't been eaten already by the birds. Once more we sample the wild raisins, biting through the shriveled pulp all the way to the great flat seed in the center. Still no flavor to speak of—leave them for the birds.

Now on our rocky pasture we separate and get down to the business at hand. Everywhere are prickly blackberry bushes hanging luxuriantly with fruit. Paths are already beaten through the brambles for us—not by bears, or neighbors, who all have their own berry patches, but by people out from town enjoying the fruit of the field on the miles of what to their eye is "abandoned" farm land. There is plenty here for all.

A handsome male oriole flashes briefly in the top of a poplar and then quietly leads his family away. Warblers in their subdued fall plumage, and in what numbers and kinds I could not guess, sift silently through the trees. I recognize the black mask of the yellow-throat but that is all.

One of my pails is full so I prop it up in a stone wall to start the second. One hand picks berries but the other picks flowers. Pearly everlasting, the favorite even of Colonial ladies, grows nearby in handsome clumps. I pick both the yellow-centered male flowers and the pure-white female flowers, and gather long spires of rust-brown dock.

Beautiful wands of goldenrod that have just opened out I pick in their prime. Where our little spring stream has dried away to a marsh I gather pale-mauve Joe-Pye-weed and white thoroughwort. I move out through the dark-brown knots of rush seeds to gather a few plump cattails. Surprisingly cold water seeps up over my shoes and cools my ankles. Only now am I fully aware of what hot, sticky, itchy work this is. A silver-spangled fritillary flaps lightly by as I sink lower into the ooze.

I gather up my harvest and slog back to join the others. Ken is over by the apple tree at the meadow corner. The cheat! He has filled his buckets with summer apples. He has nice ones—the last of the Yellow Transparents and the first of the red-and-green-streaked Early Harvest. Nothing tastes better than the first apples of the season. I bite into my second crisp, juicy apple and chuckle to myself at how easy it is to overindulge and be stricken with that malady of urgency known as "green apple quick step."

Ken and I sit and watch a pair of tiny pert wrens scolding us from the apple tree. I suppose they have young nearby that we are disturbing though we can't see them. Reluctantly we move on.

A pair of catbirds call each other names from the tangle of grapevines in the hedgerow.

Trudging back up the cricket hill the boys spot a garden spider including legs a good inch across. Its body is a gorgeous combination of yellow and black and it hangs like a pendant jewel in the center of its cobweb, a huge work of art, signed down the middle with a characteristic zigzag of silk.

Next we practically step on a white orchis, a delicate wand of white fringed orchid blooms. There are quite a few species of orchids that bloom at the end of the summer but since I usually associate wild orchids with spring, I consider these one last special favor of the season.

I head to the attic to lay my flowers out to dry while the others head straight for the pond. The attic is an inferno compared to the hot hill! Quickly I tie the pearly everlasting into bunches to hang head down from the rafters beside some herb bundles. The goldenrod will dry in graceful curves in this tapered wastebasket. It's a beautiful old Indian-made ash-split wastebasket decorated with fading green curlicue twists.

The full moon rose orange and lopsided over the hills while we swam. Those first red maples turned bright scarlet down by our marsh warned us all to make the most of this swim!

We had the season's first corn on the cob for supper, and blackberries in cream. Tomorrow I'll be making blackberry jelly. Those kitchen water pipes make a great place from which to hang the jelly bag. How nice it will be to have the froth skimmed from the jelly on our toast once again!

Out in the barnyard an animal coughs. The ducks at the pond quack—uneasily, or just at the moon? Then all is quiet except for the night-singing insects. All the insects slow the tempo of their song as the temperature drops. The temperature cricket chirping

pour in the blossoms, some raisins, and the juice of two oranges and two lemons. When the brew has cooled to 70°F. I sprinkle in a spoonful of dried yeast, cover the kettle, and put it by the porch door, which I hope will be near enough to 65° for the next five days. Every day I open it and send the blossoms whirling in a good stir. This is the first fermentation. The yeast beasts will be multiplying vigorously and they will want a breath of fresh air once a day.

While I wait for the dew to dry off the grass I strain my goldenrod infusion. I have sterilized a gallon jug to ferment it in. This will be the slow, quiet fermentation during which the yeasts will turn the sugar into alcohol. Now I want to keep the air out. We use inexpensive plastic fermentation traps that we get from a home winemakers' supplier in Ottawa. (He has bins and bins of gadgets in his cellar. The other half of his basement is his wine cellar, where five-gallon carboys gently bubble away.) The fermentation trap is an air lock. It lets out the carbon dioxide but keeps vinegar flies and oxygen from getting in. The classic fermentation trap is a glass rig comprising two bulbs and a U-shaped tube, which is filled with a sulphite solution. The plastic gadgets, a vial-within-a-vial arrangement, that we use are not aesthetically equivalent to the traditional traps, but they have the advantage of not breaking when we inadvertently bump them up against the sink. A balloon stretched over the neck of the jug would almost serve the purpose.

I pour the golden liquid into the jug and fit it with an air lock. The fermentation is going quite well. Tiny bubbles fizz up the neck of the jug and blip out the fermentation trap. I leave it on the counter until it quiets down, a day or two, and then I take it down to the shelf in the cellar.

For a wine cellar we have appropriated one side of the work bench for fermenting gallon jugs, and the upper canned goods shelves are lined with wine bottles on their sides to keep the corks from drying out. Our friends have provided us with some fancy wine bottles to refill. We also use some of the thicker-walled soda bottles for wine-for-two. We don't drink much of the stuff—soda, that is—so we are delighted when the carton of empties our friends bring contains bottles of what we consider the choicest size.

The only serious error of judgment in our personal bottle recycling program has been the elderflower champagne incident. A few weeks ago we were shaken out of our torpor one oppressively hot afternoon by the sound of an explosion in the cellar. Subsequent cautious investigation revealed the sorry sight of green glass confetti everywhere, precious champagne trickling unappreciated down the wooden shelves and sandstone rocks of the house foundation. Now we choose stronger bottles and wire the corks on tightly when we are attempting bubbly brews.

Once you have freed yourself of the idea that all wine comes from the grape, you start considering almost anything for wine. We are trying marigold wine and pumpkin. Last year's green tomato wine tasted like a dry red burgundy—if you closed your eyes. Part of the fun of homemade wine is that you never know what to expect. Even from one year to the next the same flowers may give you quite a different product. You can choose by the amount of sugar that you add whether the wine will be sweet or dry and, to some degree, how strong a wine you'll have. It must contain a certain amount of alcohol so that it won't spoil, but there is a concentration of alcohol beyond which even yeasts cannot survive.

Our mint wine was a dry, light dream. On the other hand, our rose-hip wine was awful. We may not have the touch for rose hips. We ground and dried trays full of them for tea, but they molded defiantly, in spite of our most solicitous care. Our rose-hip jelly looked and tasted like weak glue. I'm convinced that rose hips belong on the bush to brighten the winter landscape. Still, almost anything makes good wine.

GOLDENROD WINE

1 gallon water
2 pounds sugar
1 pint blooms
2 oranges
2 lemons
½ cup raisins
1 teaspoon yeast
(1 teaspoon yeast nutrient)

Bring the water to a boil in an unchipped enameled (never metal) pot and stir in the sugar. When the sugar is dissolved, turn off the heat, add the blossoms, the juice of the oranges and the lemons, and the peel of the lemon. (Grate or slice the peel, being careful to avoid the white bitter pith.) Add the raisins and cool to 70°F. (about room temperature). Stir in yeast, and yeast nutrient if available. (The raisins and lemons will probably add sufficient nutrients for the yeast so you can get along without the yeast nutrient if you have no winemaking supplier near you.)

Cover pot, put in a slightly cooler place, 65°F., and leave for five days, giving the mixture a good stir once a day.

On the fifth day, sterilize a gallon jug, strain the mixture, and pour the liquid into the sterile jug. Cap with a fermentation trap and put away in a cool (about 65°) dark place for a month.

When the wine has cleared and there is a deposit of dead yeast, the "lees," in the bottom of the jug, "rack" the wine by siphoning it off into another sterile jug. Put the fermentation trap on again, and put the wine back in a cool place for another three or four months.

When all signs of bubbling have ceased, rack the wine into sterile bottles. (By now you can tell if you are going to end up with wine or vinegar. If it tastes terrible when you rack it this time, it has been contaminated and you might as well throw it away. If it merely tastes a little "raw," you will probably be very pleased with it after it has aged a bit.) Seal with sterile corks or caps and put the bottles on their sides in your cool, dark place. Allow about six-months further aging. Cheers, santé, and all that!

*   *   *

David holds open the door to the multipurpose room of the Canton Presbyterian Church for me. His deep-blue eyes have assumed that private expression which indicates he is people-watching. Carefully we carry my entry for the annual Garden Club flower show to the registration desk.

"Name?" sweetly queries a well-groomed voice.

"Marnie Crowell."

"Entry title? That's for the newspapers in case you win, you know."

"Renew the Earth, Compost!"

The well-groomed hand writes, "Renew the Earth."

"No, comma, Compost, exclamation point," I add.

The entry formalities over, to the mandatory murmurs of "How nice . . . ," we pass into the exhibition room to the table marked "President's class—for those who have never won a prize before." That's us.

First we put down a wooden tray. In its center we stand a tall glass cake stand and ring its base with flawless rich-red tomatoes and neon-yellow summer squash. We set a plain punch bowl on the cake stand and wreathe it with red dahlias and tiny wild black-eyed Susans. On the bowl in gold stick-on letters I paste my exhortation, "Renew the Earth, Compost!" Then I fill the bowl with the most beautiful compost you have ever seen. I had been prepared to cheat on this point and had inspected the compost heap of a friend of ours who tends his compost heap more tenderly than I do mine. My compost looked as good as his, so I was spared that moral dilemma. There wasn't anything in the rules that said the compost had to be your own. There wasn't anything in the rules about compost at all.

I try one of the little black-eyed Susans poking insouciantly up from the compost but decide it isn't necessary. The arrangement is based on a triangle, the composition a sumptuous cascade in red and gold of August's bounty, the dark hue of the punch bowl's contents successfully echoed by the centers of the tiny black-eyed Susans, as they say. And the compost doesn't smell at all. We enjoy a quick peek at various floral creations in their artistic exhibition nooks before we are hustled out because the judges are ready. David grins to himself as he lopes down the steps.

We return to find a shiny gold ribbon gracing our August opulence! On the card of constructive (of course!) criticism, face down, the judges have written, "Imaginative. However, the materials are perhaps a bit beyond the intent of this class." Perhaps.

Making compost, like many a rural art, has as many variations as there are farmers—the method is the maker. Our compost pile is a casual affair in a three-sided enclosure behind the garage. On my unnecessary compost raid I observed that Dick Kepes separates his leaves into a high-rise community of chicken wire cylinders. Leaves are slow to decompose and in this way he assures that they are well supplied with oxygen I presume. In organic gardening magazines I have seen elaborate composters that provide for aeration by long handles one moves up and down to stir things up. The con-

traption resembles a back-yard sedan chair. We stir our compost
when we pull up the last of the squash and tomato vines that have
volunteered there—after harvest, of course. Our compost pile pros-
pers, so I assume it is well fed, but should it falter I am told we
can add bone meal, lime, blood, or septic tank starter. A compost
pile belongs in every back yard to take care of leaves, lawn clip-
pings, and garden odds and ends at the very least, but I wonder
how many suburban garden centers currently carry septic tank
starter.

Our compost pile is also our garbage disposal. Our kitchen scraps
are layered inoffensively under a cover of leaves. That way we
keep the nutrients to spread around the flowerbeds instead of
sloshing them down in precious clean water to a river already
choking on the overabundance of the wasted nutrients of our sewage, our processing plants—the open-ended, one-way fertilizer drain
of civilization. Is a real garbage disposal so much more convenient
than mine? It may save time, but I merely say the compost
pile, like the roadside mailbox and the hungry chickens in the
barn, invites me faithfully, day after day, into the company of the
wide sky in all its moods—to mark the last golden leaf of autumn,
to hear the first note of the chickadee's spring song over the February snow drift, to measure the second April inch of the spring
bulb's progress.

SEPTEMBER

THE WHITE DUCKS parade through the meadow picking bugs out of the grass and the Huntleys' two chestnut riding horses ignore them. We drive past the sign saying "Roger Huntley, Auctioneer," and into the yard, but no children come pouring out of the Huntleys' house. The hammock, the lumpy-cushioned old couch, and the assortment of chairs lining the rambling front porch are all deserted.

It is milking time, so we are sure of finding at least a couple of Huntleys at home. As we walk back to the huge dairy barn, a handsome rooster inspects us haughtily from atop one of the tractors in the open shed. Cats in every hue and size, easily as many as twenty, crowd around bowls of milk on the barn threshold.

Through the open door of the barn we can see the long rows of big black-and-white Holsteins, their heads through the stanchions, munching feed from the trough in front of their noses. The two oldest boys, Doug and Danny, and the hired man are doing the milking this evening. Danny gently washes the swollen udder and teats of a cow and Doug slips the shiny nozzles of the milking machine up over the fat pink teats. With alternating rhythmic pulsations the machine empties the great soft bag. The front end of the cow munches steadily on; at the back end, her tail switches away at the flies without interruption.

"The rest of the family has gone over to Potsdam getting shoes for school," says Danny, moving on down the line of cows.

"We brought some zucchini. I'll put them on the back step."

"O.K."

While the boys each give the horses a handful of presumably greener long grass from our side of the fence, and Ken inspects the Huntley pigs, I get the squash from the car and put them on the back steps.

We roll down our own driveway in the gathering dusk. A couple of frogs are tuning up by the pond. "Rivet, rrriv-vet, rivet."

On the seat of the straight-backed wooden chair by the back door is a large zucchini resting on a book we had lent to Huntleys. I see the Huntleys raise a light-green variety with long dark stripes down its side. Ours are nearly ebony-dark green. An interesting exchange . . .

*   *   *

It is a perfect Saturday afternoon for a drive. Gone is the heavy heat of summer but yet to come is the chill of frost. The grass-hoppers of this world are out singing today; only the ants are still toiling over their canning kettles.

We head up the back way to St. Regis singing silly songs and counting brown cows on each side of the road. We pass an old car pulled off at the head of a grassy swale between the woods and the side of the road. We pass two women bent over in the tall grass. Ken slows the car to a halt and turns it around.

"Did you see those two Indians picking sweetgrass back there in that ditch?"

Indian baskets are our hobby. We collect splint and sweetgrass baskets, large ones, small ones; baskets in junk shops, antique shops, and at auctions. The Iroquois have been making baskets around here for no one knows how long. They sold them to the early settlers, and we collect the ones their descendants now throw out of their attics. That is how we happen to recognize sweetgrass picking when we see it.

The older woman straightens up and smiles back at us as we walk up to her. She has a fat bundle of yellowed grasses neatly arranged in her brown hand. She pushes back a graying wisp of hair over her forehead and grins broadly as we explain our interests.

"Yes, yes," she answers with a rising inflection in her voice. She speaks slightly halting English. The younger woman is her daughter; she is pleased to show us the long coil of braided sweet-grass that she has made. It is in the trunk of her car. She opens the car door and lets out two shy children, three and four years old

I'd guess. She speaks to them in Mohawk. Their grandmother affectionately tousles their silky black hair.

We describe to her the sweetgrass that the Penobscot Indians in Maine gather in the salt marshes. "Oh," she smiles, "Yes, I have heard. They use some kind of weed. We use sweetgrass. See how good it smells when it's dry?" She raises the braid to her nose and then holds out the fragrant coil to us. "You want to come see my baskets?" she asks. We assure her we do and she pulls an official-looking envelope from her purse with slow hands. Carefully she tears off the return address and gives it to us. "You come see me up at the reservation, mmm? I am always there." And that is how we came to meet Molly Rebo.

*　　*　　*

We stopped at one of Roger Huntley's farm auctions today. Long lines of pickup trucks and cars of every conceivable make parked in the grass along both sides of the road attest to the widespread popularity of the farm auction as local entertainment.

I see jovial Mrs. Leland in a blue flowered apron, unwrapping another platterful of homemade donuts over at the food table. Gerry Ostrander, Court's wife, and Roger's wife, Ann, are presiding over the books and cash box at a card table where the bidders reckon up the price of their impulses. Gerry has a cheery nod and greeting for her many friends in the crowd. Ann has kept her high school harvest queen good looks after six children, the youngest of whom, peppy little Sandra, runs up for some money and dashes off to Mrs. Leland and the soft drinks. The three boys who pass things up to Roger at the auction table and hand them over to the successful bidders are Huntley sons.

Roger in his hallmark tweed hat is selling off the smaller farm tools left in the old barn. He sells the first of several hay forks very quickly as if to tell the crowd that they had better be on their toes or someone else will walk off with all the bargains. They get the hint, and the next two hay forks go for a higher price.

A large box of nails comes up next. No bidders. Roger throws in a couple of hammers and a plane. To the young man who buys the lot for a dollar Roger says with a grin, "Gee, I'm glad you came to the auction today." The boy smiles; he probably got a real bargain but he'll feel surer later. A flint-faced woman recording in a long black book her winning bids on junky stuff must be a downstate antique dealer. One of the local antique dealers beats her bid on a nice old-fashioned child's sled. A hand-cranked corn sheller brings a flurry of bids. A local businessman takes home a set of brass-knobbed harness hames to decorate his den.

The crowd groups itself in front of the porch when Roger starts in on the household goods. The foresighted have brought their own folding lawn chairs. An interesting array of farmers' wives, suburbanites, and retired couples settles into the front-row seats. A couple of dealers stand quietly by the porch steps. A steady line of men carrying furniture and bric-a-brac is soon weaving back and forth to the pickup trucks. Children swing on the pasture gate and bounce up and down on the beds standing on the lawn until their mothers catch them.

In his magnetic singsong Roger chants, "Four, four, four and a half. I've got four fifty, four fifty, five? Five. Six, do I hear six? Six. Mary save your dollar, I'll need it a little later"; he grins as a flustered lady raises her own bid in the excitement.

A beautiful old French doll comes up next. Her sweet, small china face smiles from a box marked with the name of a famous Marseilles dollmaker. She has obviously spent her whole long life in that faded box. Strange, precious things turn up in these old North Country homes! As the bidding quickly climbs to fifty dollars Roger looks at the doll in the box in his hand and says to her, "You're the most expensive dolly I've ever had my hands on." The crowd laughs. He turns to his wife. "Except you, dear." The crowd laughs again.

Many dishes, lamps, basins, chairs, and books later, Roger opens a shoebox and pulls out a pair of fine china bells fitted with metal hangers at their tops. "I don't know what these things are. They're real pretty, though." He hangs them on his fingers. "Now wouldn't they look nice on a Christmas tree? Anybody know what they are?"

"Roger, those are the bells they used to hang over the top of a kerosene lamp to catch the smoke," one of the front-row elderly ladies confides.

He grins and auctions them off. Then he discovers in the shoebox a small round gauge from the lid of a pressure cooker he has earlier sold, and everything stops while the buyer is found and the part reunited with the cooker.

Ken bids on a square basket with a cover, which looks Indian. Roger puts two others inside it to liven up the bidding. "Four dollars, four dollars, sold; Ken." A few minutes later a handled splint egg basket comes up, and we buy it for a dollar. A maple-sugar barrel goes too high for us.

During the lunch break we all go out to the barn to look at the cattle that are going to be sold next. The barn floor is covered with fresh clean sawdust. The cows and calves are shiny-clean and brushed. Roger carries a hand microphone out to the raised ring, which has been set up and filled with sawdust. The first cow is led out of the barn and into the ring. A good cow may bring as much as seven hundred dollars; an exceptional one, a thousand. Many of the men around the ring are carrying fat rolls of cash, hundreds of dollars, in the pockets of their faded overalls. Why do they scorn the checkbook? City ways?

"Now here's a good one, folks," says Roger. "You can see she has a good udder on her. Who'll start things off at four hundred dollars? Will somebody give me three hundred and fifty? I've got three, three and a half, four, four, five, five, five, six, six and a quarter, quarter, six and a half. Six seventy-five, bidding six seventy-five. It's a real milky herd, folks. Six and a half, six and a half. Sold, six and a half; Joe."

Not being in the market for cows, we call it a day and head back to our car. The wing-toed, high-topped shoes I discover among the items of junk Roger has tossed into the basket to sweeten the pot might fit me. They are lovely soft-as-gloves brown leather, preserved over the years from bending over and cracking at the sides by sheets of cardboard carefully cut to fit inside. I try them on; they fit perfectly. But they squeak.

I ask a friend who is of the appropriate vintage to remember these high-heeled, high-topped beauties how long it takes for such shoes to stop squeaking; she answers laughingly, "Till they're paid for!"

The square basket is Indian. It is nicely decorated on the wide splints with faded yellow and green designs that were printed on with a stamp cut from a potato. Potato markings were popular at least a hundred years ago. The color of the splints and the yellowed newspaper lining corroborate this. Even more exciting is one of the baskets inside, a round honey-colored splint basket decorated with rows of fine splints twisted into small coils. The top rim has been mended with a lacing of red yarn. Spidery handwriting on the bottom proclaims this "Ma Butterfield's basket—bought March 1879." We are elated; it has been a good auction day for us.

But one was even better—we bought our farm at an auction. For months we'd driven miles up and down country roads looking for a farm that was in halfway decent repair, for sale, and not opposite a trailer camp. We'd almost resigned ourselves to living in town a few more years when a friend told us about this place. On a raw, gray October Sunday we drove out to look at it. The foliage had fallen early that year; the old farmhouse had not one speck of paint left on it, and beds, tractors, and a wringer-washer stood forlornly in the front yard. Ken disappeared into the barn to talk to Roger; I decided that perhaps there was nothing wrong with the house that a coat of paint wouldn't cure, and went to see what the inside was like. Beyond the clutter of boxes of curtains, stacks of books, and piles of chrome dinette chairs, I could see that the house had been well cared for, and pink-purple-silver-green-and-gray wallpaper is, after all, a matter of taste.

In short, we fell in love with the place. That night we excitedly decided on our highest offer, that sum for which we thought we wouldn't kick ourselves ever afterward if it were topped by someone else. Monday morning I stayed at our apartment with baby Tom and David, while Ken sallied forth to win us a home. Fortunately for us, six miles out of town was then considered beyond commuting range, and a hundred acres too small to start out in the dairy business. So Ken stood toe to toe with just one other bidder. He came back that afternoon with five different kinds of rakes in the back of the car.

"Now where are we going to use those?" I asked with fingers crossed.

"Our farm," was the welcome reply.

*　　*　　*

The phone company man promised that it would help us get off this eight-party line if we'd let them bury their new cable along the edge of our farm. As if this weren't inducement enough, they even paid us a little money, and when their digging machine came through they most obligingly scooped out the spring in our lower meadow as they went by. Ken was a little disappointed that they broke the old wooden barrel that had bordered the buried spring (to give it good edges) for more than a century, but that was more than offset by the renewal of the fountain. Court and Alan no longer had to come down at noontime on summer days to let seventy thirsty milk cows cross the road to get a drink.

The phone man has been up the pole on the corner all morning, clipping and rearranging, and ringing us up periodically to see whom he gets. We are being switched to a two-party line! At last he is satisfied and comes into the house to show us how to dial Mrs. DeKay, who'll be sharing this line. He demonstrates our ring—it sounds like a town phone now—and tells us our service has been "upgraded."

As soon as he's gone, I pick up the receiver to try out this new service. A voice droning through the details of a new recipe for carrot cake greets my ears. I know that voice! I hang up, puzzled. That was one of the marathoners from our old line. I try again an hour later—another "regular" is on the line. Hours later I make contact with repair service. It can't happen, they tell me. There is no way all eight of us could have been moved to a two-party line. Not entirely reassured, I hang up and call Mrs. DeKay. Instead I reach Gary Cougler, the boy at the farm midway down our road.

The next day the phone man is back in the kitchen again fiddling with the phone. He has already spent an hour up on the corner pole. "Mrs. DeKay is pretty frantic," he chuckles. After a few more calls in to the office, he announces, "This should fix it now," and again the phone truck rattles down our hill.

About suppertime the phone rings. It's Joe Cougler trying to call Joe Moran. We go through the whole story again. We are still not off that line. We hang up, and he tries again. It rings here. "Never mind," laughs Joe, "I guess I'd better drive up to Morans' and see him myself."

*   *   *

Smiths' is a gas station and a grocery store at Langdons Corners, about five miles out of Canton. We always begin our directions for finding our farm from Smiths'. When people are sure they should have already reached our farm, they invariably stop at Smiths' to call us. Smiths' saves them a dime and gives them the directions.

Smiths' is an inviting place; petunias and marigolds in window boxes smile gaily, as yet untouched by frost. On the shelves above the flowers are ranked boxes of red tomatoes, the surplus from the kitchen gardens in the area. The top shelf is piled high with yellowing green bunches of feathery dill weed for the local picklers. The store also sells locally made bologna and cheese curds, little lumps of rubbery goodness from a local cheese factory. They even have tiny sweetgrass baskets—thimble cases just like the ones my grandmother had—made by the Indians.

I am on my way to Smiths' when I spot the telephone repair truck at Mrs. DeKay's. I stop the car and approach the phone man, not the one we've seen so much of lately. I tell him the whole story.

"Won't you please come back with me right now and straighten it out?" I plead, and he obligingly climbs in his truck and follows me home. I nod politely through the there-you-are-Mrs.-Crowell-it's-all-fixed-now routine; and away he goes.

The school bus disgorges my boys at the head of our driveway. It goes on up the hill, and out gets Gary Cougler. I see him go up his driveway and disappear into the house. The yellow bus turns around and thunders back down our road. I pick up the phone and dial the second party code. Gary Cougler doesn't answer. No one does. It rings and rings. I think at last we've done it! Now our friends must be ready to talk to us the first time they dial our number. The odds have changed!

*　　*　　*

All day and all night the air is filled with insect songs. Almost the only bird song—you surely can't include the racket of the ever-growing blackbird flocks—is the sweet trill of the goldfinches flitting from one clump of drying thistles to another, launching thistle-down stars out over the pond as they go, feeding or coaching their begging fledglings.

Red and brown dragonflies coupled together buzz over the pond in a last frenzy of activity that will ensure the survival of their kind before they themselves are cut down by the coming frosts.

The sun seems so warm now but the signs are unavoidable: frost glittered on the barn roof this morning; a pair of wood ducks put down for the night on our pond on their way south; and a chipmunk has been driving Belle, our beagle, crazy with its constant, impertinent trips back and forth under her very nose to stock up its larder.

Across the road the pasture seems to have special end-of-season charms for the cows. The Ostrander collie, Rex, has to come over every afternoon in the sunny glow of four o'clock to send the cows home with his barking and heel nipping.

What curious times we live in. These are the days of fence rustlers. The Couglers had to go chase their heifers last night. Someone had driven a truck down the lonely road at the back edge of their farm—and carried off their fence rails. Suburbanites are paying two dollars apiece for split rails I hear. There's gold snaking across the pastures of these hills.

Up by the fruit trees we have a pile of rails that Ken hopes to use to mend that section of our fence. Ken figures he'd better do something to make that pile of rails not quite so tempting. You can't just hide a pile of twelve-foot rails. We stack up a tall white beehive beside them. That ought to hold them for a while.

*   *   *

The piglets came. They are cute, very intelligent looking. I see why pigs so often star in nursery rhymes. They are both females, a little more than twelve weeks old and a little more than two feet long, pale-pink, haired lightly with white. Their ears are a lovely shape and stand up nicely from their heads. Their tails do a neat twist. They are Lancasters. Ken brought them home in the back end of the station wagon, each tied up in a sack. One worked its sack open in the car, which the boys thought was very funny. Ken, checking the situation in the rear-view mirror, didn't find it quite as hilarious.

After we lift out each wiggly sack and put the pigs in their stall, I climb the stairs with the pitchfork to throw down some old hay through the sliding trapdoor that opens above their stall. Ken fixes it for their bedding. I feel very pleased with myself for remembering Robert Frost's lines in "The Death of the Hired Man":

> He bundles every forkful in its place,
> And tags and numbers it for future reference,
> So he can find and easily dislodge it
> In the unloading. . . .

The hay has indeed been put in the loft that way. If I attack a bundle crosswise and randomly, it is very hard to get up a forkful, but when I try lifting out the hay in packets the way it has been put in, it is very easy. Although my eye cannot discern the separateness of the packets, the pitchfork can.

After lunch I walk up to the garden and pick a good mess of Kentucky Wonder beans. I admire them for the way they climb up our poles out of reach of the weeds and bear so many beans. As

I turn into our driveway on the way back, an oriole flashes in the maple leaves. He is still an incredible flame and handsome black, even as he dons his winter plumage and sounds his ethereal farewell for this season. He sings a few effervescent phrases and moves on down the maples. In the winter, when the trees are bare, I like to try to count the oriole nests hanging from the elms over the road on the way into town. Such a graceful long bag of a hammock they build for a nest! But the elms are dying so quickly. I look anxiously at the beautiful elm behind the barn. Is it turning yellow too early this year? Has it been infected with the incurable fungus by invading elm-bark beetles? Such a wine goblet, a fountain of a tree. Doomed. I hope the oriole is getting used to maples.

There are the two pigs! They trot out of the barn into the sunlight like a pair of secretaries going out to lunch. They look so guilty when I drop the beans on the step, run over, and say firmly, "*Where* do you think *you're* going?" They look like two little girls just about to sneak a peek in an empty men's room. They bolt back into the barn. I run after them and close the door behind us. Then it is fairly easy to maneuver them back into their stall. They must have squeezed under the gate of their stall. A log wedged under the gate will keep them till Ken gets back. My knees are weak. I couldn't hope to catch two adventurous young pigs, even ungreased, once they got started. I'd be so angry to see my pork chops go running down the road. . . .

The crows have been busily calling up a flock. The tree swallows have already flown south. Yesterday I counted nearly a dozen barn swallows on the utility wire to the barn. Today there are none.

A killdeer whirls up from the edge of the pond in a flash of white—"Killdee, killdee, killdee!" A yellow-legs, a tall sandpiper, on his way south from the tundra, stands teetering, as if on stilts, by the little beach. We are hurrying to beat the rain and bring in some alfalfa for the pigs. We park the wheelbarrow in the middle of the alfalfa patch we found between two fruit trees in our fledgling orchard.

Ken cuts the dark-green alfalfa vines with the swinging scythe. I like to watch his body balance the rhythmic strokes of the arcing blade. There is quite an art to swinging the scythe in an advancing path, not pulling it around into your shins, or stabbing the blade tip into the ground. The boys spear up great nests of trailing green on their hay forks and pile them on the waiting wheelbarrow, mercifully without impaling each other in their enthusiasm. My job is to pack down the layered pile.

At last our makeshift hay wagon can hold no more. We lumber off to the barn with our swaying load. We toss the pigs a forkful. They shake and chew it with rewarding eagerness. We run through the raindrops to the house.

*   *   *

My parents have arrived. For one small part of the year we shall enjoy the old-fashioned pleasures of an extended family. Ten years of living in sunny California have ruddied my father's Scottish complexion. His fine hair remains dark, unthinned, but silvering at the temples. David seems to have inherited the thoughtful, faraway look of his blue eyes, and Tom their merriment.

My mother is grandmother enough to have snow-white hair, and Californian enough to favor bright orange slacks and to take a ride when she feels like it on the tire swing hanging from our pine tree.

We went up to the sunflower patch this morning and cut off the heavy seed heads with stout brush nippers. There is no easy way to harvest sunflowers. The stalks are tough, but they topple over in the wind. The mice quickly strip every one they can reach.

Now we have several bushel baskets filled with heavy seed heads, and have arranged ourselves in lawn chairs to await the return of the school bus while stripping out the plump ripe seeds.

My father chews on his tongue in contented concentration as he picks out sunflower seeds. It makes no difference at all what task he is set; he is completely satisfied to be sitting in the sun in this, his favorite season of the year.

The warm afternoon sunlight casts dancing blue shadows of the maples across our white farmhouse. We could not paint this house Federal blue, or bayberry green, or Colonial gold for the same reason that the tire swing hanging on its long rope from our pine tree looks more at home here than it would on any tree in town.

A Monarch floats by, and another. I have brought out a plate of cookies and some milk. As I pour the first glass I am startled by a Monarch settling down on the lip of the milk bottle. It moves unhesitatingly, at once unrolls its long proboscis, and calmly inserts it like a drinking straw into the drops of milk on the bottle's edge. As we stare in amazement, the butterfly drinks its fill, taps its long tubular mouthparts on the edge of the bottle, coils its long "tongue" up again, and tucking the coil under its chin, takes off! If only the boys could have seen that.

We hear the big bus grinding up the hill and see the yellow giant swing ponderously around our corner. The driver eases his noisy cargo to a halt. The red lights flash and the red stop sign semaphores out from the side of the bus. The doors swing open and our towheads tumble out, trailing a line of jackets, papers, and sneakers, calling one more jibe or promise over their shoulders to their schoolmates.

Scarcely a minute after their snack the boys are rolling down the grassy slope in a fight. But by the time the warriors reach the back door they have established a cease fire, thanks to a praying mantis. David carefully carries the large green insect to his entomologist grandfather. All elbows and knees the creature seems, a rough definition of *arthropod*. In the hush of observing the mantis slowly stalking up a branch, the whine of a nearby silo being blown full of fodder momentarily penetrates our consciousness. One becomes so used to the sound of blowers filling the neighborhood silos at this time of year, dawn to dusk, that it barely registers any more.

We need some potatoes for supper so we collect a burlap sack and a digging fork and head for the garden. Potatoes are more than brown lumps in net bags stacked in supermarkets. Potatoes are also dark, dark-green, two-foot-high plants bearing delicate white-ruffled candelabra flowers with yellow candle centers. The potato has a pirate heart. When the potatoes are ripe the vines yellow away and die, leaving only the faintest map to the buried treasure. Moving down the row to the part we have not yet dug, we press in our fork and lift out a radiating network of rootlets and potatoes. Some of the pale, slender stalks bear peas and marbles at their tips but there are a few good-sized baking potatoes to each hill, and handfuls of the golf-ball size, which are our favorite. One of the paramount pleasures of the season is eating field-fresh new potatoes, scrubbed, boiled in their jackets, and coated with melted butter. The little new potato is a very distant cousin to the sprouty nubbin of the February vegetable bin!

We pull some carrots by their leafy tops, wipe off the dirt and crunch one, bitter and sweet. They have a fragrance in the field that doesn't last beyond the bin. While the boys make sculptures out of purplish-green burdock burs, I gather an armload of feathery, pale-lavender wild asters.

We head for home, past the butternut tree, trying to count the nuts still hanging on dark branches against the sky. Butternuts do not make a very satisfactory lawn tree because their leaves shrivel yellow-brown early, and drop off. Next down come the sticky dark-brown butternuts. If you can beat the squirrels to the nuts, gather them, dry them, and hull them—dyeing your fingers a good rich, old-fashioned butternut brown in the process; you can then hammer out the sweet, rich kernels, preferably on the flat of an old iron wedged handle down between your legs on your lap.

Since the nuts are still hanging high in green husks, that day is a long way off. We trudge home, up the back steps, past a surer crop, the sunflower heads spread to dry on the back porch.

The screen door bangs after each of us. The ducks at the pond quack hopefully at the first bang or two but then go back to dabbling for their own dinners.

As Grandfather settles in the kitchen rocking chair, Grandmother slices fresh tomatoes for our supper. The boys present tonight's corn for inspection.

"Grandpa Chief is going to show you how to make fritters tonight," says my father, rising from the rocker.

Taking the corn from David and Tom he eyes each full, ripe, perfect ear with satisfaction. (But I can remember that even when he was a top entomologist for one of the largest agricultural chemical companies in the country, he used to say, "Any ear of corn that isn't good enough for the worms isn't good enough for me." He never bothered to spray our own garden—unless he had some new idea he wanted to try out.)

Corn fritters, or oysters, as they are sometimes called, modern cookbooks notwithstanding, are flat fried cakes of pure milky corn that has been lightly grated off the cob; the tough skins of the kernels should remain on the cob. Chief adjusts the wooden grater with its row of metal teeth set across a round hole over a bowl.

"There, deer jaw all set," he announces, picking up the grater. He has always been fascinated by Iroquois culture, and the fact that this is a way corn was prepared for the chiefs of old no doubt contributes to the fact that corn fritters are his favorite food. The

Indians grated the corn—green corn they called it, as opposed to dried—on the teeth of a deer's jaw bone. "Fritters are chewed twice," the Indians joked.

"Marn, pass me the bear oil; the stone looks about ready," he says, accepting from me the corn oil and pouring a little onto the griddle. He drops the grated corn in silver-dollar-sized cakes onto the sizzling griddle. When the cakes are golden brown on the bottom but still moist on top, he flips them one by one, hands me the flipper, and retires to the rocker to supervise.

"See boys, that's the way it's done," he grins.

At the big kitchen window Ken, watching the swallows skimming the pond, calls us all to come quietly and see the bluebird sitting on a wire, its rusty breast agleam in the golden light. Each year, and always this time of the year, we see just one or two bluebirds. I wonder where they spend the summer.

When we have eaten all the garden's bounty we can hold, we clear away the dishes. Through the window over the sink we see our neighbor Walter Bowers throwing cornstalks to the heifers. The hills are a deep blue tonight. The dishes rattle, the boys squirm over their homework at the kitchen table. The men rattle their newspapers and the rocker squeaks on the narrow floorboards. The kitchen here is still as kitchens were nearly everywhere in Victorian days.

We put the best sunflower seeds in warm salted water to soak overnight. Dried and crisped for fifteen minutes in the oven at about 300° they will be our winter treat and the rest will be for the birds. I hear my father telling my sons of the secret language he had with his brothers. "We called robins pleurs, house sparrows were zeerds, and the nuthatches we called yanks," he says recalling his own farm boyhood.

The last light of the long day gleams on the polished butternut wood of the staircase as we make our way upstairs to bed. The boys each swing the light chain as they pass, carrying it partway up the stairs and dropping it behind them. This chain—made up of the tiny metal balls that are often used in key chains—goes all the way up to the light in the upstairs hall ceiling, a clever but outlandish two-story pull cord that lets you operate the light from the lower floor.

David's room is at the head of the stairs. His door, like all the upstairs doors, bears the marks of Ryland's renovations on its white paneled front. Where clearly once was the bar of an old iron drop latch, now is fastened a brown, very Victorian doorknob. David's windows face the pond and barn and sunrise. And he has closets— added on to be sure, but three full doors of them.

Past the white stairwell railing with its graceful turnings, the wide painted boards of the hall floor slope downhill slightly to the front of the house. On the sunset side of the house are Tom's bedroom and ours. These front rooms, once the guest rooms, have flowered wallpaper—but no heat. (Both back bedrooms are painted and heated.) Company was to come only in the summer? And lest the guests should stay too long, Tom's room has no closet at all, and we have a token only, the merest triangle of a closet, formed by a tongue-and-groove paneled door across one corner of the room. Tom's room does have a floor ventilator with fancy scroll work whereby one could rob Peter of heat to pay Paul, the parlor below in this case.

At the end of the hall, on the front wall of the house, is a windowed door opening out onto a small porch. We open the door to let in the evening breeze. The top and bottom of the window frame are elegantly, if incongruously, carved in a Grecian dentil molding. It must have been very pleasant in Uncle Ryland's day, when this door opened out onto a piazza roof that ran the whole length of the front of the house.

The hills tonight are aglow with the orange sun and the rival brilliance of the first notes of autumn color. I hear a robin singing, "Pleur, pleur, pleur." He says we will have rain tomorrow. His last brood of youngsters is ready now to join the flocks and head south. We will probably have to use a different barometer for the next rain.

* * *

The robin was right; it looks as if the long gloomy days of autumn rains are setting in. Rain is pouring down, spangling the pine, bringing down golden maple leaves, painting tree trunks black, and soaking the silver barn boards dark.

The pigeons have plastered themselves on the vertical side of the barn roof hip, defying gravity in the slight curve where the roof flares out for the gutter. Now that is proof of how stupid pigeons are. Granted it is more sheltered there than on the upwind side of the barn, but they could go back inside the barn through the same window they came out earlier this morning. Pigeons are smart, I suppose. They have adapted to man's world. I just don't like them.

Secretly I welcome rainy days. I need them to make a dent in all the things I am supposed to do but keep putting off. I always have a huge backlog, for at the first ray of sunshine I can find some excuse to be outdoors. After all, we don't get that many sunny days up here. Given that philosophy, I would probably not make out very well in those parts of the country where they get their weather practically six months at a time. A half year of obeying my conscience would be quite a strain.

Today we have a pleasant job to do; we are making applesauce. We miss being able to cut the apples on the back steps in the sunshine, but we are not sorry to do without the yellowjackets, which would quickly broadcast to all their kind that we were peeling fruit for them. The irascible yellowjackets sorely lack the good manners of the bees.

From the kitchen we can hear the rain water trickling into the cistern in the cellar. You can imagine yourself in a cave, listening to water running into a secret cavern far off in the darkness of a lower level.

As we sit and core and quarter, we diagnose the various blemishes on the fruit. This mark, aptly named scab, is caused by a fungus organism. Here is the scar made by an egg-laying coddling moth; we will find that apple tunneled by the wormy larvae eating their way out. The artist who drew the fruit in an old volume of engravings we have included all these blemishes as characteristic of the varieties he drew; he considered them part of the nature of the apple. The modern housewife would probably not accept such apples as these we've plucked from long abandoned trees were she to find them wrapped in plastic in her grocery store.

We cook the apples soft and press them through a food mill, one pot of sweet pink and glossy Wealthy applesauce and another of yellow Black Twig applesauce. We sweeten and taste and blend until we have the combination of flavor and texture that pleases us most. We pour the perfected mixture into jars, and process them. The tall jars rattle companionably in the boiling water of the old blue agate canner. If only we could also bottle the warm, spicy fragrance of the kitchen! My father takes the apple trimmings out to feed the pigs. He does not return for quite some time; he likes to watch the pigs.

After lunch Ruby Latimer stopped by on her way into town with a cardboard carton full of ripe tomatoes. We add them to a basket of our own and set ourselves up to can a batch. We are making the most of the rainy weather; the canning kettle never cools the whole day through. This would be a tiresome job alone. Together, we form an efficient assembly line, each racing in friendly rivalry with the one next in line. One washes tomatoes in the sink. Another scalds them briefly—oh, so briefly—so they don't develop a taste well described as the flat-sours, and drops them to cool in the other sink filled with the well's coldest water. Next the rich red globes are deftly peeled, quartered, and packed into gleaming hot jars. Add a dash of salt, of pepper, of sugar, and pass the jars down the line for lids and rings. Another batch is ready to rumble around in the canner. The cooling jars make an impressive line. The red tomatoes go to the top, floating over an amber inch or two of juice. It always seems to me that they should sink. The domed lids of the cooling applesauce snap in, "ploink," and "ploink" again from farther down the line, as the sealing vacuum forms beneath the lids.

The rain has let up, the pigs have had a course of tomato peelings, and the first of the cooled jars have been squirreled away on the hoarding shelves in the cellar. The phone rings. It's Ann Huntley. "Today is primary day." What could she mean? I know it's not the Presidential primary. "It's for Pierrepont and we weren't sure you'd heard about it; Roger's running for councilman you know. . . ."

"Of course," I say. "We'll be down to vote."

I explain to Ken, and we go out into the silvery, dripping evening.

At the white, wooden town hall we find our neighbor, Mary Moran, seated at a small table in the center of the large room with two other ladies. They check off our names in their big yellow books and hand us little slips of paper on which we are to mark our choice of the candidates. These we then fold and drop through a slot into the appropriate box, REPUBLICAN or DEMOCRAT, while the ladies studiously scrutinize the ceiling. Ranged around the edge of the room in folding chairs that are attached to the wall sits a smiling assortment of Huntleys and four generations of Ostranders. We buy some brownies and cupcakes from a card table set up by the Husky Harvesters 4-H Club, and chat with our neighbors.

The little lady who guarded the voting machine our first year

here had gotten quite flustered trying to get the blue velvet curtains back on the track of the little voting booth after Ken had
pushed the levers and cast his ballot. (Do you suppose he tried to
vote Democrat on a North Country machine?) But he had won the
ladies' hearts at the covered-dish supper downstairs in the town
hall basement; he ate three kinds of pie.

We walk to our car parked in front of the abandoned gas pumps
of the long closed grocery store. Pierrepont Center today looks
better from a distance, but it must have been charming in its heyday. The ex-Vermonters of Pierrepont laid out their town in
proper fashion, with schoolhouse, town meeting hall, and church,
all in a row. Both the little schoolhouse and the church stand silent
and closed now. I wonder if the bell still hangs in the church
tower, inscribed: "This church bell was presented by Mr. H. E.
Pierrepont, of Brooklyn, New York, 1854." The enterprising building committee had convinced the wealthy New Yorker to donate
the bell to the little upstate town that bore his family name. He
was consequently rewarded with their esteem and gratitude and
a box of local butter, cheese, and honey.

Driving out of Pierrepont we pass a once-handsome brick house,
the small home of the town clerk, a lot where a cheese factory
once stood, some very spruce-looking farms, and some tenant farmhouses not quite as prosperous-looking. We are going to visit
neighbors, who want Ken to look at some giant puffball fungi
that have appeared in their yard. Mr. Millard leads Ken to a puffball fully two feet across, surrounded by several smaller ones—
basketball- and softball-sized.

We bring home some of the prodigious puffballs. Everyone
marvels at the biggest one. We cut open a smaller one. It is snowy-
white clear through, springy like a sponge. We cut up small
rubbery strips and fry them to a rusty golden in butter. What a
fantastic taste! Truffles couldn't taste sweeter. Even Ken, who
doesn't like mushrooms, agrees it is good. He still forbids us the
largest of the giants; he wants to take it in to the University.

I can feel that cold, clear air has been moving in this evening—
tomorrow will be a sparkling day. As I lie in bed mentally inventorying the possibilities of the new day, my soul practically
leaps out of me; I hear the call of the Canada geese for the first
time this fall! Very close, very clearly, I hear them; they must be

winging low over our ridge. Perhaps they will spend the night in our corn field.

When you try to describe that call of the wild geese to anyone else, you are really telling them about yourself. To someone old enough to have known a real loss, their passing cry in the night is the sweetest, saddest, most heart-piercing sound in the world. To untouched youth, it is the most thrilling call to vast adventure. What the geese are actually saying to each other, I cannot say, but no one can hear their cry and remain unmoved.

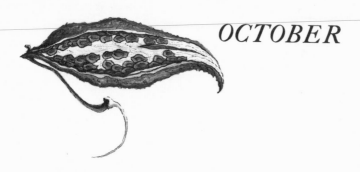

OCTOBER

THE MAN WEARS white coveralls, long white gloves stiff with newness, elastic at the elbows, white headgear that makes allowance for vision in the front but carefully covers head and shoulders, fitting down over his chest in front, extending across his shoulders in back.

"Hive tool," he mutters. His assistant places across his gloved palm a steel instrument slightly curved at the end.

"More smoke," he murmurs. "Now over on this side." Louder: "More smoke!"

At an angry buzzing he draws back. A misplaced step sends Ken —for the man in white is he—crashing back into a tangle of grapevines. We are trying to get the beehives ready to remove the honey.

It is the middle of a windless sunny day. Most of the bees are off in the fields at work and those still in the hive should be in a good mood. They don't like rain or wind or cold; that shows you what eminently reasonable creatures the bees are. We have to pry up the top box of honeycomb frames, known to the practitioner of the art of apiculture as a super, and insert under it a board fitted with a small metal bee escape in its center. This is a one-way gate that should empty this level of bees by tomorrow so that we can, unmolested, lift out the frames of honey. Propolis, or bee glue, cracks with a sharp report as we pry up the super with the long crowbarlike hive tool. Bees like neither sharp noises nor bumping on their hive, both of which we manage to supply in abundance.

I am wearing a somewhat less impressive costume than Ken's. My bee veil hangs over my face from a round hat brim and is tucked deep into my dark jacket collar. Bees supposedly dislike dark colors, but I have not noticed much reaction on that score. I insisted on bona fide bee gloves after my initial outing—my short gloves kept pulling out of my sleeves every time I reached over the hive to hand something to Ken. I wear ordinary faded blue jeans (not the ones with holes at the knees, which I once to my sorrow wore) and my heavy socks are pulled up on the outside of my pant cuffs.

My responsibility is the bee smoker. This is a little box fitted at one end with a nozzle and at the other a bellows. It sounds very picturesque and it is. The lady at the antique shop where we bought it was horrified that we intended to *use* such a quaint country artifact. It was in perfect condition, however, and even at conversation-piece price a good deal cheaper than a new one.

Inside the smoker box is a wad of rags or bits of rotten wood that we hope will burn and smoke the whole time we are working. I apply this anesthesia by puffing the little bellows and pointing the head of the nozzle toward the top of the frames, from which a line of bee eyes are somewhat hostilely surveying us. My job is to give the bees enough smoke to calm them, not enough to smoke up the honey or asphyxiate Ken.

Eventually we get the bee escape in position and move on to the next hive. In front of this hive buzzes an active crowd of bees. If the bees feel crowded they will take the queen (especially if you have been so foolish as to fail to provide your hive with a queen excluder, that piece of screening designed to imprison her highness in the brood chamber while allowing free passage to her subjects) and swarm, or fly off to begin a new hive. These bees are not clustering at the hive entrance so they may not have swarming in mind. They are not fighting, so the hive is not in the throes of repulsing an attack of robber bees. These are young bees, and they are playing! I find it reassuring that this highly regimented society still affords some of its members the opportunity of play.

In general, foolishly anthropocentric as it may be, I find the bee society disconcerting. Only the queen bee has any sex life. The males, or drones, do none of the hive work. The extra drones will soon get their due when they are unceremoniously tossed out of the hive as the colony gets ready for winter. The ordinary females are the workers. They begin life at cell cleaning. They graduate to nursing, caring for the young, and feeding the queen. The next duty they draw is ripening the honey and ventilating the hive with the beating of their wings. Then they become the masons, who build the combs, constructing the beautiful hexagonal cells for brood or honey from wax secreted from special cells on their abdomen. After two or three weeks of hive duty they are liberated to the fields. They spend their days as field hands gathering nectar and pollen and generally work themselves to death within a month and a half!

Our clumsy efforts at inserting the bee escapes cut short the busy lives of some. No matter how carefully we apply the smoke and the long, bristled bee brush to wipe them gently away, a few are inevitably squashed when we lower the supers back into position.

* * *

Today we are ready to take off the honey. Once more we approach the hives in our bee-proof costumes, being careful not to come between the bees and their front door. We lift the roof off the top super. It is not exactly deserted, and we wonder if the bee escape did any good at all. We decide to remove the honey anyway. Ken lifts up a well-filled frame. The cells are nearly all capped over with wax; the honey is ripe and ready. Gently he brushes off the bees and hands the long, heavy rectangle to me. I quickly wrap it in newspaper to keep the bees from continuing their labors on it and put it in the back of the waiting jeep. The bees are most persistent. Frame after translucent frame is wrapped and stacked in the jeep. Bee after bee tries to make her way back into the stacked honeycombs. Occasionally one of the bees gets angry and buzzes shrilly about our heads. This is very disconcerting. If too many bees change to this song, it is better to go away and come again another day. In general, as I have said, our bees are quite good-natured. I painted these hives with a fresh coat of white one day while the bees were busy in the meadows. The workers returning laden from the fields paid me no heed at all. These, by the way, are not wild bees, but gentle Italian bees of sunny disposition. The Caucasian variety are said to be the gentlest of all, and the black bees of the American South a very nervous sort. If the queen fails and the bees raise another to take her place you may get a hybrid population and these will be very cross bees indeed.

Bees communicate the location of honey sources by means of a waggling dance. It has also been demonstrated that Italian bees, for example, have their own distinct way of dancing and that mixing types of bees in a hive does, in fact, produce a tower of Babel.

We are tempted to apply what we see in the world of animals to the world of man by transferring it directly, or under the interpretation that suits our prejudices, or to reject it entirely. The pendulum swings all the way from the belief that man is not an animal at all to the feeling that the study of baboon societies can solve all the problems of today's teen-agers.

Nowhere are these tendencies more apparent than when it comes to a discussion of races. For plants and animals a fairly clear-cut and satisfactory definition of race exists: it is a group that has evolved into a genetically distinct population.

But ethnic man? Scientists from various disciplines are able to agree only that the number of human races today probably lies somewhere between the number one and a hundred.

Animal biology does indeed have relevance to human behavior, but the "truest" interpretation? If we can ever recognize when we have found it, it will probably lie not as far removed from old Aesop and his fables as one might think. Even science is metaphor.

At length we have dismantled the hives down to the brood chamber at the bottom and the food chamber above it which contains the honey left to see the bees through the winter. We drive carefully out of the meadow with our precious cargo. As we unload the sticky packages in the shed at the end of the garage, we calculate that from the three hives we have removed a hundred and thirty pounds of honey.

*　　*　　*

A sparkling, flawless noon! The maples are more gold than green. I would like to serve the sandwiches to our guest on the back steps in the precious autumn sunshine, but I'm not sure I dare. How could I explain the line of a few thousand bees streaming in and out of the cracks of the dark green shed door? They have found yesterday's honey. Even though the combs are still wrapped and hanging in extra supers I know they are taking back as much honey as they can. Did one of the sticky hitchhikers fly back with our secret, or were we betrayed by a clever scout this morning? We'll just have to wait until they have returned to their hives this evening, move the honey to the screened porch, and check our screens!

A small corner of the big woods over the hill to the west of us belongs to this farm. We decide to go check the apples that grow in the rocky pasture in front of the woods. The trees don't bear a crop in every year, nor do the worms invade the apples every year. Good cider is made from a blend of tart and sweet, hard and soft varieties, so off we go to see what this year has brought us.

This hillside once belonged to Oringe Crary, "The Pierrepont Poet," and his son, George Lucian Crary, who styled himself "The Adirondack Poet." Although today but a few gnarled trees remain, at the turn of the century the younger Crary wrote:

> On the Pierrepont hills a fine orchard stands
>> Where one hundred and twenty kinds vary
> In color and flavor and always command
>> The highest price when shipped by Crary.

Somehow the Adirondack Poet had also acquired the nickname of Skunk Crary. There are those in Canton today who remember the old man with his flowing white beard and extraordinary skill at grafting fruit trees. The bard of our hills does not mention, but folks recall, that he was apprehended shipping to select customers in Boston barrels of his choice apples, the centers of which were packed with plump, illegal partridge!

The fall foliage is nearing its peak of brilliance. Where once-green hedgerows murmured "trees," the species now wave bright-colored banners of their individual identities. The two golden-brown trees at the head of the line are ash; the short ones in reds and purples nearly blue are dogwood. Our northern species is modest in spring compared with the showy flowered southern species with its crosses of white bracts, but in the fall the little alternate-leaved dogwood easily rivals the southern one in splendor.

The sugar maples are a blaze of golden orange; the red maples true to their name, a bright, clear red. The birches rain yellow droplets in the breeze. Behind this bright parade stand the dark spires of the ancient hemlocks in the woods.

As we walk through the remnants of the apple orchard, we talk of hunting grouse, or partridge; how one would expect to flush a bird from the hawthorns into the open corridor at the wood's edge. Then suddenly, with a heart-stopping whir of wings, a ruffed grouse explodes from the leaves at our side, another, and then another! We were partly right—the grouse were there, but evidently we weren't expecting them enough.

The North Country is schizophrenic about hunting. The division between hunter and nonhunter partly parallels the division between the idealizing back-to-Mother-Earth movement of the young and the attitudes of the farmers who have long coped with Mother Nature. The issue stirs the passions and politics of both the bird watchers and the Chamber of Commerce.

The hunter is a harvester, needed to keep nature in balance; or the hunter is blood-happy—a shoot-at-anything-that-moves idiot. The conservation department shall manage our deer herds. No, the gun clubbers know they know more about deer. No, the politicians in Albany will tell us whether we will shoot the does, Mom, and apple pie.

Just leave the animals alone, let them do their own thing. God will provide. But we've taken their habitat; crabgrass, two-car garages, and backyard barbecues have moved in on them. We haven't left much room for the predators—bobcats, wolves, and coyotes—and we bounty them, besides. If we didn't shoot Thumper and Bambi, we'd be up to you know where in little animals—and then they'd all starve. Man the manipulator is going to have to get a whole lot cleverer.

We step into the dark of the tall trees. The hemlocks softly sigh above us. A gnarled old beech tree looms out of the shadows, its silver trunk twisted into a grotesque, enchanted rhinoceros form. We scuffle across the leafy carpet to Fox Rock, the great split boulder near the foxes' den. In a shaft of sunshine at the gray granite base curl a pair of brightly striped yellow-and-black garter snakes. They slide off into the beech leaves. The boys crawl through the tunnel in the rock. Polypody ferns and crustose lichens crown the boulder's brow. The shrill, angry birdlike call of an invisible chipmunk tells us we've outstayed our welcome in his dining hall.

Once more in the sunshine of the rocky pasture's slope, we read the summer's history in the apple trees. It's been dry; there's practically no scab. Leaf rollers have earned their names in the curled leaves. Here is a fruit spur with five little knobby green apples instead of one good fruit. Back when the trees were snowy with blossoms, the stings of the rosy aphis tricked all the blossoms into setting fruit instead of just the king bud in the center. Curculio have dimpled and gnarled these apples and apple maggots have railroad-tracked the flesh of others.

The new crop of bug men will have to learn the sounds of the leaves of the orchards—when they rustle with leaf rollers, when they are wet enough to be threatened with scab, when to spray and when not to spray. These creatures who would preempt our harvest are the most adaptable on earth.

I rob the grouse of a small bouquet of brilliant red hawthorn apples and gather the little bird's nests of the blossoms of Queen Anne's lace starting to set seed.

We climb the hill toward home, mentally mapping milkweed plants so we can find the new shoots for the kettle next spring. The brown pods, split at their center seam, are fringed with silvery floss. Every breath of wind sends hundreds of the seeds with their shiny parasols dancing away up into the blue.

As we clamber over the last hedgerow we discover some sweet wild grapes of almost Concord flavor. Most of our hedgerow vines bear beautiful bunches of grapes, but unfortunately grapes of unpalatable acidity. We purple our fingers and fill a bag with this precious find. Soon, all harvest-laden, we tramp through the meadow grass and into the golden light of our maples.

A car stops at the brow of the hill. Are they woodchuck hunters? No, they are leaf-lookers taking a picture of our golden maples. They turn and focus on the flaming sumac bush. We'll soon have to pick some of the red fuzzy spires of berries to soak in water to make Indian pink lemonade.

We pull our seedy little grapes off their stems and heat them just enough to perfume the kitchen and make the purple juices flow. We strain the thick rich juice, sweeten it, add water, then bottle it, and give it a short turn in the canner. This wonder fluid is still so strong we'll again have to dilute it by half when we serve it through the winter!

* * *

The grandparents have gone off exploring the countryside for a vegetable stand with some late-maturing sweet corn. I am taking a catnap. Thump! Something bangs into the front wall of the house. I look out the window and see on the golden leaves the brown, striped body of a ruffed grouse. The poor bird has broken its neck. I go out and gather up the still-warm lifeless bird.

As everyone is out, I put the bird in the bush by the walk to see if anyone will notice it. No one does. Ken and the boys return and go out to the barn for chores. My parents return and settle themselves, grating corn for fritters and reading the newspaper. Out in the barn I tell Ken about the grouse. After thinking a minute, he grins and sends me up to the ell attic by way of the back stairs for the old shotgun.

I smuggle the gun out to him, and the boys on cue call their grandparents out to see a line of gabbling Canada geese that have just this moment cooperated by winging slowly, deep in flying conversation, low over the barn. As my father reaches the door, he sees the dark line of geese and Ken grinning and holding the shotgun in one hand and a very dead ruffed grouse in the other. Most amazing! We all laugh and explain.

My father offers to show his grandsons how to dress the bird (odd expression for what is surely a most thorough undressing!). We put a large kettle of water on to boil, spread newspapers on the kitchen table, and lay the bird on them. Long square-knuckled fingers and short boyish ones reverently stroke the soft breast feathers. The boys save the jet-black feather ruffs at either side of the throat. They remove the wing feathers at the joint—old-fashioned lady's hat ornaments—and the fan of brown tail feathers banded elegantly with black.

Then they dip the bird in hot water and pull away handfuls of wet feathers. Soft gray down clings to their fingers. Such a tiny body under all that fluff! They remove the viscera; one boy chokes at the warm gamey smell but stays right there at the table. They admire the white-ringed trachea, the spongy, shiny lung sacs. They sort out the little heart, the hard-walled gizzard with its tiny stones, the soft-walled crop full of grapes. We've had no frost yet so the grapes are not yet fermenting. We have heard people say that the grouse get intoxicated feeding on fermented grapes and fly drunkenly into things. There's obviously more to the grouse "crazy season" than that. Whatever it is that triggers the dispersal of these young birds it is an effective, if bizarre, mechanism for regulating population density.

We wrap up the little bird to bake. It is sweet and delicious, remarkably meaty, with no shot to crunch on.

*   *   *

I have said that Steven Crary paid fifty dollars to have a picture of our house put in the 1878 *History of St. Lawrence County*. Several of his well-to-do neighbors paid an additional fifty to have portraits of themselves included. Steven Crary had the pictures of General Custar (sic), aged seventeen months, and Bullet included —his horses!

Here on the flat meadow that is now a corn field once stood the Crarys' trotting track. Across the road I can see the pile of rubble that marks the site of the caretaker's peripatetic house— it was once the north wing of our house. It must have been satisfying indeed for Ryland Crary at the height of his success to come up and lean on the fence watching his bay, Ryswood, trot by. Like his owner, Ryswood also cut a wide swath: he was for some time a record holder at all the area fairs.

Today we've come to fill the jeep with corn gleaned from the harvested field. Our jeep is fitted with a homemade wooden cab, jaunty and square, and painted bright red. The back panel lifts off easily—a summer convertible of sorts. Al Ostrander's tractor with its cutter-chopper-blower and wagon rig has finished cutting the corn here. At the ends of the field some of the tall stalks have been flattened by the tractor's wheels, putting those plants out of reach of the harvester's blade.

We walk the rows of stubble and gather ears of corn, tossing them into the back of the jeep. It hurts me a little to see the bare, stripped ground; corn is such a selfish crop. It tolerates no company of weeds. The farmers spray the ground with weed killers that let the corn grow in lofty isolation. Jim Latimer says he couldn't farm without the herbicides: He couldn't raise enough corn to feed enough cows to make any profit with today's lack of hired help. All the nutrients offered up by the soil are chopped up and hauled off to barns and silos. For a year or two this field will sway gently with a sea of oats, then timothy and clover. It will be hayed for several years before being plowed back to corn.

We'll have to husk all these ears, pull back the husks to let the nubby kernels dry so they won't mold. For our few animals it will be an easy chore, but I groan to think of doing it for a larger number and for a whole long winter's feed. I think probably we are always robbed of something in the Faustian name of Efficiency. A husking bee, with the merry companionship of young and old, when a young man found a red ear of corn, entitling him to a kiss—it may not be quite the trade we thought it was to ride the harvest rig alone, to stand and watch the whining blower fill your empty silo up.

There are frost warnings again for tonight—a frost watch, they call it. The sky is clear and far away. With no clouds to wrap the heat around us the night will probably grow cold. Our corn gathered, we bounce across the next field to pile the jeep with the winter squash and pumpkins. We find the butternut squash by following their long vines through the grass. We stagger under the weight of the big jack-o-lantern pumpkins and pat the bright, round sides of little pie pumpkins.

We drive into the barn with our precious load and pile the pumpkins by the colorful feed bags. We felt we were really accepted in the community the first time the Couglers gave us matching feed bags; you have the possibility of making so many more things with matching cloth.

We toss the pigs some corn, and with their approval we unload our knobby cargo. Alas, the alfalfa we cut with such pleasure the other day has begun to mold. "Make hay while the sun shines" must mean not scything it, but drying it in the sun to cure it. You can't feed stock spoiled hay.

We cover the tomato plants with blankets and burlap, pick the last of the dahlias, and go in to dinner. We're having fresh chicken tonight. We fill our freezer with the tender young cockerels culled yearly at this season from our neighbor's flock. It may be unkind to feed my boys such fare, because the day of the farm-fresh chicken has largely passed. At the supermarket meat counter the "fresh" bird in the plastic bag has the tag of a faraway place dangling soggy on its leg. Tom and David are going to have too fine palates to eat those, or chicken TV dinners, or soybean "chicken." Actually, it may be better for us all to forget our costly habit of eating meat. All the easier then to move down a step in the food chain—a more efficient way to keep an outsized population from starving.

*　　*　　*

Warming sunlight streams through our picture window. Mare's-tail clouds streak the sky and rising mists swirl over the pond. A blue-winged teal has joined our big ducks, dabbling in the shallows with them as though he'd always been there.

We are eating breakfast with three myrtle warblers this morning. They take turns clinging to the lichen-sprinkled shingles of the shed roof. These tiny birds look neat and trim in their blend of olive, black, brown, yellow, and white—a sort of mix-and-match with the shingles and the gray, green, and white lichen circles. When the little warblers launch themselves into the air like aerial stunt men, they flash a dazzling lemon-yellow rump patch, and their dark tail feathers fan out to reveal a pair of white spots at the margins.

"Confusing fall warblers," as the bird books so accurately call them when they are all wearing their drab, virtually identical winter plumages, are confusing enough. That is why, I suppose, the white underfeathers on the tails of the myrtle warblers are never mentioned. That would confuse them with the more prominently spotted magnolia warblers. Only if you were eating breakfast with them, marveling at their acrobatics, would you be most impressed with the way the morning light flashes through these white crescents.

Again and again the little birds rocket over the mock-orange bushes picking invisible insects out of the air. Occasionally a daredevil brushes his feathers against the window glass in a sharp turn. Even more rarely one of the little birds clings briefly to the narrow window molding, which affords scant purchase even to those incredibly tiny dark feet. For one quick wink the bright-eyed, white-chinned face peers in at us, inches away from our coffee cups.

Virginia creeper with leaves half turned to red has hung garlands of blue berries to ripen in the end-of-summer sun. One of the toy-sized birds reaches up and plucks a berry, a giant mouthful. Along the coasts the myrtle warblers feed heavily on bay-berries—which are more their size!

Reluctantly we clear away breakfast. The sun makes us lazy. Oh, to have the conscience of a cat!

*　　*　　*

The Kepes and Carlisle families, friends from the University, have arrived for one last apple-picking outing before a killing frost. They bear clanking cartons of empty wide-mouthed jars for honey, wine bottles of several types (some with gorgeous gilded labels), and soda bottles of our favorite size. Good friends!

Armed with boxes and bags we head for the apple trees. The children, and we are many, from tots to teens, are soon clowning in the tree branches at heights according to their daring. Apples rain down on the unwary to peals of laughter and joyous shouts from the trees. One soon learns to avoid the apples buried under the long grass; they taste of the ground. Bag after bag is filled.

We bag the Wealthies separate from the Black Twigs. Wealthies are sweeter but don't hold up as well as the Black Twig variety does in winter storage. The McIntoshes are our favorite munching apple, and the small green ones on the farthest tree make the best pie. Another tree, probably a wild seedling, bears hard red knobs that taste like sawdust. Everyone revels in the exhilarating autumn afternoon.

In every direction majestic new vistas are opening up: distant royal-purple hills appear between the golden banners of trees. Only a few hardy crickets still sing in the grass. Winter is not closing in; something is draining away—the birds, the leaves, the flowers, and the fruits. We hardly notice in the bright October days, as blue as the eye can see.

In the field below us a mare stands patiently by her yearling colt and this spring's sucking colt, napping side by side on the ground in the sun's warmth. Already the young ponies have grown shaggy coats for winter. The little ones get up and, kicking up their heels, frisk away as we draw closer.

We gather our retinue and apple bags, and make our way, Pied Piper style, still crunching sweet apples, back up the hill. The dark triangles of a pair of fighter jets scream by—look how low—over the barn. Our farm is in the path of practice bombing runs. Occasionally we see these planes heading out to "bomb" Lake Ontario as the radar facility boys score them. There's a serpent in every Eden.

We put our fruit gently in through the back windows of the station wagons and follow the children into the cool dimness of the barn. We feed the pigs, and gather up the warm brown eggs. The threatening eye of a hefty Rhode Island Red hen still sitting in her manger nest in the stall peers out at us through a wide crack in the wall.

"That one's going to lay an egg any minute now!" one of the girls announces with due excitement.

The children choose their Halloween pumpkins from the harvest heap, passing over the merely perfect to choose the funny, long thin one, the warty one, the smooth yellow one. The wives hand their husbands small, sweet, dark-orange pie pumpkins, and take one of the odd green squash to try. These are the mysterious offspring of the monstrous Blue Hubbard-type squash that appeared on our compost heap last year. Even if they don't taste good they are decorative. The huge, lopsided blue-green-orange parent squash spent most of last winter in the kitchen by our telephone. It made a good seat.

Reluctant children are gathered for the ride back to town. "I know she'll lay that egg if we could just wait a few more minutes!"

*　　*　　*

Venus came to breakfast this morning. The days are growing darker now. That lovely planet hangs glowing in the dark band above the golden horizon. We watch as we eat.

The rising sun outlines the frost feathers etched inside on the kitchen window. The long-anticipated frost glitters in icy needles on the grasses. Columns of mist steam off the pond; the sun glints on a film of ice at the water's edge. Lumpy snow granules and perfect flakes lie cupped in red and yellow leaves. Does the cold need practice?

The tiny warblers and the phoebes—and the occasional bluebird —who have been such good company this past month as they enjoyed dining on the insects of the air virtually without competition, will have to be moving on now. The blue jays will soon be leaving their summer home in the woods and come to dine at our feeders.

Blackened, cold-killed leaves hang limp on the dahlias like the dark oily rags of a garage mechanic. The dooryard button chrysanthemums, Oriental symbol of long life, and the sturdy mint patch nod brightly to the morning sun.

The frost has turned some of the leaf gold to mellower tones of brown, but the reds are more brilliant than ever. In winter we hear reports of the snow conditions at ski resorts in the area, but today the radio gives us the foliage reports for the touring leaf-lookers. The mountainous areas to the south of us have passed their prime—30 percent off, 30 percent brown, and 40 percent color. The High Peaks region and the Northern fringe are 50 percent red, 40 percent other colors, 10 percent past. Sounds so official, but I'll bet it all begins with a "guesstimate."

The mystic call of a line of Canada geese has brought me hurrying out into the fast warming sun. They are circling down over the hedgerow up by the old trotting track. Faithfully every fall they stop by up there. Do they, as we do, always stop at their favorite places? We will need to consider that when we work out a refuge system for them, I should think.

Weatherman says the full moon will bring a hard frost tonight, so we dig the beets. All the smaller ones will cook with their sweet greens tonight. The bigger beets will store well in the cool cellar.

We uncover the tomatoes, breaking off those vines that are still green, bearing handfuls of unripe tomatoes. We are engulfed in the smell—like no other—of the vines as we carry the trailing bundles to the house and up to the attic stairway. The vines hanging here in the dry darkness will ripen these golden globes, not to the juicy redness of the ones from the field, but they'll be good enough for November.

* * *

Our radio station from Ottawa tells us that today is Thanksgiving Day in Canada. We will feast today with our northern neighbors because the grandparents are leaving soon and won't be here for the Yankee holiday. Our harvest is gathered in; we are ready for giving thanks. Frost has come to the North Country, but Washington says we must wait till the end of next month—ours will be a root-cellar Thanksgiving.

Couldn't we have Thanksgiving zones like time zones?

*   *   *

The trout truck has had to wait for cool weather to make its rounds from the hatchery. A postcard informed us of the hour and place of our appointment to pick up the fish for our pond. Our allotment is eighty-one trout according to the card.

With three large milk cans of cool clean water in the back of the jeep, we follow a trail of water dribbles and puddles into the parking lot behind the grocery store where the hatchery truck waits. The very official pickup truck is outfitted with a tank, a chugging aerator motor, and a very starched and pressed officer. The multicolored patches sewn on his khaki shirt gleam as he dips out wriggling brook trout, four or five inches long, from the tank in the back of the truck. He passes buckets of fish down to the owners of the motley assortment of pickups—and one red jeep—that surrounds him. We hand our card up to him. He mumbles, "Twenty, thirty, five, fifty, seventy, eighty, one," barely audible above the chugging, jiggling motor. I never dreamed the card would be taken literally. He tells our boys to splash their hands in the water occasionally to keep the water well oxygenated. They are glad to oblige as we head for home.

We ease our way down the pasture, letting our jeep, but not the curious heifers, through the gate, and lift out the heavy milk cans to the water's edge. Slowly we lower the long cans in on their sides so that the pond water mixes gradually, reducing the shock of temperature change. The young fish eye us calmly, and after a while their dark forms stream slowly, effortlessly, out into the pond.

The fisheries officer said we need expect no mortality. The next morning we find no still forms floating belly up. Four quick shadows dart from the sunny shallows off to deeper waters. The pond has a new personality.

*   *   *

I pull on my shiny black rubber Wellingtons and slog out to the barn to take care of the pigs. As soon as they hear me coming they heave themselves up from the straw where they have been slumbering blissfully, leaning against each other. They stretch themselves up so that their front feet rest on the edge of their stall and their intelligent faces lean out eagerly. They seem to "oink" on the inhale. Since I cannot pour their food into the trough while they are standing over it, I walk over to the pile of husked corn and choose two ears. "Pork Chop" and "Bacon" jump down at once; they know this game. When I throw both ears to the far side of their stall, they gallop over and jostle each other to see who gets which ear.

Quickly I dip out a ration of their feed, which has been mixed with water and left to soak to a puddinglike consistency. Reaching over the side of the stall I pour it into their trough. Now they will be occupied so that I can clean their quarters a bit. Contrary to reputation, pigs are not smelly or dirty. They deposit their excrement in neat cylinders in one corner of their stall. I open the gate, let myself in, and prop the gate open far enough so that I can shovel out the manure and wet straw into the large, flat pan that stands just outside. It was once a maple syrup boiling pan, then a cement mixer. Now we have threaded a chain through the horseshoe handles on it and use it sled-fashion behind the jeep as a manure spreader. "Pork Chop" or "Bacon"—we never try to tell which is which—comes up behind me and starts to chew on my boot top. I let myself out and slam the gate. That busy-body chewing habit and their ever-increasing size are the only things I don't like about doing the pigs. I like to stand and look at them. They have nice long backs, a sign of a meaty pig.

Ken has been considering the fate of "Pork Chop" and "Bacon." He has decided that we will smoke the meat ourselves this time. Not being sure how he felt about smoked pork chops, he decided to try some before he is confronted with three hundred pounds. Against my better judgment he climbed up on the roof and suspended a rack of chops (the Latimer pork from our freezer) down the chimney. It is so windy that the power lines have been down all day, but we are sung and warm in front of our fire. The boys have roasted potatoes, squash, and apples in the coals. We baked scrumptious golden-browned biscuits in the little tin reflector oven facing the flames. There is more to hearthside cookery than novelty. Unlike an oven with a thermostat, the shiny surface of the reflector oven casts an unwavering heat down on the biscuits or corn bread or coffee cake, browning them to tender perfection. The smoked pork chops are a real treat, but I don't think I can be persuaded to become an ardent advocate of rooftop chimney cooking.

*   *   *

It is the custom of the neighborhood to put out decorations for Halloween. When the leaves have fallen from the trees, baring the branches to the windy skies, porches and piazzas bloom with jack-o'-lanterns and scarecrows.

Leaves from the yard now stuff blue overalls and the tattered jacket of a booted dummy, complete with red neckerchief, pumpkin head, battered brown felt hat, and corn cob pipe. He sits in a lawn chair by the mailbox or sprawls on the porch steps.

Sheeted ghosts flutter in the trees at the Huntleys'. Across the road the biggest jack-o'-lantern from the field smiles back from the shelter of a corn shock tied firmly around the porch post. Nearly every place the school bus stops there are paper cats and bats and witches in the windows and lines of pumpkins on the porch.

By six o'clock it is already dark. A double row of lighted jack-o'-lanterns shines on the Latimer steps. The oldest boy condescends to stay home to hand out treats. Might as well, he shrugs. His eyes reveal how much he really likes the job. Dad is in the milkhouse; Mom loads her hobo, witch, and princess into the car to make the rounds of neighbors and kin. In the poorer sections of the countryside, battered Fords and Chevies have long since left for town. Disheveled children, expressionless behind the garish plastic masks that are their only costume, will dutifully hold out pillow cases at every door, trudge up one street and down the next, periodically unloading at the car waiting at the corner the cheap candies to which the townspeople, angered at the annual anonymous invasion, have resorted. And that is how you kill a custom.

Trick-or-treat begins at Grandma Latimer's down the road in the little green house. She is looked after by her sons and surrounded by their Hereford cattle in her pastures. She passes out luscious chocolate bars by the handful. Next comes our road, with just four families. First, Walter and Emma Bowers at the corner for beautifully polished McIntosh apples and whole packages of Life Savers in shamefully generous quantities, then our house, then the Couglers. Here's Norvelle, called Budge, and Oswald, called Joe (they run the feed store twenty miles away in Heuvelton). Budge Cougler hands out homemade bright-orange frosted cookies. Then up to Joe and Mary Moran's candy bowl. Joe sold his cows the same time Walter Bowers did; they gave each other moral support when Roger auctioned off their cows for them. Roger's wife is Grandma Latimer's daughter—she makes the great popcorn balls in their candy bag. Across from the Huntleys' is the Al Ostranders' farm, but Al is up milking with his dad. His wife, Rita, and his daughter, Cheryl, are probably getting treats over at our house about now. We go next door to Ostranders, senior. Gerry does the honors for the family, dispensing little bags made up with peanuts, pennies, and every kind of candy you can imagine.

Around the corner toward us lives one of Grandma Latimer's boys, Bob, who owns the Herefords. We stop to let their big boy, Monty, guess who our boys are and hand them treats. The twin blue silos at the next corner (emblazoned Latimer and Sons—there are three of them—aged fourteen, eleven, and eight) mark the farm of Grandma Latimer's son Jim and his wife, Ruby. Jim gives the boys some teasing and some delicious brownies that Ruby and Patricia made. The brownies are especially tender and moist because they are made with chicken fat. The boys sample some on the spot and carry more home. Behind Jim's place live the Lelands. Alyce, who sews shirts for the boys, is Rita's grandmother. Her husband, Babe, lets the boys dig into the candy corn, and Alyce gives us all cupcakes.

How could we eat so much and still come home with brimming bags? We don't ration it out in this household. The boys can gorge themselves until it's gone; and then we don't hear much teasing for sweets for a while.

RUBY'S BROWNIES

The Latimers are a large family, so you could cut this recipe in half and bake it in an 8" x 8" pan. The brownies are so unusually good that you really ought to bake the whole batch.

To get the chicken fat, you will need the fat from the body cavity of four or five chickens. You can freeze the fat from successive chickens until you have enough to render (or ask your favorite local restaurant to save some for you). Melt the fat over low heat, and it is ready to use or store. If you are culling a lot of plump young birds from your flock, you render the fat in the same way and store it in the refrigerator for a month or so, or in the freezer if you have so much that you need to keep it longer. Chicken fat is excellent in cookies—simply reduce the amount of butter called for in the recipe to two thirds. You may have to add a little liquid (milk or water).

The Brownies

4 ounces (4 squares) unsweetened chocolate
½ cup melted chicken fat
4 eggs (unbeaten)
2 cups sugar
1⅓ cups flour
1 teaspoon baking powder
½ teaspoon salt
2 teaspoons vanilla
(1 cup nut meats)

Melt the chocolate in the chicken fat over low heat. Remove from heat. Mix eggs and sugar, and add to chocolate mixture. Stir in the remaining ingredients, including nuts if you like them. Spread in a greased 13″ × 9″ pan. Bake at 350° for 25 minutes. Do not overbake. Frost when cool.

The Frosting

1 ounce (1 square) unsweetened chocolate
4 tablespoons butter
2 cups confectioners' sugar
2 tablespoons hot water
1 teaspoon vanilla

Melt the chocolate slowly with the butter. Remove from heat and stir in remaining ingredients and beat until smooth. Spread on the brownies.

This makes a thin, crisp frosting that is a marvelous addition to the chewy, rich brownies.

NOVEMBER

THE MAPLES in the front yard form a golden aisle no longer. We hardly have to rake the leaves; the wind will blow them away before the first heavy snow, but we like to have some leaves for covering the bulb beds and for tucking in around the shrubs. Most of all the boys like a big pile just over the garden wall. They camouflage the brink and take turns scuffling through the leaves and off into space, to sink laughing into four feet of rustling maple leaves. Then they cover themselves with the pungent leaves, and only the gentle sighing of their breathing and the undulating of the leaves above their squirming bodies give away their hiding place. It could be my brother and I playing in the leaves when we were kids, except that now the all-pervasive fragrance of burning leaves, once the hallmark of autumn, is missing. That is the one form of pollution I can think of for which we all feel nostalgia.

We keep a watch for our lone remaining guinea hen. Yesterday we saw the three big birds teetering absurdly on a wire above the hen yard and then they were gone. Mrs. Leland called to report that two of the mad adventurers had been killed on the road at her corner. But they were gone before we could get down there. Guinea hens are good eating.

We don't see any of the heifers in the meadow. They're always getting out at this time of the year—looking for greener pastures— so we go down to our pasture to check. There they are, all of them, dolefully eying the empty water trough down behind the pond. One of them bangs the trough with her knee and the hollow gong reverberates across the short-cropped meadow.

Ken is gone, the Ostranders are off for the day, and so are the grandparents, but David says he knows how to fix the plugged-up siphon, so we slide down the bank of the pond to the trough. Tom watches from the safety of the bank while we inch under the electric fence.

"First you unhitch that silver clamp."

I unhitch the clamp and water pours out of the black plastic hose. David holds the gushing pipe on the edge of the trough, and the heifers jostle one another to reach the stream and lick the bottom of the trough. We find refuge on the uphill side of the trough, being ever so careful not to back into the electric fence as my father did when he came down to pull a polliwog out of this mechanism. Court had not exaggerated his polliwog story!

I unscrew the shut-off valve from the side of the trough. This ingenious gadget contains a block that floats on the surface of the water in the trough and shuts off the flow when the tank is full. I poke at the clogged valve. "Back off, you heifers, you." Eventually I remove yet another polliwog, and prepare to hook up the hose again. Now I understand why Ken returned soaked from head to toe when he did this: there is no way to stop the water gushing out of the pond through this pipe while you are trying to screw it back onto the shutcock. The heifers get squirted on their big silly heads. Serves them right for butting in. We get squirted; I do not have enough strength in my hands to force the pipe and valve together long enough to engage the screw threads.

"Watch out! I don't think we'd better squirt the fence."

Then it occurs to me to kink the pipe under my foot. That does it. I screw the valve hastily onto the barely gurgling pipe and we are back in business.

That evening we entertained the clan with the tale of our turn with the polliwog. "All I had to do was kink the pipe to stop the water," I said innocently.

"You *didn't* kink that expensive plastic pipe!" Ken roared.

I changed the subject.

*　　*　　*

A light snow has dusted the ground during the night. It is roundup time. The morning milking must be finished; here is Court at the foot of our meadow, with pickup trucks and a car full of hired hands and recruited friends. Alan rides up on a brown-

and-white cow pony, his dark collie trotting happily along. They
are unhooking the fencing at the gates in order to drive the
heifers from our pasture across the road into the Ostrander pasture
on the other side. From there they can herd them through the
cut in the woods to their own barn for the winter—they hope.

As usual the heifers come right over to see what is going on.
Their coats have begun to thicken up for the winter and they are
sleek and fat from their summer's grazing. They look good. The
gates are open, no cars are in sight on the road. The men move
slowly up behind the cattle. And then those heifers bolt and trot
off across the meadow! Alan gallops after them to head them off.
They turn and trot back to the corner. A heifer breaks away but
the dog cuts it off, barking and nipping at her heels. The men
wave their arms and yell. The heifers that have lately been so
eager to cross the fence line now look as if they will have to be
dragged across.

Again and again they wheel, and Alan and pony take off after
them. The group races and turns with skidding speed. They brush
against a section of rail fence; horse and rider roughly graze a
tree in the melée. They stagger, but fly on unhurt.

Three of the heifers trot across the road. A line of cars is
waved on while horse and dog and men regroup the remaining
cattle. Another pair crosses over, and a third. One heifer tries to
bolt up the highway but an approaching pickup truck changes
her mind. More arm flapping and shouting and pounding, and the
last of the heifers is safely across.

The cowboy and his dog expertly work the little band of heifers
across the field and down the path through the woods. The men
and trucks head back to the barn by way of the road. The turmoil
and pageantry are over.

Our pasture looks very empty.

*　　*　　*

We have a roundup of our own this frosty dawn. It's time to
bring the ducks up to the barn for the winter. Ken and the boys
sneak around the back edge of the pond to appear suddenly behind
the ducks sleeping on the bank. They drop a net over Biggy
and pounce on Brownie and Blackie. Tucking Biggy under one
arm, Ken nets the fleeing Semi with the other. It's quite a chore
for the boys to carry these heavy flapping bundles with the wriggling feet. Tom trips and a duck flutters loose. Pinioned ducks

quack and the indignant drake hisses his complaints. The frightened duck is easily recaptured and the procession makes its way to the barn.

The ducks are released in the fenced-in hen yard with the chickens where they can all enjoy the sunshine and dust baths a few more days while their winter quarters are being readied. The chickens' summer home is the corner stall that communicates with the hen yard by a little door. The stall is equipped with a large round feeder, an automatic waterer, and straw for nests in an orange crate and the wall mangers.

Outside, the hen yard has been scratched and nibbled nearly bare. In one corner are the hollows that the little black Cochin bantams have scooped out for their dust baths. They scratch vigorously, and then settle into the depression, casting up clouds of dust with their ruffling feathers, just as a robin would bathe in water. A big Rhode Island Red hen stalks by, her feathers shining a beautiful even rust color in the sun. Another scratches the dry ground with her yellow feet. She stirs up something— her head flashes down and the insect disappears into her sturdy beak. "Puck, pucka-Buck!" issues from inside the barn. A hen struts out through the low door into the sunshine, having duly announced the laying of a large brown egg.

The woolly gray sheep on the other side of the fence stands immobile, chewing on a mouthful of grass. He's not impressed.

*   *   *

"Go on home, Rascal!" I pick up a corn cob and throw it at the retreating dog. That's the third time today I've sent that dog home. He is a sandy-colored, raw-boned, blue-eyed, part-Samoyed dog that was given to Gary Cougler. The dog is rambunctious, still a playful pup, but too rough for my taste. As he runs off up the road I hear the school bus pulling up the hill.

The boys tumble into the kitchen and head for the refrigerator. David flashes a blue and white and orange ring. "See what Margaret gave me today," he says. "She got it from a penny gum machine." She probably thinks it means true love; he thinks it will make a dandy collar for Dimetrodon or Allosaurus, his plastic dinosaurs.

The phone rings. It's Gary; he sounds miles away. He asks if all our ducks are here. He just found a big duck with a green head out in the shed where Rascal lives. It must be Biggy. Poor ducks. Poor Gary!

Ken pulls into the driveway and I go out to meet him with the story. He goes into the barn and returns a few minutes later, his face pale, shaking his head. "Rascal got them all, except for one bantam and the ducks. One of the ducks is pretty badly chewed up," he tells me softly so the boys don't hear. "If only we could have had them moved into their winter pen. . . . He must have jumped over the fence and squeezed in through their little door. I didn't think he could fit through there."

Ken calls the boys and takes them in the car up to the Couglers' to reclaim Biggy, who apparently has survived his strange odyssey. In the car Ken tells the boys about the birds, and sends them, quiet, into the kitchen on their return. David stands staring thoughtfully out the kitchen window; his usually irrepressible little brother sits still in the rocking chair by the stove while their father takes Biggy to the barn alone.

After a while Ken comes in tenderly carrying the wounded Brownie. She has a gaping tear across her back that exposes a large red section of flesh. We spread newspaper on the kitchen table while Ken sterilizes a needle, and thread is located. We are going to stitch poor Brownie up. I lean down on the big bird, passing my arm around her soft neck and up across her wings. With my other hand I try to hold her feet immobilized.

She doesn't struggle much. Occasionally she shudders and starts at the needle prick, and from time to time she shifts her weight. Ken sews on. I stroke her dappled breast and look sadly into that dark unblinking eye of hers. How tough these "lesser" animals are! Many are the animals we've sewed up like this—a whole procession of rabbits, once before a bantam, and a cat-mauled chipmunk. Each of them looked like a hopeless case, but as far as we know, they all survived.

So there is hope for Brownie. She squirms again. The boys are still watching, but I'm sure they're wishing at the same time that they could look away. "There," says Ken fastening off the thread in a surgeon's knot, "that's all we can do for now." He takes her back to the remnants of the flock in the barn, and boards up the little door to the hen yard.

We never saw the dog who was too well named again.

I have never understood before how "blue" could mean something different to each beholder. Now that I have to buy our eggs from the store I understand. The white things in those cartons are "eggs" to other people but to us they don't taste much like the eggs we gathered from our flock.

It didn't take Ken long to decide to go see our neighbor Dick Briggs, who has a good-sized flock of chickens and raised the ducklings we gave him last Easter. Ken has admired the coloring of Dick's bantams. He loads burlap sacks and boys into the car and off they go; just for a visit, they tell me.

Next morning it is suggested that it is my turn to feed the chickens. I oblige and enjoy the surprise of a pair of guineas, two new golden banty hens, a chick, and a young rooster. "Cock-a-doo!" he greets me. I hope he learns the rest of the phrase when he grows up.

Brownie is healing well and two more black bantams and a Rhode Island Red have reappeared from hiding places in the upper reaches of the barn. Fresh eggs again!

* * *

The bees did not find their way into the honey on our porch. We bring in the heavy frames of honey to warm over the registers. We are going to extract the honey today. Once upon a time you had to put the combs of honey in the oven to melt all the beautiful little wax cells. The honey would then settle in the bottom of the pan, and the wax float to the top. When it cooled, you could lift off the wax to claim the honey—an arduous and even messier job than what we'll do today, thanks to the invention of the honey extractor.

The large tin cylinder Ken is roping firmly onto the top of a white wooden hive box is a honey extractor. He lowers into the extractor a metal mesh basket and tops it with some gears fitted with a knob handle. Next he fits a pail with a milk strainer. Across the mouth of the strainer he places a scrap lumber board, in the center of which there stands the sharp end of a nail. He puts the long capping knife in a pan of hot water on the stove to heat the blade. Grandmother covers the counters with newspapers. The boys line rows of shining jars down them.

The honey on the registers has warmed up, so we can begin. Ken takes a frame of honeycomb and balances it on the nail. Sawing upward with the hot capping knife, he opens the gleaming honey cells. He holds the frame angled slightly toward him so that the wax cell caps fall into the strainer in jagged sheets of light-colored, brittle wax. He twirls the frame around and uncaps the cells of the other side.

We lower the oozing frame into the basket of the extractor and balance a second bar of honey opposite it. The boys finally reach agreement as to which of them will have the first turn, and the knob of the extractor is whirled faster and faster. Thrown out of the cells by centrifugal force, shining flecks of honey sparkle down the drum walls. The empty combs are lifted out, light now and translucent. We suspend them in an empty super to return them to the bees, who will clean them up and refill them with much less effort than building a new comb.

Over and over, the knife is heated, the capping wax drops away in softly clicking sheets, the frames spin, the extractor clatters to a halt, and the sparkling drops silently coalesce into a growing pool of honey. Again and again we put pots under the spiggot at the bottom of the extractor and open the honey gate to the sluggish flow. We try to separate the light, minty basswood-blossom honey, the redolent clover honey, and the molasses-dark buckwheat honey.

We heat the honey carefully to 150° and strain out bee legs, bee wings, and bits of wax. Heating makes the honey less apt to crystallize later and more apt to pass through the straining cloth now.

Tom applies himself intently to pulling out the supporting wires from a frame of honeycomb without breaking the cells, while David cuts square pieces of the comb to put in the best-looking jars for decoration. We have tried putting 4" × 4" plywood frames for comb honey in the hives, but our bees have never deigned to fill them.

Last comes the sticky job of pouring the golden treasure into the waiting regiment of jars. Tiny air bubbles rise, the caps are screwed down, and that part of the job is done. We put the pail of sticky cappings aside to drain.

By now we all have honey in our hair, honey on the counters, honey making crackling noises of our footsteps and an absurd fly-paper game out of all our newspapers. The kitchen air is cloying; we can no longer taste any difference between the honey flavors. We have plenty of honey to send back to California with the grandparents, and for all the relatives along the way!

We clean up and sit down. Aahhh!

*   *   *

Ken and the boys have spent a lot of time in the hedgerows
this fall, cutting dead elm trees and thinning the basswood, ash,
and red maples, which will eventually replace the dying elms.
They hitch the felled trees to the jeep and haul them back to the
barnyard to be sawed and split. Ken is anxious to teach the boys
the art of splitting wood and the joy of physical work.

Cutting wood is something Ken is always about to do for exercise. Piles of logs and branches build up across the back walls
of the garage and accumulate in the barn from our roadside
gleanings after storms or highway department devastations. Ken
finds that his small bow saw makes slow progress through the
seasoned rock maple (a far cry from the times he used to saw
up waist-high fallen Douglas firs in Washington with the Forest
Service). Handsaw and pride yield to an electric chain saw, which
is quiet, easy to handle, and readily chews through the limbs the
boys feed over a sawhorse.

However, an electric saw limits one to the fifty-foot radius of
a heavy-duty extension cord, so we borrow a gas chain saw for
the hedgerow work. Ken says that when he uses the electric saw
he cannot keep the image of a power plant somewhere else,
belching smoke, from the back corners of his imagination. With
the gas saw there is no somewhere else—the dense blue smoke
billows around, and the air is rent with an insistent whine.

Whether or not you use a power saw, an element of woodsman-
ship remains. Ken shows us how to undercut a log on the far side
so it will break off cleanly, to put in a wedge or block up the butt
end of a log to keep the log from pinching and binding the saw
blade.

Today we have a dead ash with a straight grain, unlike that
of the twisted, iron-hard elm, so the splitting is fun. Ken shows
the boys how to turn the piece to find a natural crack for the
beginning split, and to deliver a blow with the double-bitted ax.
However, the logs are too large, and the boys' aim leaves something
to be desired. Ken turns to a steel wedge and an eight-pound
sledgehammer, or maul. Choking up on the handle of the maul,
Ken taps the wedge into a crack until it sticks; then he takes a
full swing. If he misses, he will knock over the whole works,

perhaps splintering the handle of the maul on the wedge. If he strikes a sound blow, the ring of metal on metal will resonate in the splitting wood. As John Henry sings:

> I'm aswingin' nine pounds from my hips on down
> Listen to that cold steel ring. Lord, Lord.
> Listen to that cold steel ring.

The ash cleaves in one clean blow; the frosted fields ring. The pieces are tossed into the wheelbarrow. Load after load is trundled to an open cellar window and tossed in to join its fellows in limbo. The split logs and branch lengths make no neat pile in the cellar—the wood stays where it lands. When winter weather confines them indoors, Ken and the boys will rearrange it into piles—homes for the field crickets that still sing in the cellar.

With a little practice you can tell ridge-barked slow-burning elm logs from the silvery, quicker-burning maple. You can distinguish the fine, regular grain of hardwoods such as apple, maple, or cherry from the coarse, open grain of the soft pine or spruce or poplar. Softwoods burn straight away to ashes; hardwoods produce a good bed of coals.

To build our fires we always start with a big log placed up on the andiron legs across the back of the fireplace. In front of it we nestle two or three pieces of kindling—split pieces of a resinous softwood, or maybe some maple branches no bigger around than a child's wrist. Under the kindling, we tuck scrap paper—our junk mail—from the hickory splint basket beside the hearth. Then we put another good-sized log across the andirons at the front and, reaching under it with a single match, light the blaze.

To keep the fire burning brightly there's one easy rule: Keep the two logs together, near enough to keep each other warm, and far enough apart—about a finger's breadth—for breathing room.

Good fire, good marriage, same rule.

*　　*　　*

We are going to see Molly Rebo, the Indian basketmaker, at the St. Regis Reservation before the snowy weather closes in. As we pull into town at the edge of the reservation, we note a sign that still reads "Hogansburg." Not long ago the Mohawk braves made headlines by repainting the signs to read "Akwesasne." The original Mohawk name, which means "where the partridge drums," has been reinstated by the Native Americans in a pointed gesture of ethnic identification. Now we need some help locating the address on the envelope Molly gave us.

We stop at a small building with a big sign indicating that lacrosse sticks are made here. Entering what is both showroom and warehouse, we are confronted with lacrosse sticks hanging from ceiling to floor in long rows across the entire room. The proprietor is happy to give us what directions he can and tell us about the manufacture of his sticks. The long handles are split out of hickory wood, but it's getting harder to find decent hickory, so plastic has already begun to replace it. The sticks are steamed and bent two times to shape the crook; then they are sent to various Indian families in the area who lace in the net pockets.

We are shown a series of oil paintings of Indian lacrosse games, done by a reservation artist. Thousands of braves used to gather for the games, we are told. They played the rough game for days, carrying dead players off the field without interrupting the game. Some sport! Some story!

The boys in mock innocence nudge the lines of sticks into swinging motion as they pass them. The sticks are marked with the flashy decal of a well-known sporting-goods manufacturer. They will be shipped out to colleges and prep schools to owners who will never guess that they were made by Mohawk hands.

We follow our directions through the Indian settlement with its large Catholic church, its community hall bearing a Mohawk name. We pass some shacks, some small but comfortable homes, and a few that look very prosperous. The Mohawks of St. Regis are among the best high-steel walkers in the world. Perhaps they have no fear of heights; certainly, working high on the girders of rising skyscrapers, they make excellent money. Supposedly the tradition began some eighty years ago when workers on a bridge job on the Quebec side of the reservation found Indians calmly looking over their shoulders as they worked out on the narrow girders. Although these Mohawk steelworkers can only get home for weekends, about half of the working force of the reservation is so employed.

Electricity came to the reservation in 1951. Although the traditionalists, or Longhouse people, have adopted cars and television, a modern life style is a problem they have to come to terms with. And there is also the problem of money—the Indians cannot get mortgages because it is reservation land, which is owned by the tribe; hence there is nothing a bank could repossess. As progressive Chief John Cook says: "It's very difficult for a child to have flush toilets and drinking fountains at school and then go home and have to carry water from a little hole in the ground."

When we finally reach Molly's modest home, the old man who opens the door tells us to come back in an hour; Molly has not yet returned from her weekly shopping trip to Massena. Standing in Molly Rebo's yard, we can see the graceful International bridge to Cornwall, Canada, arching up over the little unpainted building.

We decide to go watch the big tankers and freighters pass through the locks in the St. Lawrence Seaway. Freighter traffic is very heavy since all the captains are trying to get their vessels out of the system before the Seaway freezes up for the winter. The great ships pass one at a time into the lock; they sink slowly as the water level is lowered in the lock, just the towers and turrets visible against the skyline, and sail out the other side to the sea.

The hour passes quickly, and our boys are now glad they chose to come. We head back past the sprawling gray aluminum and automotive plants—another odd juxtaposition to the island refuge of the Indians. Many Mohawks resented industry coming to their island, but the ugly plants mean jobs, and more men can live at home.

The Seaway and concomitant industry have been a mixed blessing: some of the Indians have given up raising dairy cattle because of the fluorides raining down in the plant emissions. The Mohawks have seen their fishing and guiding business fall off because of oil spills and effluent discharges. Of course the industries themselves have become aware of the problems and work to alleviate them, but when you believe as the Indians do that the Earth is your Mother, the white man's heavy-handedness in dealing with delicately balanced ecosystems is hard to take.

This time we have better luck at the Rebos'; Molly herself invites us into her home. We step into an enclosed porch heaped with baskets and splints, fragrant with sweetgrass braids—her workshop. The little place feels tropical in spite of the raw November

day. The other room has a wood stove on which is sizzling a
pan with one pork chop remaining. Molly and her aged uncle are
just finishing their dinner at the little table, which is the only
piece of furniture in the room besides some chairs. The old man
retires to the sleeping alcove at the far end of the room and
composes himself, sitting upright, hands resting flat, palms down
on his knees, in meditation.

Ken produces the jar of honey that we have brought for her.
Molly serves us sweet, strong tea that has been brewing in an open
pot on the back of the stove, probably all morning long. Indian
custom demands that the host offer what food he has, even to
strangers or enemies, in the sanctuary of his home. And the offer
must not be refused.

Molly settles her round, aproned figure on a chair amid the
clutter of splints and we talk baskets. She shows us how she peels
the long, flexible ash-wood splints in a wooden vise held between
her knees. She cuts the strips with a gauge in her lap; the gauge
is a wooden-handled tool fitted with points of scrap metal that
divide the splints evenly into widths for weaving. She makes a
six-strand star on her generous lap, and her nimble, smooth brown
fingers fly around it with a narrow weft. She stops and steps outdoors into the cold yard for the bottom of a basket that she has
out there being kept flat and damp by board and weight. She will
turn up all the strands, perhaps around a wooden form, perhaps
not, and weave up the sides to finish this basket.

Molly fingers an old coil of sweetgrass that is hanging on a
nail on the wall behind her. "I remember when I made this . . . I
was in the jail. I had a fight with this woman and they put me
in there, you see?" David's eyes widen and Tom listens attentively.
Molly laughs and shows us a decorative twist, the Indian name
of which means something like the ends of your fingers. It looks
like a row of fingertips.

She tries to describe an old honeycomb form of weaving. "A
sieve?" Ken suggests.

"No, no, something you put the corn in and shake it through
like this," she demonstrates. Ken should have said "strainer." Reaching behind her, she pulls out a long chain of pale, knobby, large-
kerneled hominy corn. The husks have been stripped back and
braided ingeniously together, exactly as untold generations of

Iroquois women before her have done. It is complicated to fix this hominy, she tells us. "You have to boil it with lye, and do everything right or the corn will make you sick." We have had the delicious *o-nen-sto,* corn soup, staple of the Iroquois culture, made with rich broth, afloat with kidney beans, chunks of meat, and lumpy puffs of hominy, presumably prepared correctly.

An old car pulls up in the yard and Molly's daughter and her family come in. They converse in Mohawk, but the girl's husband says laughing, "Indian beef steak," as he puts a package of venison down on the little worn table in the kitchen. Molly hugs her infant grandson on her knee, a round baby with solemn dark eyes.

We purchase some of Molly's fine pale splint baskets with green braids of sweetgrass woven in, and thank her for her hospitality. We must come again, she assures us as we step back out into the other world.

Long after the boys have fallen asleep in the back seat of the car, Ken drives silently down our road, passing our own empty cornfield, flat and desolate under the leaden sky, and I ponder: the soil here is rich, the corn grows well. Before that it was a trotting track, and before that? Even before the Onondaga were the Guardians of the Central Fire, the Seneca Keepers of the Western Door, the Mohawk Keepers of the Eastern Door of the proud and mighty Iroquois Confederacy, did ever laughing Indian women with dark-eyed children come with their digging sticks to plant their corn on our sunny hill?

*   *   *

We have one more basket trip to take, to see Art Einhorn, an anthropologist in Lowville who is a specialist and student of Iroquois culture and craft. He told us to look for the only red house in Lowville.

We drive into town, passing seven red-brick houses; they apparently do not count. Ken consults the phone book and the fire department. We are directed to turn at the next corner, go down that main street until we come to the triangle parklet with the Civil War statue, then turn off there and go down two more blocks. We do all that and find a barn-red house on the right side of the street—that must be it. Two doors down the street on the opposite side stands a scarlet house! We can hardly suppress a laugh as we finally walk up to Einhorn's barn-red house.

When we reach the house, Art leads us to a back room beautifully decorated with an Iroquois braided corn-husk mask, a braid of corn like the one we were shown at Molly's and a wonderful assortment of Indian artifacts and photographs. His lovely daughter, Winona, is introduced and withdraws. Our boys disappear with his son, Victor; his quiet, dark wife joins us for a while. Einhorn himself looks as if he might be Indian, but he doesn't say. This is the man who, we were told, once came upon a wounded deer in the forest, and lacking any weapon, he put the animal out of its misery with his bare hands. This is the man who, with his wife, gave family life, respect for their culture, and education to an Onondaga, a Seneca, and two Mandan Indian foster children.

We admire his fine old beadwork and basket collection, especially a very old round basket with a square base, the splints of which have been printed with an elegant leaf design, and tell him of our visit with Molly.

"You have seen one of the best of the Iroquois basketmakers," he replies. On hearing that Molly identified the Maine sweetgrass as some weed, he laughs: "Mohawk chauvinism."

We are joined by Louie and Allen, friends of the Einhorns, who have just returned from a day in Ottawa. Louie, short and classically Indian, helped prepare a recent exhibit of Indian art at the Whitney Museum in New York City. He holds up the baskets of ours that he likes, murmuring softly with satisfaction. The discussion turns to an Algonquin woman in Canada who has agreed to make knee-high moccasins for the two men from outlines of their feet. Our host tells us that she once made a dozen pair of moccasins in a single day.

Now I remember where I have seen Louie's smiling face before. He is one of the men in the wall photograph in the room of Indians playing the venerable game of snowsnake. They are bending over a groove in the snow, intently watching a long wooden shaft, the snowsnake, which they send hurtling along the track in the snow. They are obviously enjoying themselves. On the wall below the photograph hangs a snowsnake close to six feet long, smooth and brown, shiny with the indescribable patina of age.

As we rise to take our leave of the pleasant gathering, Louie says he will see us again when his group, the Thunderbird American Indian Dancers, comes up this way to put on a performance of Indian dances in the spring. Molly had told us that she doesn't approve of revealing sacred dances to the white man. But these will be sufficiently secular for her.

*　　*　　*

The turkey steams in golden majesty upon the platter. There are potatoes and squash from our own fields, and the last of the tomatoes ripened in the attic stairway. We have a choice of our own pumpkin pie or fragrant mince pie made from our apples and the venison we'd been given.

We hold hands around the table in silent grace. I am swept by the memory of the first Thanksgiving dinner I ever cooked, bride uncertain, and we had invited guests. Peas and creamed onions were traditional to Ken. My family always had baked potatoes, acorn squash, and lima beans. Our Southern guest longed for a good old sweet-potato casserole. So we had them all. When we sat for grace, the table howled and wailed! It was Belle, forlorn little puppy we'd brought home the night before, voicing her insecurity beagle style.

I look now at Belle, the dog who likes turkey more than anything else, lying on the rug, at Ken and our golden-thatched boys descended from a long line of Cape Codders. I think of that first feast near the Cape, of Molly Rebo, of the fruits of our land. And I give thanks.

MINCE PIE

Homemade mincemeat is easy to make, and a real treat. This is the recipe for people who think they don't like mincemeat. It is easy to digest, and so gently spiced that children love it.

Mincemeat

- 1 tablespoon butter
- 1 pound ground beef or venison
- 2 pounds tart apples (about 10)
- 2⅔ cups raisins
- 2½ cups currants
- 2 teaspoons salt

1 tablespoon nutmeg
2 cups granulated sugar
1 tablespoon powdered cloves
1 tablespoon cinnamon
1 cup liquid (cider, coffee, wine, orange juice, etc.)
1 cup meat liquor

Cook the hamburger (or deerburger!) in a heavy kettle. Add enough water to make 1 cup of meat liquor. Put apples through a meat grinder with half of the raisins. Mix all the ingredients and simmer for 1 hour. Bottle hot in sterilized jars and seal. Makes 5 pints. Allow 1 pint for a small pie, 1 quart for a large one.

Crust

2 cups flour
½ teaspoon salt
⅔ cup lard
6 tablespoons cold water

Mix flour and salt, and cut in lard. Add water. Roll out the dough and line pie plate. Fill with mincemeat. Add cranberries or applesauce if you don't have quite enough mincemeat. Add extra juice if it seems dry, dot with butter, and cover with the remaining rolled-out dough. Bake at 450° for ½ hour. Serve warm or cold with cheddar cheese or vanilla ice cream.

Some General Tips on Making Pie Crust

For tender, flaky pie crust, you need to keep the shortening firm and cold. For this reason, lard, with its firmer consistency than vegetable shortenings, gives better results. Cut the shortening into the flour with two knives, a fork, or a pastry blender until the pastry resembles crumbs. Add only enough water to make the dough hold together. When making a two-crust pie, add just enough water to form the top half of the dough into a ball. Take that out and add a little more water for the rest of the dough. Chilling the dough makes it easier to handle. Do not stretch the dough. Prick the bottom of the crust in several places if you are baking an unfilled pie shell. It is important that the oven be pre-heated so that the crust cooks before the shortening melts and makes the crust soggy.

*　　*　　*

The moon stands behind the pine tree. The deep chuckling, barking call of an owl sounds again from the dark branches, "Keeyow, Keeyow, Youkkh." I can't see the bird. Should I waken Ken? The barnyard lies silent under a light sifting of silver snow. I cross the cold moon patches on the floor and crawl back into the warm bed.

We woke to our first real snow of the season this morning. You didn't have to get out of bed to know it: the air has a different sound, a different smell to it now. It may be nearly five months before we see brown ground again; sometimes half a year is white here in the North Country.

The boys are ecstatic; snow is so useful! They haven't set foot inside since they got off the school bus. Ken has his ornithology class listening to bird call records in front of a crackling fire in our living room.

"Keeyow, keeyow."

"There it is again—that's what I heard last night, Ken," I murmur as I bring in a plate of cookies.

He scowls murderously at me. "A short-eared owl, and you didn't wake me up. I've always wanted to see a short-eared owl."

Short-eared owls come through New York State in the late fall. They feed almost exclusively on meadow mice, and bark in our pine tree. Next time I will wake up my husband.

DECEMBER

WE GET UP before dawn like our neighbors with herds to milk. In these short winter days the boys are getting on the school bus in the darkness.

The farmers eat at least four meals a day. First they have a bite of breakfast before milking—how bravely the kitchen lights break the darkness here and there in the black hills! After milking, it's eggs and bacon aplenty; there's a lot of bacon on a pig. At noon comes dinner, the biggest meal of the day. If it's harvest time there may be several extra hired hands to feed. At four, the children home from school, the family sits down to supper. Then it's off to the barn again for evening milking, and, when the men come in from milking, they will probably want another dessert before they go to bed.

Milking, spreading manure, plowing, planting, harvesting, fixing fences, tractors, a hundred other things, trips to town, milking—it's all in a day's work; fair weather or foul. At least the farmer is his own boss; but is he, when there are a hundred acres of corn out in his fields crying to be cut before the frost, and every dawn, every dusk, a hundred cows are waiting to be milked?

The butcher's truck lumbers into the yard at 8:00 A.M. Out steps a pleasant-looking man in old green work pants and a faded red, hooded sweat shirt, and together with his helper begins unloading his paraphernalia. Slaughtering and butchering, fortunately, are no jobs for amateurs. The quality of the meat is directly affected by the expertise with which both operations are executed.

As they lower a fifty-gallon black iron pot off the back of the truck David says, "See that, Tom? That's the kettle they're going to scald the pigs in. They're going to kill 'em and dunk 'em in there so they can scrape off the hair." It was just a matter-of-fact statement. I was relieved. "Pork Chop" and "Bacon" had not become pets.

Ken has pulled the station wagon up to the back porch. He lowers the tail gate and slides out on to it three large cardboard cartons. The largest box is filled with pork roasts, hams, and slabs of what we will soon try to turn into bacon. Another box is filled with ground sausage meat, a bag with leaf fat and trimmings for lard, and the remaining box is filled with pork chops. I've never seen so many pork chops at once in all my life!

This is a moment of truth of sorts. Had we fed the pigs properly so that we get nice meaty hams and chops with a large tender eye of meat, or were those pigs mostly fat? The chops look beautiful. I prod a lean, round ham. They look just as the extension service bulletins say they should.

"He said they were the best-looking pigs he ever did," Ken grins proudly. We have been much amused that every time any of the neighbor menfolk were anywhere near our barn, they managed to give the pigs an appraisal.

"Good-looking pigs," they always said. We were pleased but suspected that it was just something you are supposed to say, like, "My, that's a cute baby."

We carry the meat into the kitchen, and sort out half a pig for the Latimers. We took half of one of their pigs at the end of the summer so that we would have real pork when my parents were here. Jim had declined to be paid in cash, said he'd wait until our pigs were slaughtered. So Ken has been especially anxious that our pigs be big enough and lean enough. Jim said he'd always wanted to try smoking his own hams and bacon instead of having it done at the slaughter house. With what I consider inordinate faith in our as yet unproved curing skills, he has cast the fate of his share of the ham and bacon with ours.

I put the big canning kettle on the stove and dump in the fat trimmings. The sheets of so-called leaf fat that lie just inside the body I break up; it almost seems a shame, so elegant a free-form wax sculpture each of them makes.

Lard must be rendered over a very low heat. Gradually the white solids melt into a watery clear liquid, leaving only tiny browned scraps of residual tissues—the cracklings to be baked into cornbread. Carefully I pour the clear, warm fluid into several large cans and put them out on the back porch to cool. The rapid chilling will produce a snow-white shortening of fine grain that will keep us in perfect pie crusts for a year.

The sausage meat is about a third fat and two thirds lean. Not usually much of a spice man, Ken has reveled in creating the proper aroma of this blend for twenty-five pounds of sausage:

¾ cup salt
⅓ cup sugar
10 teaspoons sage
 4 teaspoons each pepper and thyme
 2 teaspoons each cinnamon, poultry seasoning, and parsley leaves
 1 teaspoon each ground clover, nutmeg, mace, and rosemary
 3 bay leaves, crumbled

He spreads the sausage out in a large flat roasting pan, sifts on his special mix, and folds it in with his hands. When he is satisfied that it is thoroughly blended, he takes a few pounds of it and retires to the kitchen table.

From a bag he produces some lengths of pig intestine that he carefully washes. These are natural sausage casings, thin and clear long lengths of tubing. After a few false starts he is able, by fastening down one end of the tube, to stuff sausage meat in the other end and work it down to the far end. Ken, the anatomist, observes that the thin-walled jejunum section of the intestine, where digestive enzymes are secreted, makes better casing than the ridge-walled ileum, through which food is absorbed into the bloodstream. I suspect any of the older farmers around here could have told him that in different words. At appropriate intervals he gives the tube a twist and ties it off into links with knots of thread. Triumphantly he holds up a very creditable length of sausage links, cuts off a section for Jim, and heads down to the Latimers' for the first installment of rendering our account "paid in pig."

*   *   *

Our barn feels the loss of its cows. On the back wall hang
reminders of its bovine heyday, pin-up posters for the cows. They
are charts with photographs of champion bulls that tally the merits
of these prospective sires with such names as Airytop Sir Seely
Pabst, Ellbank Admiral Ormsby Pride, and Council Rock Ivanhoe
Worthy Barbara. Beside the bull charts, a Heat Expectancy Chart
tells us that "cows noticed in standing heat from 12:30 noon
through evening will be bred at the appropriate time the next
forenoon if called by 8:30 A.M.," with appropriate dates for artificial insemination penciled in for Sheba, Dolly, Speed, Nancy,
Bertha, and 8831. The rows of empty stanchions now function as
a sort of slalom course when we chase the chickens back into
their winter quarters.

The well and pump that supply drinking water to the house
are also located in the barn—an interesting commentary on farm
priorities. Without the congregation of warm cow bodies, we found
to our dismay that the water system was subject to freeze. It
seemed the simplest solution to build and insulate a small room
around the pump, but there is nothing we can do about the
buckling and cracking of the concrete floor as it freezes and thaws.

The well room turned out to be the ideal temperature for curing
pork, about 38°. We are spared the warm weather problems of
flies and spoilage, but we do have to keep 150 pounds of curing
pork from freezing for the next month.

We have decided to try both the dry, or sugar, cure, and the
sweet-pickle brine method. To dry-cure fifty pounds of meat Ken
mixes: 3 pounds of salt, 1 pound of brown sugar, and 1 ounce of
saltpeter. Half the mixture we put away for a second salting of
the hams a week from now. We spread a sheet of plastic and line
up the meat. We sew through each piece a loop of bailing twine
to serve as a handle. We pat the mixture onto the chunks of bacon,
pack it into the shanks, and spread it on the faces of the hams.
One of the barn cats comes to the door and peers in hopefully.
We wrap the pile of meat safely in the plastic and turn our
attention to the cold pickle for another hundred pounds of meat.

In a large tub we dissolve 9 pounds of salt, 2–3 pounds of sugar,
and 2 ounces of saltpeter in about 5 gallons of warm water. We
lower the big hams into the solution and fit a few bacons in

around them. Weighting the meat down under the surface of the pickle solution with an old stoneware crock lid, we fasten on the tub lid.

We mix a weaker pickle for most of the bacon: 3 generous pounds of salt, 1 scant ounce of saltpeter, and 1½ pounds of sugar, and dissolve it all in 2 gallons of water.

Gratefully we put our gloves back on; that is a cold job. Once a week we will have to hoist up the meat by its rope handles, stir the solution in the tubs, and repack the meat.

The hams take three days per pound to cure by the dry method, four days per pound in brine pickle. The bacon will be ready to take out of the pickle in two or three weeks to wait for the smoking, which we expect to start in a month or two.

*   *   *

I consider it the epitome of luxury that I can put on my ice skates in my kitchen. I place our dinner in the oven and go down to the pond for a spin. As I step out onto the ice I think about how the pond came to be. A young man from the Soil Conservation Service came with an augur to make test drillings all over the hillside. We noted that the clumps of wetland plants probably indicated where there were springs under the meadow. He explained that if we put the pond too far down the hill we'd have so much water in the spring run-off that we'd have to install an expensive flood gate system. I hoped it could be where I could see it from the kitchen window. He said that fish would need a hole more than eight feet deep so it wouldn't freeze clear to the bottom in winter, and the dirt from the hole would go toward constructing a horseshoe dike around the downhill side of the pond.

The bulldozer came in August during the dry spell. From the back yard the ducks watched their new habitat being constructed. At first it looked like a bomb crater. Gradually the autumn rains and the springs, which were indeed where we had hoped, began to fill the pond.

One morning at breakfast we were astonished by the pterodactylian appearance of a great blue heron slowly flapping down to the raw hole in the mud. He stalked carefully around the water's edge. Deciding his visit was a trifle premature he no doubt made note of future frog meals, and flew off. He was right in theory—frogs were among the first to colonize; raccoon tracks soon marked the muddy shore.

We had an early snow that winter, so the ground did not freeze. When the little pond iced over, more water seeped out of the hill and made the edges soggy. A new freeze came, but the seeping trickle made the ice a poor fit time and time again. The skating was not very good.

This year the autumn rains had raked the full to brimming pond from end to end. The water's surface had borne the marks of dipping swallows, circling beetles, dimpling trout, and the wakes of the duck armada.

Freeze-up had come one morning while we watched. Ice had formed at the edges during the night; by breakfast half the pond was in its grip. When next we looked the water left was still unfrozen, but very, very still. In one more hour the little lake was frozen fast in a shimmering skin that wrinkled like wet silk.

Tonight the whole pond is smooth. The pond tells me how I am going to skate. Sometimes the surface is pebbled with teeth-rattling lumps except for a spot just large enough for a figure eight. Another day there may be only one long narrow strip of smoothness that says: you'll practice rolls. So I ride one edge of the blade and then the other, up and down that rink. A row of crystal mouse tracks ran along the edge of the white ice that day.

Tonight the pond says: ride the wind! As I glide from bank to bank, singing to myself as I skate, I catch a glimpse of Ken watching from the big kitchen window. A few minutes later he appears, takes our picture, the pond and me, and disappears off to his barn chores. I sing on, to the scratch, scratch, rhythmic scratch of my blades.

I stand a minute, very warm. The clouds in the all gray sky recede like a dizzying camera-dissolve shot in a movie. The moon comes up and I fly down her path.

The kitchen light calls, and I make my way up the hill to dinner. I stamp inside, where dinner smells good. As a thorough wave of warm fatigue sweeps over me I unlace my skates, envying no one in the world.

The other evening a town friend apologized for calling us at six. I assured him it was all right, we'd finished eating our supper some time ago.

"One day a woman was commenting to my wife about the crazy hours those Crowells keep. She said they get up at dawn and fade as soon as the sun goes down. And then she remembered with considerable embarrassment that we do too."

I laughed, "What's *your* excuse, Bernie? You aren't farmers either. Why are you so out of schedule with society?"

"I just think man is supposed to be awake when it's light and asleep when it's dark," he answered.

In the North Country in winter, that makes a pretty short day!

* * *

Last August it occurred to me how nice it would be if we could store up some of the heat to save for use about now. We have done that with our brandies.

For the impending holiday we put out on the little cherry table in the dining room a decanter of red brandy and one of green. As I admire the tall, slender one sparkling with ruby red choke-cherry brandy, I can easily recall stripping the plump pendants of chokecherries, cascades rattling into my pail, the August sun baking my back. When all the leaves and a pretty little green-and-white crab spider had been picked out, we put a little water in the pan and cooked the tiny cherries just enough to make the dark red juice flow. To the strained juice we added sugar and brandy, and put the mixture away on the bottom shelf of the dining room cupboard to bring out, clear and spicy rich today.

The cupboard is a most unusual one I think, dating back to the modernization of the house, not quite a hundred years ago. The top half has doors opening most conveniently both on the dining room side and on the other side of the wall in the kitchen. It is made of alternating boards of golden maple and dark red cherry woods, as is the wainscoting that runs around the lower half of the living room and the main part of the kitchen, as well as here in the dining room—North Country Baroque. Around the top edge of the paneling runs a cherry chair rail, charming in its irregularities from having been hand planed.

I have learned that our paneling was the work of two brothers from Crary Mills, Aaron and Prosper Barrows, who were described to me as "cabinetmakers of consummate skill, the local Duncan Phyfes!" Where they got the style of alternating red and gold woods I do not know, but from about 1880 on, it appeared in Adirondack guideboats, canoes, and the small pleasure steamers that plied the lakes, as well as in the best rooms of North Country homes.

So far Ryland was the only one I know of around here who chose it for the parlor, the dining room, and the kitchen. I have seen an old photograph of a room in the Prospect House, *the* glamour resort of that bygone era at Blue Mountain Lake, in which the paneling not only alternates light and dark woods but also is installed on the diagonal! I am glad that Ryland did not have that done here.

The dining room is a very small room, created, I suspect, when the north wing was taken off and moved up the road past the Couglers' house to become the caretaker's cottage for Uncle Ryland's trotting track. There are several houses in this area whose core was once a wing of another house across the way. North Country men of a century ago apparently thought nothing of splitting their houses amoebalike to conquer the uncivilized wilderness up here beyond the Adirondacks.

The green brandy is mint. Our dooryard mint patch produced a wealth of aromatic leaves that we gathered one morning while an oriole sang. We added water to as many leaves as the pot would hold and brought it to a boil. À la Euell Gibbons, we put a pie plate filled with ice cubes on top of a boiling pot to condense the minty steam and send the aromatic oils back into the infusion. This we strained, added to it yet another batch of leaves, and repeated the distilling for a brew of double strength. To the hot mint essence we added sugar and brandy, and a further ingredient that only those who reproduce this on their own shall know. Then we put it in the cupboard, to see the light of day only when called forth for this holiday cheer.

Not only the brandies carry a secret of the summer sun. The table too has a secret memory of green days. On the underside of its center leaf some unknown artist of many years ago carved a willow, a slender birch, and three small shrubs.

The candle sconces wear red ribbon bows and we have put a skating scene on the dining room table. On top of a cracked mirror ringed with cotton snow, roly-poly snow babies, inch-high china figures from my childhood, skate, sled, and tumble in little hooded suits of pebbly white.

In the living room we hang our hemlock greens across the gold tops of the old Victorian picture frames, and set up a little crèche on a table. The boys go out to our barn and bring in trailing handfuls of real hay for the scene.

One of the little mâché sheep has a broken leg, which we fix with a lump of clay. The other sheep is kneeling down. We now recognize what that means—he's about to squeeze under the fence and run away.

Ken has had the figures since childhood. Somehow neither of us can abandon anything just because it has seen better days. The angel in particular is a bit battered. Our first Christmas out here was David's first year at school, kindergarten. During the pre-vacation excitement he came home one day and demanded, "Mommy, would you be afraid if an angel came down from the sky right now? Know what I'd tell him? I'd tell him all farmers need manure spreaders!" The school bus is a mighty instrument of acculturation.

FRUIT BRANDIES

You are actually flavoring brandy that has already been distilled (unless you want to tangle with the "revenuers") unlike the fermenting of homemade wine, which is perfectly legal.

The basic proportion of fruit syrup to inexpensive brandy that we like is 2 parts of juice to 3 parts of brandy. This stretches and flavors the brandy, but it is still strong enough so that it will not spoil. You will have to taste a small amount of syrup and brandy mixed together to adjust the sweetness and strength to your taste.

Chokecherry Brandy

Crush 4–5 quarts of berries and bring to a boil. Strain off the juice. Add 1 cup water to 1 quart of juice and boil gently for

20 minutes. Strain the juice through a jelly bag. Do not squeeze the bag or you will make the juice cloudy; just be patient.

Heat the juice just enough to dissolve about 4 cups of sugar in it. Cool, and add to about 1 quart of brandy. All these amounts are necessarily approximate—the amount of juice in the cherries will vary, the amount you reduce the liquid by boiling also varies, as well as the amount of sugar and brandy you like. Just keep in mind the ratio of 2 parts juice to 3 parts brandy.

Put the mixture away for at least a month. This is a rich, spicy cordial.

Raspberry or Blackberry Brandy

Heat 5–6 quarts of berries in just enough water to keep them from scorching. Put the juice through a jelly bag. To 3 cups of juice add 1½ cups sugar (and 6 whole cloves if you are using blackberries). Boil this mixture gently for 20 minutes, cool, and add to about 3 cups of brandy.

* * *

One of the most exquisite joys of rural living is cutting your own Christmas tree. Here you can even do it without feeling that you are decimating the wilderness. Acres and acres of rocky, scrubby pasture land have been planted to Christmas trees by the prudent farmers of the county. Their sons now enjoy booming tree businesses that amply finance their own Christmas shopping sprees.

"Scotch pine, spruce, or balsam—you cut or I cut," their signs advertise.

Our rocky Christmas tree meadow climbs up to the forest patch of ancient hemlocks. We snowshoe back to its darkest heart to view the trees we'll never cut. A single file of tracks marks the path of the fox whose den is near the boulder where we saw the pair of yellow garter snakes a few months back. The low-hanging branches of one hemlock have formed a cave. We take turns snowshoeing down into it, and laugh at our clumsy efforts to back up and out. Snowshoes are fastened to the foot with a harness that joins boot to snowshoe at the toe only. You walk by scuffling, as if you are wearing bedroom slippers that are too large. If you try to go backward the long heel of the snowshoe drops down into the snow and trips you up. If the snow is very deep and light, you can be in for quite a scramble trying to get back on top of your big webbed feet.

Near the edge of the woods we find the tracks of a more agile snowshoer—the ruffed grouse. The feet of these birds in winter bear a fringe that helps support them on the snow's surface. Even more exciting than the tracks is the discovery of the marks in the snow that show us where the grouse spent the night. The bird had dive-bombed itself down under the snow for shelter. On arising next morning the grouse had exploded out of the snow, leaving the hole with graceful parallel rows of wing-feather marks penciled on either side.

We pick our way out through the last of the hemlocks and cut a few boughs for greens. Discussion begins: Is the prettiest Christmas tree the one by the pasture gate where we left the jeep? Or is the one by the big rock better? It is a pine, maybe we should get a spruce this year. How about that one over there? Much too big, remember they are always so much bigger when you get them in the house.

Our tracks lace in and out the warp of trees as we look for the best one. Finally, we all agree on a perfect pine with tiny cones sprinkled through the branches. Homeward bound we sweep our tracks behind us with our precious load.

It will probably snow some more tonight; there is a special silence about the sky. The soft swish of our trailing tree, the squeak and slap of our snowshoes, and then the meadow is silent.

* * *

The honey that drained off the wax cappings has crystallized. It forms a grainy spread with a flavor all its own, which the French appreciate even if most Americans do not. Honey that has granulated can be reliquified by heating the jar in a pot of hot water, more's the pity in my estimation. I scrape the sugary paste into a honey pot and lick the spoon.

Ken rinses the capping wax and puts it into a can to melt on the stove. We are going to take care of our Christmas list by making candles. Ken has fitted the six tubes of the old tin candle mold with string wicking. The wicks are pulled through the hole at the point of each slender mold and secured by a few drops of melted wax. Match sticks across the wide mouths of the mold hold up the other ends of the wicks.

The wax that the bees make for capping honey cells has a higher melting point than that used for the honeycomb walls, so these will be very fine candles. Undyed and unscented, they will have a pale-gold color and a sweet scent of their own. Ken pours in the melted wax and puts the mold aside to cool.

He scrapes away some brown, gummy propolis, or bee glue, from the side of the melting can, and pours the hot wax into a tall narrow can; the boys are going to dip some candles. They coat the wicks lightly with wax and pull them out straight with their fingers. When the wax has cooled enough to begin dipping they take turns plunging in their wicks, just long enough to add another coat of wax, not long enough to melt off the last layer. Gradually the little candles assume, albeit somewhat irregularly, a respectable girth. The boys are very pleased with their gnomish tapers.

Ken adds a bit more wax to the sunken hollows that have formed around the wicks in his candle mold.

The sweet smell of the kitchen reminds me that I have honey bread to make. I choose a jar of strong, dark buckwheat honey and mix the bread in the jolly companionship of the candlemakers. If all the claims made for honey were true, what wonder food! Eat honey for your heart, for fewer cavities, for quicker energy. It's better for a baby, easier to digest, and an aphrodisiac when it's fermented. Honey unquestionably does keep baked goods fresher, being hygroscopic, or moisture-absorbing. You can substitute it for part or all the sugar in many recipes, perhaps cutting down the other liquids in cookie and cake recipes.

The grandparents, now back in California, have sent us walnut meats for our Christmas baking. The squirrel instinct runs as strongly in them as it does in us.

After dinner the boys spread the kitchen table with the fragrant greens we gathered from our woods. They shake out the flat hemlock boughs and the shaggy pine trimmed off the base of the Christmas tree. They each arrange a swag of greens and David helps Tom wire on some of the long curving cones that have blown off our tall white pine during the windy fall. We tie on red ribbons and go out to deck our doors.

Stars sparkle high in the sky and the town lights of Canton

glitter on the horizon. Christmas lights framing our front door cast blue, green, gold, and red glow-shadows on the snow. We hang one swag at the center of the window of the front door and tramp around to the back door. The house looks very cozy and welcoming in the snowy dark.

Even a barn window casts a cheery glow out onto the snow. Our town friends have told us that they like to see the light in our barn when they come down the Pierrepont road at night, and they picture Ken and the boys out in the barn at their chores. I don't think I should tell them that what they see is usually the chickens' light, which turns on automatically to lengthen the daylight hours so that they will continue to lay eggs.

We tie the second bunch of greens around the cow bell hanging at the back door. The warm bouquet of beeswax and honey bread engulfs us as we come back inside. Ken brings his candle mold in from the porch, and gently removes the cold candles. Burnishing them with his finger tips he asks, "Who would like to go for a ride? Let's deliver the walnut bread to the neighbors before we eat it all."

We gather the shiny-wrapped loaves tied up in red ribbons, and crunch across the driveway to the car. The cold air tingles the hairs in our noses and paints our words in clouds before us. A shooting star flares down to darkness over the barn.

Making the rounds of our neighbors' cheery hearths, we deliver the bread, and in turn acquire a box of frosted Christmas cookies, a plate of fudge, a batch of peanut brittle, and a new Red Rose feed calendar. We admire the life-sized wooden Santa and reindeer in the Latimers' yard that Mike made in shop at school. The younger boys have made a wonderful bird feeder standing on a stout post in the yard—a slightly surrealistic creation with a line of corn ears standing vertically along its roof, cobs impaled on a row of nails, reaching long fingers to the sky. The Huntleys' windows glow with electric candles; Cheryl Ostrander made a snowman for the porch; her grandparents have outlined their porch in all-blue lights. From the multicolored outlines of the roofs to the garland of twinkling white bulbs in a naked cherry tree, Pierrepont is aglow with Christmas cheer. The lights are such a friendly comfort in the long, cold northern nights.

HONEY NUT BREAD

½ cup margarine
½ cup sugar
½ cup honey
1 egg
3 cups flour
3 teaspoons baking powder
1 teaspoon salt
¾ cup milk
½–1 cup chopped nuts

Cream the margarine and sugar together. Add the honey and the egg and beat well. Stir in the remaining ingredients and mix well. Bake at 350° for 45 minutes in 3 greased 7″ × 3″ × 3″ pans. This gives you three very pretty loaves of a nice size. You can also bake the whole recipe in one 5″ × 9″ × 3″ pan if that is all you have. In that case, you will have to increase the baking time to about 1¼ hours.

*   *   *

Tom and I have a pretty good pile of cranberry and popcorn chains heaped up before us on the table. David, holding the old-fashioned corn popper over the coals in the fireplace, is popping one more batch. Our popcorn crop this year was not as bountiful as we had hoped, but it did produce enough of the short, tapered ears (a mere three inches long) to fill one tin cracker can. David rubbed off enough of the translucent teardrop kernels to cover the bottom of the corn popper basket. Shake, shake, the hard kernels of unpopped corn rattle in the little wire cage at the end of the long wooden handle.

Stringing cranberry and popcorn chains is a real labor of love. The popcorn kernels keep splitting, and the needle has a treacherous habit of poking out of the cranberry where you do not expect it, stabbing your fingers mercilessly.

But we are nearly finished now and Ken has begun the master-of-the-house ceremony of hanging the lights on the tree. When he has them arranged to his satisfaction, each bulb clipped just so, he fastens the Christmas angel to the topmost branch. Her wings and carol book needed a fresh coat of aluminum foil this year, but her starry gown still looks fresh after thirty years of seasonal glory.

We garland the tree with our cranberry–popcorn chains. (Ken says the tree now looks perfect as it is, an observation that has lost some of its originality since he says it every year at just this point. It still sounds new to him, however.) In the safety of the upper branches I hang the oldest glass ornaments: a horn that toots, a red bird whose tail we have reconstructed with a curly, speckled guinea hen's feather, a golden owl, a clown, a German church, a blue tea cup and a pink tea pot, a silver pine cone, an iridescent fish, and the clear glass balls and bells from the World War II years.

There will be no tinsel icicles this year. Ken doesn't like them, so we use them only every other year in compromise. I don't believe the boys will let him get away with that much longer. We hang the lower branches with plain metallic balls and ornaments we have made over the years. There are Pennsylvania Dutch paper stars and origami birds, both of which we've long since forgotten how to make. Nesting somewhat incongruously on the needled branches is a silver-painted crab with pipe-cleaner legs, made from the carapace we found on the beach one summer. Gilded halves of milk-weed pods frame tiny feathered birds or golden angels playing musical instruments. The candy canes are spread around the tree now with greater sophistication than in former years. There was a time when the boys hung them all on the same branch, for convenience sake, I suppose.

When the last ornaments have been hung we admire the most beautiful tree ever, as we sit by the dying fire sipping homemade eggnog. Around the room on the rail above the wainscoting, the Christmas cards from our friends smile at us. A very pleasing number of them have been made by hand this year.

At last "the stockings are hung by the chimney with care" and we go up to bed for what children will assure you is the longest night of the year, in spite of the fact that astronomers have placed the winter solstice a few days earlier.

* * *

Long before the lazy winter sun has shown us any signs of day, the family is out of bed. Four pairs of feet hit the cold bedside floors nearly simultaneously. Ken exercises his paternal authority by going down the dark stairs first, to turn up the heat, turn on the lights, and plug in the Christmas tree lights, which twinkle brightly on the pile of presents that has appeared around the tree.

The stockings are taken down from the fireplace, and a warm blaze soon routs the winter dark. We unwrap the little joke presents in our stockings and pull out the orange we always know will be found in the toe.

A welter of ribbons and wrappings and boxes soon covers the floor. The prettiest papers are rescued and carefully folded aside for future use. The happiness we feel is almost palpable in the bright confusion; these are the tokens of love in a family close in spite of geography. The opened presents are arranged in various chairs by their new owners, who will admire them there for the day.

As the sun comes up, we go to the kitchen for breakfast. The sky glows shell pink, shading imperceptibly into the blue above. A golden shaft of incandescence gives the clue to the place along the line of dark hills where the orange-gold orb will show itself.

"I see it first," Tommy crows a minute later as the glowing rim of the sun edges up over the hill. The snow glitters pink; hoarfrost has touched the trees and outlined every branch and bush and blade with feathery crystals; the nutcracker's sugar-plum fairy world. As we watch, pink turns to gold, loose flakes of snow on the drifts glitter like strewn mica. The breathless dawn of Christmas day even has the grace to come at a civilized hour here in the North Country.

Since everyone wants to go tobogganing to work up an appetite for the Christmas feast, we do the morning chores together. The ducks are delighted with their Christmas double feed ration. We fill their water dish and put it back on the warmer, the barn-style hot tray that keeps the water from freezing.

The chickens have their own apartment in the cold barn. Ken has hammered up some old wallboard to make them a cozy corner under the barn stairs. The hens' room is decorated with a cross-stitch lettered poster on the wall proclaiming Dick Kepes's slogan: "An egg a day keeps the ax away." And nearby is their pinup poster—a lushly frosted candy Easter egg photo I cut from the farmer's wife section of an agricultural magazine.

The guineas hop down from their roost and make their way over to the feeder as the brown bantams move aside for them. The black Cochin bantams with feathers on their feet also consider themselves above the brown banties in the peck order. I can't tell the three black hens apart so I don't know who is head Hickety-Pickety among them. The young brown bantam rooster is still awed by these ladies, but the tables will be turned by spring, I'm sure.

David and Tom reach under a black hen in the nest in the orange crate, and hold the warm brown eggs up to their smiling cheeks. If the big Rhode Island Red had been sitting on the eggs I'm not sure they would have reached under her; she might have glared them down with her fierce eye. Although the banties fluff up their feathers and warn you off with a rasping cluck, they only feint their passes at your hand.

Having exchanged our Christmas gifts with the animals, we put the eggs in the house and pull the big toboggan out from under the back porch. It is eight feet long, and striped in alternating light and dark woods. The toboggan was purchased for half price the first winter the department store had opened in the new shopping center. They never again made the mistake of assuming that winter is nearly over here in January.

We line up the long toboggan and seat ourselves. Tom tucks his feet under the curling front, David slides in behind him with his legs straddling Tom's waist. I do the same behind David, and Ken fits on behind me. We all paddle with our mittens, grab the rope strung along the edges, and we're off! We hurtle down the chute, roller-coaster over some moguls halfway down, and streak out across the meadow.

"Lean left!" Ken shouts as we slip out of the track and head toward the only fence post we left in when we rolled up the section of fence last fall. We slide back into the track and glide to a whispering halt in a shower of flying flakes. Tom rode down "no hands," his mittens pasted over his eyes to ward off the showering snow; his parka hood is white. We rest on each other, laughing.

Chickadees scold us from the feeder as we arrange ourselves for a second slide, my turn to ride in front. We push off, the moguls slap my breath away. We whip down the track, body-English a few more feet at the bottom to pass the sere thistle plant that marked our previous record.

The sun warms us from the dazzling sky. I hear the Latimers' snowmobile and see it snaking across their meadow. What a glorious day to be out! Next time Jim urges me to try their snowmobile I think I'll offer him a ride on our toboggan.

JANUARY

AH, THE SEED MERCHANTS are canny ones. They send us their gaudy catalogues while Christmas tinsel, gay wrappings, and bows still blossom bright in our minds.

Dear Sirs:

Please send us a window box of bright petunias like the ones the Latimers grow in the huge black hog kettle on their front lawn. Walter Bowers has his petunias nodding brightly from a ring of silver-painted tractor tire. How are we to choose between your ruffly colors? We like them all.

We'd like a field of nodding sunflowers, bushels of carrots, and shining rows of beets. Send us whatever green beans you think are best—we never can remember which kind we tried last year. If the tomatoes grow at all we're sure to end up with too many, although the canned-goods shelves are always empty by spring.

David wants a bed of marigolds and one red rose. Tom says he wants hollyhocks that reach up to the sky. We'll have larkspur and sweet peas in candy colors, pepper-sweet nasturtiums, an armful of snapdragons in all the new shades, a wallful of morning glories in old-fashioned blue.

Last year we couldn't fool okra and peanuts into thinking this was Georgia. We'll try some toy tomatoes and seedless watermelon this year. We need miles of jack-o'-lantern vines, and piles of winter squash for the cellar. We're not sure whether we prefer the Butternut or Acorn squash, depends which kind is on our plate.

Your zinnia page charms us with its bright fiesta, and oh, the dahlias fairly glow! Do you really think we could grow such grand-opera lilies? We do know where we could put some smiling pansies, and a row of shasta daisies, and carnations, and. . . .

We'd better meditate on hoeing before we mail this order.

*   *   *

Snow lies two feet deep upon the pond.

"I'll take the jeep down and plow it off," says Ken. "David and I went out and drilled it in the middle. There's eight inches at least. That jeep's awfully heavy but you'd think that would be enough ice."

"Why don't you call Arlie Parker?" I suggest. "He could tell you all the fine points of plowing a pond, I'm sure."

Arlie is a high school teacher and house painter. He painted our house for us, even the outhouse. All through the job he kept asking when we were going to take the outhouse off the back of the house. We assured him we weren't going to. "First time I ever painted an outhouse," he said, but he finally did it. It makes a great place to keep the lawn chairs and toboggans. And it's a perfectly good two-holer; it even has wallpaper on the walls.

Arlie lives in a big new neo-colonial house he built for himself back in the maples just before you come to Smiths' store. He has a pond back of his house with floodlights on it; he used to be a big hockey star at St. Lawrence University.

Ken phones Arlie. "Have you ever fallen through?"

"Sure, three or four times, but I only had three or four inches of ice. Eight'll be fine."

Arlie is the only one I know who would ever fall through the ice while plowing more than one time in his whole life. Arlie is a pretty hefty guy; I imagine he just jumped out and lifted whatever he plows with out of the hole.

A carful of our town friends, the Kepeses and Carlisles, has arrived to skate. Dick Kepes goes down to the pond with a shovel and begins to clear a rink. The snow has settled enough in the field that Ken decides to try to get the jeep down to the pond. With snow-plow blade held high, the little red jeep pushes its skidding way across the snowy field and out onto the ice. The ice groans. Will the jeep get enough traction on the ice to move the snow, or will it just sit spinning its wheels? "You can always sand it," the audience wisecracks.

Dick keeps on shoveling; it looks like a race between man and machine. When the jeep starts plowing, it works like a charm. Dick skates over and begins to clean up after the jeep, which is clearing wide arcs across the pond. The ice cracks loudly, but the jeep does not go through. Soon everyone is skating on the cleared end.

It is warm and snow is falling, dusting skaters and ice alike with a fluffy powder, a scene from the paperweights of my childhood. When you shook the liquid in a little glass globe, white flakes would swirl in a miniature storm around tiny winter figures.

Dick is working at pushing the plowed-up drifts of snow off the edge of the ice. He is afraid the weight of the snow will bend the ice down and water will seep over at the edges. A hole about the size of a penny appears in the ice; fiercely water bubbles up through it. In seconds the hole enlarges and dark water gushes up onto the ice. The snow piles, pressing down around the pond's edge, have buckled the ice at the center of the pond up into a dome.

In time the boys leave the snow fort they have built from the plowed-up drifts; the girls stop their circles and spins; the pond is left alone to the quietly falling snow.

Next day the phone rings. It's Ruby from the farm down below. "We wondered what on earth Ken was doing with the jeep. We saw him go plowing down across the field yesterday forenoon."

"He was plowing the pond."

"Well, we never would have guessed that!"

*　　*　　*

I was standing at the window by the sink just now, admiring the way the wind blows the brown leaves across the slope of the snow, which glows with a golden luminescence. The waning sun is not visible through the low gray sky, but the light reflecting on the snow field affirms that it is there.

One of the tumbling leaflets turns and heads back up the hill. How can that be? I pull myself up onto the sink counter to have a better look. The leaf is a mouse, a small brown meadow mouse tumbled by the wind across the glowing plain. It runs like a wind-up toy; there is no undulation in its gait. Tiny feet I cannot see propel it up the hill until the wind again tumbles it down the other way.

I pull one of my slipper heels out of the porridge pot soaking in the sink. I start with dismay as the mouse circles a little fruit tree we had carefully wrapped against the hunger of such a one as he. But, no, he isn't interested in nibbling our apple tree today. The little brown form scurries on. There is another mouse a few yards farther down the hill! A strong gust carries it far down the slope.

A group of milkweed pods sways in the wind; dried grasses tremble, a tangled skein of spun gold laid out to dry. The first mouse just vanished in a blink, down a hole I cannot see. I get to see the trick again; the second disappears.

"Mom, do you know where my paste jar is?" asks David, walking in with scraps of colored paper in his hand.

"I think it's on the shelf in the paint closet," I reply.

"Thanks," he says, leaving the kitchen.

The wind rattles the milkweeds. I wonder what it says about us that neither of us mentions that I'm sitting in the sink.

World, Ken invented a better mousetrap. It is for winter trapping, and it is an extremely humane contraption. The heart of it consists of a 5" × 5" wooden box known to the trade as a nest box because a mouse can be induced to enter the small round hole in its side and build a nest in the cotton quilt batting thoughtfully provided inside. To the front of one of these boxes Ken has attached an aluminum box trap so that it forms a tunnel, like the mobile hall units that accordion out from airplane terminals to the entrance of the plane.

Inside the nest box he put a pocket handwarmer; yes, the shiny little metal kind that has inside a wick to be lighted, and that comes with a little blue suede drawstring bag to keep it in. Surely this is the ultimate in winter trapping. He wants his mice alive so he can give them a numbered ear tag by which he will know them the next time they meet.

The traps made their debut in the garden under the kitchen window. Ken demonstrated them proudly to his sons. They all came into the house quite pleased with themselves. Unfortunately, when they went out to collect them one trap was overlooked. It was not missed for several days. Alas, when the oversight was remedied, the trappers found they had been all too successful; in the no longer cozy little apartment lay a frozen-stiff meadow mouse.

Tommy insisted they bring it in and stuff it and study it. This means they measure it from here to there, and there to here, weigh it, and dissect it for various anatomical facts of interest. (We once had a funnel-mouthed Plecostemus fish, also known as a window washer, or sucker cat, in our aquarium as a scavenger to keep it clean; we called it Hoover. It was the ugliest fish I ever saw. When it turned up dead one morning David could scarcely be dissuaded from stuffing that too.)

The mouse was duly stuffed and committed to Science. I just passed it in the hall on my way to the bathroom. I jumped.

* * *

This is the January thaw. Today the snow just can't seem to melt fast enough. I hear water trickling down into the cistern in the cellar so I know it's melting off the roof. Rivulets of water are streaming down the sides of the driveway. The brown fields are appearing through their white covers with a speed that indicates the snow is sublimating. It just can't wait to pass from frozen to liquid state—the snow evaporates directly into the air. Dark maple leaves frozen in the pond's surface seem to burn their way down through the ice. A flock of house sparrows is busy cleaning up the seeds on the bared ground beneath the feeder.

This is the warm spell Ken has been hoping for. It's time to begin smoking the hams and bacons. Wet maple branches should be just the wood for it, so we walk down the road gathering soggy arm-loads. Last night's wind—hurricane gusts of seventy miles per hour according to the radio this morning—has strewn the ground with maple prunings. At the far end of the line of trees Tom discovers a bit of mouse fur on a rock, the dinner of an owl, or a weasel perhaps?

Wind rattles the branches above our heads. It looks as though the sap is running from a mossy crack up in the cleft of one grand old maple; everything's so wet it's hard to tell. The boys take turns tripping each other with trailing branches, and as we trudge back up the hill Ken spots a foreign woodpecker at the suet holder on the biggest maple. We freeze. It is the red-bellied woodpecker that visited the feeder last week. They are rarely seen this far north. It looks almost like our familiar standbys, the hairy and smaller downy woodpeckers, but it wears a scarlet hood instead of a red cap spot. Do you think he will stay around long enough for our birding friends to come and see him? Not a chance.

We pile up our sticks on the sandy floor of the garage. The car will spend the next few days outside—this is the smokehouse now. The hams and bacon slabs have been scrubbed to remove the excess pickling salt and carefully dried so that they will smoke evenly.

Ken is very proud of the rig he has assembled for smoking. The extension bulletins give plans for making small smokehouses or setting up barrels that inconveniently communicate with the smoking fire by an underground ditch. Our smoker consists of an enormous tin box, at least four feet square, which hangs suspended from the garage ceiling. It is connected to the chimney pipe of the chunk stove we used last year for boiling sap. A rickety ladder enables Ken to climb up and hang the meat inside the enclosure. (He doesn't know what the tin thing is; he found it in the attic of the stable.) The whole thing looks like a tree house made by Boeing Aircraft Corporation.

When the hams and bacons are properly arranged, suspended from a crossbeam by their bailing-twine handles so that no two pieces touch, Ken climbs down and lights the fire. He has it arranged Indian style, the sticks radiating tipi fashion. This arrangement cools as it burns down so that the fire won't get too hot and scorch the meat.

A little experimenting and he has figured out how to keep the fire going just enough to maintain a steady haze of smoke. The meat should be just about 100°F. Unfortunately he cooked his new thermometer when he lit the fire; he had forgotten it was lying on the stove top.

Throughout the rest of the day Ken slips out about every half hour to check things and put a few more wet sticks on the fire. Belle sneaks out past Ken on one of his trips and streaks for the pile of rocks behind the garage where the woodchuck lives. How does she know he was out today?

Ken walks up to check the bees. The hives are wrapped in heavy paper to insulate the bees against the cold. They don't need much, their own body heat keeping their chamber warm. One hive seems a little damp, so Ken loosens the papers. Walking back toward the house Ken watches the wind riffle the water on top of the ice on the pond. He collects his dog from the woodchuck pile, and checks the smoker once again. A sweet-smoky smell accompanies him to lunch.

Sitting at the kitchen table, we see Gary Cougler head down

through our melting meadow on his snowmobile to Monty Latimer's house. He'll have to walk back home, we wager. We are reminded of Calgary, Alberta, where we lived for awhile. The city sits on the edge of the Canadian prairie in sight of the Rocky Mountains. In winter a warm wind they call the Chinook blows down out of the mountain passes. When the Chinook blows, a great dark cloud archway forms over the mountains; pale gold light shines through under the arch, and the wind blows warm as spring. It happens so often that they don't even bother with snow plows in that northern city. Calgarians love to tell of early settlers stranded in the prairie when the Chinook melted the snow out from under their sleigh runners; no matter how they'd whip their horses they couldn't keep ahead of the melting wind.

Belle's barking at the window from the top of the living room couch brings us all in, just in time to see a skunk scuttle down the road. "My first live skunk," breathes David. I'm sure he's seen them in summers gone by, but I know how he feels. Skunks not infrequently venture out for a winter jaunt. Perhaps they get restless; many a North Country resident gets cabin fever about this time of year. The animal has an extraordinarily beautiful, glossy black winter coat. The white stripes are barely visible. He holds his dark tail high and full, a banner in the wind. The hairs along Belle's backbone are raised, her bark is deafening. I'm glad she can't chase him. In an awkward gallop the skunk disappears around the corner.

The sun is glowing—pearly pink, low on the western horizon. Maple branches stretch black lace across a satin sky. In summer the lazy sun goes down well to the right of Walter Bowers' barn. Now it sets far to the left of it. If you live where you can see the sun go down you cannot help but notice its peregrinations. The subtle lunar and solar calculations made by the men of Stonehenge become more believable; you appreciate why they gave such monumental effort to the study of the heavens. You know there is meaning; a day without a sunset is a letter without a signature.

There goes Gary, trudging home up the hill.

* * *

Ken brings in the slabs of bacon, a dozen in all, each a foot or two long, six or eight inches across, and two inches deep. They are well streaked with lean—Pork Chop and Bacon really were good pigs. He trims off the skin that forms a rind on the outside of each slab. The hide is smoked a soft golden color, delicately marked with dots in groups of three—the hair pattern.

Ken steps out of his overalls. His uniform for bacon slicing consists of a plaid flannel shirt covered by a men's blue denim apron, tied butcher style in front. (Not too many years back Tom called it Daddy's nice little cooking dress.) I note with amusement that down below he is clad in long johns, gray wool socks striped with red and green, and a very veteran pair of high-topped shoes.

The slicer Jim Latimer has lent us hums into action at the flick of a switch. Ken puts a slab into the black triangular holder and pushes it past the whirling circular blade. Strips fall away in a pile behind the machine. Bacon! Getting bacon slices all the same length for monotonous little windowed packages in the store must be a wasteful process. I find the machine awesomely efficient. Its lethal precision makes me nervous. I notice that when Ken uses it he wears a gay look of derring-do so it probably is as dangerous as it appears.

The lean meat of the dry-cured bacon is a darker shade than the bright beef-red of the meat pickled in brine. We cook and sample slices from a few different slabs; smoky, sweet, amazing. The dry cure is perhaps too salty. Our homemade bacon seems tastier, crunchier, more easily burned than store bacon. I can see that Ken is going to make some data sheets so we can sort out the variables and arrive at a reproducible result. The blessing of being married to a scientist!

What was that noise? The clock on the bureau glows 1:00 A.M. It sounded as though it came from the back porch. Is something chewing up all that bacon or trying to eat our precious hams out in the garage? Ever so carefully, so as not to waken Ken, I quietly quietly creep out of bed, across the cold floor of the bedroom, and out into the hall. The moon is bright behind the maples, casting long shadows on the snowy lawn.

I hurry downstairs. I do hear something out there—a porcupine or the skunk again probably. What if it turns out to be the bear Mrs. Paul says was seen back in her woods? He can have the hams. I fumble for the kitchen door, open it, and there stands Ken, a ham in either hand.

"It got so cold after it cleared up I was afraid the hams would freeze," he explains. He puts the hams on the counter and goes back out into the glittering cold night for the others. He'd been smoking them one last time (three days in all) and he figured that when the fire went out they'd be all right hanging where they were in the smoker for the night. But our warm spell of weather has broken, so he came out to get the hams.

"Those old pioneers sure must have been upset when a bear got into their smokehouses," announces Ken, bringing in two more hams. So he has bears on the brain too.

The last three hams he brings in are the ones we are going to age Smithfield or Virginia ham style, so they have had extra smoking. We admire their dark mahogany color and decide that since we are both wide awake we might as well rub them with ground pepper and cloves, the next step in that process. The pungent smell begins to irritate my nose. We rub in as much as we can. It will be nearly a year before I take a bristle brush and water to scrub it off again.

Tomorrow morning we will wrap the hams in greaseproof paper and push each one into a tight cotton bag. We have one bag printed with a Virginia Smokehouse label—that ham should taste authentic. The others are well washed feed bags marked Red Rose Porker. They are at least appropriate. We have decided to hang them in the "linen closet" upstairs for the aging. This is a closet that was built around the chimney flues where they pass through our extra upstairs bedroom. I thought it would make a good linen closet but we have never gotten as far as putting up any shelves. Henceforth it will probably be known as the ham closet.

The hams will hang for eight to twelve months while the enzymes, or ferments, in the meat give it the characteristic flavor—if we've done it right and they don't all rot. Then all you have to do is scrub one, soak it for a day, boil it, glaze it, and bake it. But Smithfield ham is truly worth it all.

We admire the hams once more over a cup of cocoa, and go back up to bed. I fall asleep with my nose burning, but my head is filled with sweet dreams of paper-thin slices of Virginia-style ham sandwiched between layers of feather-light baking powder biscuits, platters and platters of them.

* * *

Dawn finds the mercury well below zero. From the chimneys of the five farmhouses we see from our kitchen window, smoke curls up through the chill air in pale wisps against the nacreous sky. A

tractor rolls along a side road trailing three white plumes: the tractor's breath, the driver's breath, and the steaming load of manure
in the spreader.

The morning sun intensifies the blue of the hills, but they retain
a powdery cast. This opaqueness in the air is caused by swirling ice
crystals, which glitter almost menacingly in the forbiddingly cold
air.

The snow-spread meadows against the dark forests and the white
roofs of the dark hipped barns mark the scene with interesting ge-
ometry. Jim Latimer's black-and-white heifers frisk into a loping
gallop down their meadow hill, heads bobbing gaily with the exercise. Through a frame of elms, gracefully gaunt, Jim's three giant
green harvesters wait in frozen line outside the big barn up behind
the Lelands'. The wind has blown snow onto the pond in wavy
riffles.

White meadows also checker the woods over toward Hannawa
Falls. Tamed now are the forests of the "Great Northern Purchase."
I remember a story about Hannawa Falls, then called East Pierrepont, at the provision camp of the men who were surveying this
uncharted wilderness into townships back in 1799. As the season
wore on the men became anxious to return to their homes, whether
they finished the surveying or not. Catching wind of the mutiny,
one of their leaders, a Judge Raymond, prudently hid the compass.
The band of weary, disgruntled men were loath to tackle the route
through the Adirondacks without that compass, so he was able to
convince them to complete their labors and return home honorably.

A large billowing smoke rising just this side of Hannawa Falls
must be the Pierrepont dump burning again. The sight of that particular smoke always disturbs me; I see it as a symbol of our environmental double standard. That small dump and dozens like it
across the country burn, spontaneously or otherwise, in defiance of
our hard-won air pollution laws.

What are the small upstate towns to do with their trash? Our
neighbor, Babe Leland, supervises the dump and does the best he
can. Into his waiting pickup truck on dump day, every Tuesday
and Saturday, he piles the tied-up newspapers, the scrap metal, the
aluminum, the perfectly good this and that discarded by the people
of our section of this heavily welfare-subsidized county. His wife,
Alyce, has neat piles of good, clean, salvaged clothes that she dis-
tributes or remakes for those who will use them.

The elderly matriarch of Canton society recently delivered her saved-up brown bags and a scolding for wasting our paper resources to the young man in charge at her supermarket. "Foresters" around here have a passion for planting pines in neat rows, block after block. It makes a fine crop, but then they put up signs to persuade the public that this is a forest. The pure needle carpets in these plantings are scarcely closer to being true forest floor than the artificial turf at the astrodome. We may produce pulpwood for brown paper bags to spare this way but we will be the poorer for it. Nature is complete, complex, unregimented, to be loved with the romance reserved for an enchanting, mysterious woman.

Must Progress be so immodest, so inevitable that we should raise our sons only to enjoy her, without requesting of her discipline and foresight? We are not crazy atavists longing to return to the mythical quiet of a cave. It may be dangerous to raise our boys in this country idyll. May they find we've given them the resources to take and shape what tomorrow brings, and not sit stunned by what yesterday lost!

* * *

In the kitchen there is a hot-air register that should be awarded a special medal for feeding us, clothing us, and otherwise looking after our creature comforts. Above the register we have suspended a plastic dish drainer to hold drying mittens. However, we also put into it our gloves, scarves, hats, goggles, sweaters, and cross-country ski wax. The snowy mittens end up on the register itself. Under the heap of things that fall onto the register you can often find a pot of incubating yogurt.

It took us quite a few tries to learn to culture yogurt. We tried an expensive dried Bulgarian culture but ended up with a quart of scalded milk that tasted a little flatter than when we began. We tried using the yogurt in the plastic cups from the grocery store dairy counter; we ended up with sour milk slightly thickened.

In one of Ken's scientific journals appeared a series of letters to the editor prompted by a report on the effects of feeding rats wholly on commercial skim-milk yogurt. (They developed cataracts.) From the scientists we learned of the Tricky Turkish Towel Technique, whereby the pot of yogurt is swathed in towels and incubated overnight, and that the only yogurt fit for an Armenian is temperature-tested by dipping your elbow into the milk until you feel neither hot nor cold. Another Armenian, a microbiologist, explained that you scald the milk to kill off the competition and then introduce your yogurt culture; the optimum temperature for the multiplication of the yogurt-forming bacteria is between 40° and 50° Centigrade. The microorganisms *Lactobacillus bulgaris* and *Streptococcus thermophilus* ferment the lactose and other sugars in the milk and the resulting acid formation curdles the proteins in the milk.

We gathered that yogurt making is both an art and a science—and that we should buy a good cooking thermometer.

We were spurred on in our yogurt-making efforts by the story a friend told us of a Middle Easterner who had parlayed a delicatessen business into a fortune by selling homemade yogurt to Americans. He made his yogurt in his bathtub! This conjured up an interesting vision for me until I finally realized—it took an embarrassingly long time to figure this out—that of course he must have lined up glass jars of milk and culture in his tub and then turned on the hot water.

We are now expert yogurt makers thanks to a charming Egyptian we met at a party. I told him of our trials with yogurt.

"By all means, make your own," Fadel said, and, waxing nostalgic, he continued, "I can always remember the pot of yogurt my mother made for us every day. All you have to do is stir some yogurt into milk and put it somewhere warm. But you know, I think you Americans do something to the yogurt in those little boxes you sell. It is so weak you have to keep it out on your window sill, or some place nice for a few days to let it get back its strength. Then you use it."

That is the secret it seems. Now we have no trouble culturing our own sweet, creamy yogurt to eat with granulated honey, with fruit and drizzled-on honey, or to make into a creamed cheese or use in any other sour cream recipe. We use our fancy thermometer to determine which register would keep the yogurt at 100° Fahrenheit.

If we forget and eat every bit without saving any for culturing, we go to the store, buy a little cup of yogurt—even the flavored kind will do if that's all they have—and put it in "some place nice" to recover enough to grow us a new batch.

We subsequently met Fadel's wife and asked her to convey our thanks to him for the secret. She looked surprised. "Fadel has never made yogurt in his life," she murmured.

YOGURT

1 quart milk
2 tablespoons powdered milk
2 tablespoons yogurt

Scald the milk. Cool to lukewarm and stir in the powdered milk. Mix some of the milk with the yogurt, and then pour it all back into the rest of the milk. Put this mixture in a covered nonmetallic pot, and set it any place that will incubate it at 100° for 2–6 hours until it coagulates. (If you try using a hot tray you will need to put a hot pad under your pot, cover the whole with a towel, and use a very low setting.) Then store it in the refrigerator.

Usually you will get a wondrously creamy, sweet yogurt. However, occasionally even the best-laid yogurt goes awry, so here are two recipes that make delicious use of the products of the two most common failures (you can also use good yogurt in these recipes):

1. The yogurt remains too thin—you didn't cool the milk enough and killed the culture, or the incubation temperature was too low.

Nearly Yogurt Rolls

1 cup thin "yogurt"
1 packet (teaspoon) yeast
¼ cup butter, melted
¼ cup sugar
1 teaspoon salt
1 egg
3 cups flour

Mix the ingredients, let rise 1 hour, until double in bulk. Punch down and pat out ½ inch thick. Shape into desired style of rolls and put them on buttered pans. Brush tops with melted butter. Let them rise until double in size. Bake at 425° for 15–20 minutes.

2. The yogurt separates into cheese and whey—you incubated it at too high a temperature. Strain. Use the whey in place of water

or milk in baking recipes—especially with the biscuit mix recipes (see p. 133); it is good for you. Use the cheese as a cream cheese-type spread or flavor it as a dip, or bake it into a cheese cake.

Yogurt Cheese Cake

Use the pie shell and filling of your choice with this recipe. A graham cracker crumb crust is good, canned cherry pie filling an easy topping.

3 eggs
2 cups yogurt curds
1 cup sugar
1 teaspoon vanilla

Beat the eggs until frothy. Beat in yogurt and sugar. Add vanilla and pour into a baked pie shell or crumb crust. Bake at 350° for 1 hour, or until filling is set. Add topping as desired. You will never have to admit that this started out as a mistake!

*   *   *

Belle is barking, barking, barking. We stir uneasily in our sleep. Barking, barking, barking. We wake up, open a sleepy eye. The room is orange? The Couglers' barn is on fire! Ken runs to the phone; it isn't working. He dresses and rushes out of the house. The barn is a glowing holocaust—their house is still all right. The wind is blowing this way, and we may be next.

My heart pounds wildly as I pull on my warmest slacks and sweater—it's a cold night to have to leave your home—and I begin to outline in my mind what I will do. Great fistfuls of fire are shooting up from the blazing building, showering down on our barn, outbuildings, pine tree, and house; fiery meteorites hurtle through the snowy darkness. A terrifying sight—I'd better not look, just get down to work. I don't need to wake the children yet. Gather warm clothes for everyone. Shut extra doors. Check the roofs again, so far so good. I can see the Couglers' barn frame, a skeleton consumed in flames. It glows a minute more in ghostly outline and then falls crashing in. The wind mercilessly drops flaming jetsam on the pine tree, the house; better check the roofs on the far side again.

From the sewing machine I grab a green flowered feed bag (I've been meaning to put a drawstring in it), and stuff in a few small things I'd like to save. Crackling, barking . . . must keep calm. I am conscious of the acrid smoke burning in my nose.

Fire trucks pull up in a blaze of red lights, followed by a line of smaller trucks—volunteers with yellow lights flashing, blue ones too. Forms of running men are silhouetted in headlights; trucks line the road from the Couglers' down the hill and past our living room. I recognize Al Ostrander's pickup, and the Huntleys'—it's a crazy, macabre hell fair in the middle of the night.

I see Ken returning, stopping to exchange a few words with some of the firemen, then he disappears into our barn. If it goes I think we'll lose our house. Why must the wind everlastingly blow this direction?

Better not wake the boys until I have to. If we get out of this all right they will be cross that they missed the excitement, but I don't want this glowing, screaming fiend-fire burned into their memory, making FIRE! ever after too real.

I walk through the downstairs. Since I've got time I'd like to save a few paintings. I take them off the wall and stack them by the other things on the kitchen floor. And maybe I'd like to have just one chair—my little bird's-eye maple desk chair.

The fire's bright—still those damned meteors. Shooting stars! Fourth of July! It would be pretty if it weren't so awful. Fascinating fire, like a deadly snake. The line of trucks has grown longer.

Tom stirs. "Is it morning yet?"

"No dear, go back to sleep."

There seems time for another round; what else would we like? Ken's slides and a box of papers from his file; I don't suppose there are any valuable ones here but he might be glad I got them. They say you always save the wrong ones. I take the old tin box that contains his grandfather's Indian mementos, and the boys' baby books, and a photo album.

I go upstairs and look out at the porch roof and the ell again. Maybe we won't need to go. Pack a few things in a suitcase just in case. My wedding dress; married in blue, always be true.

Down in the kitchen I survey the pile on the floor again. I step out the back door a minute. The smell! The crackling! The fire shower has pretty well stopped; snow is falling lightly through the orange sky. I hear it sifting down in little beads. It's very cold.

What are the Couglers doing I wonder; it looks like their house will be spared too. I step back in.

Ken comes into the kitchen. "I don't think you'll need these," he says eying my pile. "It was pretty close though. It's interesting to see what things you value," he smiles, picking up the Civil War cane from the small Navaho rug draped over my desk chair. "When I got up there the Couglers were just calling the fire department. They must have wakened just about when we did.

"The sparks were falling right through that broken window at the end of our barn. I climbed up and put a piece of plastic over it." The ladder he means is more than thirty feet of rungs—if you can call flat old boards that—nailed up between two studs on the dark wall. I shudder. "About the only hay left in there was right under that window, wouldn't you know it. It's a good thing I saw it when I did. Roger came in and helped me check around. I don't think that roof is very likely to catch, but there were such big chunks of stuff flying around! It's lucky there's snow on the ground. The pieces just kept burning like torches where they landed. Without the snow all that tall grass by the barn . . . The Pierrepont fire department is keeping a watch on our barn. The Chief wants to check out our pond for water in case they need it. I guess I'll go out and look around the barn again."

A half hour later Ken comes in and calls Belle, gives her a big tidbit of ham. "Good dog," he says, patting her. "Good dog for waking us up." I hug her and smile at Ken. That means we're safe now.

Ken pulls his coat on again and goes back out to the barn. Some of the trucks pull out and head for home. It is 3:30, not much over an hour since we woke up. The concrete silo still looks like an airport tower with a search light on it, but it's not lights—flames are still shooting up quite high, but it's lost the Judgment Day look. The dark form of the hay bale elevator reaches up to the high barn window that is no longer there. There is a big blue-white flash; the power company man is working up on the pole.

I decide to hang up the pictures and put back the chair; the boys don't need to know how close it was. The party lines will soon be buzzing—remember the night the Couglers' barn burned, we'll all say. But not now. It's still that night.

*   *   *

The radio this morning reported:

> A large barn was destroyed early this morning at the farm of Oswald Cougler on Route Four in Pierrepont. Sheriff's deputies say they believe the blaze may have been caused by faulty wiring. A dog, two calves, a snow machine, and a large amount of hay and farm machinery were lost. Damage is estimated between fifteen and twenty thousand dollars. Canton and Pierrepont fire departments responded to the alarm. Sparks blew on a neighbor's barn but firemen saved that by parking a pumper next to it and keeping it wet. High winds blew sparks over a large area and the blaze could be seen for many miles around. The neighboring barn is owned by Ken Crowell.

It didn't say that the snow on the hill this morning is gray. Large black cinders stare at the house from the ice on the pond, the yard, and the meadow all the way to the Pierrepont road. Ken brought in a six-inch square of burned wood that he found in the grass by the barn. The cars of the village sightseers have already begun to drive by slowly. And Gary Cougler stayed home from school today.

FEBRUARY

TODAY IS Ground Hog Day, sunny and cold. This morning we took the boys and drove over to see Court Ostrander. A pretty flock of snow buntings flew up at their corner. It is so bleak and barren there it must remind the snowflake birds of their home tundra. I am always thrilled by the whiteness of their flashing wings as they wheel away in a group.

Court gave us a very old Indian basket he had hanging on a nail in his barn. The little egg basket is about to fall apart; it has a lot of character, one would say. We admired the geraniums blooming inside his barn in the windows. Court slept right through the fire. Lucky him.

Our woods beckon us for a short walk before we head home. As we leave the car at the pasture gate we observe that everybody still smells like cowbarn. There is not much snow after the big thaw; a fresh dusting of snow makes ideal conditions for tracking. We follow a single file of fox tracks, which lead us to a tiny set of prints—those of a mouse. The deer mouse and the meadow mouse are the two species most likely to make mouse tracks around here in winter.

The deer mouse, like other tree climbers, leaves his footprints in pairs. As he hops along the ground, his long tail leaves a line, and his larger hind feet leave prints in front of the tiny paired forepaws with each bound. The tracks we see now are not his. The meadow mouse often tunnels under the snow but does venture out on top from time to time, as I saw not long ago from the kitchen sink. His short tail does not register, and his footprints alternate in the characteristic track of the walkers and the waddlers. The little tracks before us then are his, but they end abruptly. We read in the snow that our fox dined recently on meadow mouse.

At the wood's edge we come across a mysterious set of tracks a little larger than a mink's. They look like marten tracks! The prints are blurred; a marten's feet are heavily furred in winter. The marten and his larger brother, the fisher, seem to be making a come-back in the Adirondacks.

Suddenly from behind a rock at our right a mink-brown animal streaks out. It is the marten! Bounding like a cat, it disappears among the boulders and birches behind us. We climb the knoll in hopes of another glimpse, but we lose the tracks in a bare patch on the sunny slope. The shy marten could have slipped safely back to the heart of the woods while we search around the separate boulders we have each marked in our minds as the very one behind which the beautiful animal has disappeared!

Fringed partridge tracks lead us to a snow patch where glistening red partridge berries with neat, round glossy-green leaves peek out of the snow. We admire nearby miniature parasols of *Lycopodium*, or ground pine, which cast lacy shadows on the snow crust. David rightly calls it the dinosaur plant; its giant relatives are the trees pictured in primeval swamps of the Great Age of Reptiles.

I pick some birch and alder twigs to take home for forcing. They don't look very promising now, but spring rewards the faithful by turning dead sticks into wands of incredibly perfect, shiny, tiny green leaves. I pass up some pussy willow twigs; I prefer to wait for them.

On our way home our car scares up a flock of evening grosbeaks eating salty gravel in the road. Two of the birds do not fly off with the others. Ken stops the car and goes back for them. One is dead, but the other is only stunned. We take him home to recuperate, if he will, on our back porch. The other goes into the freezer for ornithology class.

Ruby Latimer stopped in after lunch. "Doesn't the smoke smell awful!" she says coming up the back steps. The pile of black timber debris that once was the Couglers' barn is still smoking three days after the fire.

We trade observations on the fire.

"My mother—she lives down by Smiths' store, you know—she

saw the red sky that night and called me up about three A.M. She was afraid it was us," Ruby tells me. "This morning when I got up, I looked up the hill and saw something shining. It was the moon of course, but oh, it gave me quite a start."

"Ken said the same thing happened to him last night when he got up to open the bedroom window wider and smelled all the smoke. I really didn't think I wanted a fire in the fireplace today, but I guess it's like getting back on the horse after you've been thrown," I laugh. "I'm glad we've finished our ham smoking!"

Ruby is kind, friendly, soft-spoken, and reliable. She and Jim share the good partnership of so many farm couples. Her domain is the house and his the barn, but if something should happen to the help, Ruby is perfectly capable of helping out with the milking. In ordinary circumstances Ruby wouldn't think of leaving Jim to get his own supper before he goes out to the barn, but neither does she hesitate to ask Jim to take her into town for a round of errands when the chores are done.

After Ruby leaves I go down cellar and bring up the last of the acorn squash to bake for supper and some wrinkled but otherwise sound apples for an apple cake. I take the apples to the sun room to peel them.

We have two living rooms at the front of the house; we don't quite know what to call them. One of them, with a hardwood floor, was obviously the parlor, but we can't call it that. We call it the living room—the one we don't live in. The other room, with wide pine floorboards and wide pine cracks, gets the afternoon sun, so we call it the sun room.

The windows are fitted out with plant shelves. No North Country farmhouse is without its jungle windows mocking the wintry landscape outside. Ours came filled with geraniums, glowing firecracker red, all but one dainty pink one. A tiny red ladybug keeps me company, making her way along the fragrant leaves.

A flock of yellow evening grosbeaks at the feeder outside the window plays the parrot to our indoor jungle. These golden birds with heavy yellow bills and neatly folded white-and-black edged wings have such a tropical look that they always seem to me misplaced in the winter landscape.

A black-and-white checkered and striped hairy woodpecker backs down the pine tree to the suet feeder; the male has a red cap spot. A group of house sparrows edges in around the grosbeaks at the seeds. Something spooks the group; they wheel up to the pine tree's sheltering boughs. The black-capped chickadees are the first to return, dropping nearly on top of one another in their perpetual game of "Flinch." A white-breasted nuthatch, ambassadorial in pearl gray, black, and white, comes head first down the tree to the suet. Winter is indeed the formal season at the feeder.

The stunned grosbeak from the road has recovered. We open the porch door and he flies off to rejoin the flock. A dozen sparrows are resting in the mock orange branches, twelve fluffy balls muffled in gray down against the cold. Brown caps pulled down over their eyes, they take the sun. Behind them drip the hanging icicles at the elbow of the gutter, melting in the sun—drip, drip, and drip again.

Out in the field the sun warms the woodchuck's rock pile doorstep. Has our ground hog come out to see his shadow, bringing us six more weeks of winter? We are certainly not likely to have less in the North Country.

KNOBBY APPLE CAKE

This very old recipe, like the early settlers of Pierrepont, was transplanted here from Vermont. It is a treasure.

2 tablespoons butter
1 cup sugar
1 egg
1 teaspoon vanilla
1 cup flour
½ teaspoon cinnamon
½ teaspoon nutmeg
½ teaspoon salt
1 teaspoon baking soda
2 cups diced apple

Cream shortening and sugar. Add the egg and vanilla and beat well. Add dry ingredients, which have been sifted together. Add a few drops of milk if necessary, but batter should be very stiff. Stir in apples and bake in a greased and floured pan at 350° for 35–45 minutes. Serve warm or cold with cream, whipped cream, or ice cream.

* * *

Ken pulls into the driveway, gets out of the car, leaving the door open, and comes in calling, "Who wants to help me take what the janitor found to our marsh?" As we all pile into the car Ken explains: "It's a muskrat. The custodian saw it on the campus with a dog harassing it."

"May I look?" I ask, stretching toward the cardboard box.

"Don't open the box!" Ken orders. "I don't want it loose in the car. You should have seen how it lunged with its teeth bared when I tried to grab it." An insecure muskrat can attack quite viciously.

We drive down through the line of silver-trunked maples, their tops a red haze against the gray sky, the branch tip buds coloring up in spring promise. Dark brown cattails sway over grassy snow clumps in the silent marsh. A few drops of rain spatter us as Ken gingerly opens the box. A subdued little animal, not much over ten inches long, exclusive of tail, peers out beaverlike. Its smooth, black, naked tail curls around its body; its lustrous brown-black fur invites stroking—but not its yellowed chisel teeth.

"Why, it's a beautiful little thing! He is just a young one," I exclaim.

Ken laughs. "It certainly looked bigger when I was trying to get it into that box."

I'd never seen a dry muskrat before—wet muskrats look so ratty compared to this elegantly furred creature. We tilt the box and watch as the little animal snowplows away like a mole, leaving a snow-ridged wake behind him. He scoots away, slowly, steadily, out into the marsh.

What caused this little wanderer to stray so far from home? A muskrat does not willingly exchange security for adventure. Muskrats manage quite well in the winter marsh as long as there is moving water beneath the ice. It does not seem likely that this muskrat's marsh was frozen up; more likely his passageways through the snow and in his lodge were flooded by this sudden thaw. Muskrats' territorial social structure strictly regulates the number of animals in a marsh, but this glossy, well-fleshed young creature does not look like one of the 'rat society's extras, an outcast without a territory, scarred by life's losing battles.

The youngster will probably find himself alone here. What does life have in store for him?

* * *

We hardly needed the radio to tell us that there is no school today. The rain turned to snow early last night, dumping nearly two feet of snow from the skies by morning. Dawn brings only a lighter shade of gray. The wind is highballing through like a midnight freight.

It sculptures dune drifts across the driveway. It pastes snow on the porch screens, fits the windows and long gutters of the barn with white caps. At times the whirling white erases the Latimers' house, the Pierrepont road, the pond, even the barn. We see nothing but flying snow and two tiny bird forms in the snow-draped tangle of bushes beneath the window.

One of the birds flies up to the feeder. I fear the wind will smash him against it, but the bird safely overshoots the feeder and tacks accurately back upwind to it. The little birds are redpolls from the boreal forests of the north. Usually they travel in flocks but here are only two. A devoted couple braving the storm together? Not quite; these two spend more time squabbling than eating.

Ken surveys the driveway drifts and decides he'd better hurry out to plow while he can still get through. It is Tom's turn to ride with him. We have learned to park the jeep in the garage with the plow facing out the door.

The little red jeep punches with its yellow plow through the first drift. In the swirling wall of snow Ken misjudges and backs into the edge of the drift. Shoveling, sanding, rocking, they break free and plunge ahead a few more feet. Again and again they back and plow, and back and shovel in the choking blast once more. Plowing has to be planned. You must move the snow back far enough to give yourself room to put the snow from the next storm, but if your eyes are bigger than your plow you grind to a wheel-spinning, impotent halt against the too-big drift. Back off and try a smaller corner.

Father and son stamp back into the kitchen. The little boy's face glows with exhilaration from the bronco ride. One or two more times they will have to plow again today. We are having our annual worst blizzard since 1947.

In the warm kitchen we peel two small pumpkins brought up from the cellar. We slice it into chunks and simmer them in a little water to make pumpkin pulp for cookies. The boys rub the slippery seeds between their palms to remove the bright-orange rind threads. They melt a little margarine in a heavy iron skillet and gently fry and stir the seeds until at last they rattle crisp and golden brown in the pan. Then they salt the seeds lightly and spread them out to cool.

The snow dashes between the icicles hanging from the porch. The barn is a pale, blurred lithograph. Our kitchen smells cozy with cinnamon and clove. With a bowl of toasted pumpkin seeds and a plate of warm cookies on the hearth, a maple log crackling in the fireplace, and every rocker filled with reader and book, the storm may rage, but we don't mind. The beagle stretched out on the rug, belly toward the warming blaze, sighs contentedly in her sleep.

Late in the afternoon the wind drops and the sky lightens. A flock of redpolls throngs the feeder. Many years we see no redpolls all winter long, but all this week people have been puzzling over these tiny strangers at their feeders. Their pale breasts streaked dark, the males flushed with raspberry sherbet and sporting berry-red caps, the redpolls are a welcome ornament at the winter feed trays.

The blue and yellow State plow roars down the Pierrepont road in a spray of flying snow. They must keep the roads plowed out for the big silver-tanked milk trucks. The power company men are also out tending their lines. It's nearly milking time. Some fifty thousand cows in the county must be milked tonight!

PUMPKIN COOKIES

What to do if you grow pumpkins and can eat just so many pumpkin pies? Make these great cookies. If you do not have a pumpkin patch but recognize that these are outstanding cookies, you can probably scrape enough meat off the inside walls of your jack-o'-lantern—when you first carve it—to make one batch of cookies. After Halloween, use canned pumpkin.

If you do have pumpkins from the field or the root cellar, cook the meat slowly in just enough water to make a slush. Freeze in packages of premeasured size. Drain off any extra liquid resulting from thawing before using in recipes.

1 cup sugar
1 cup butter or margarine
1 cup cooked pumpkin
1 egg (unbeaten)
1 teaspoon vanilla
1 cup all-purpose flour
¾ cup graham or whole-wheat flour ⎫ (or use another cup of white
¼ cup wheat germ   ⎭ flour)
1 teaspoon baking powder
1 teaspoon baking soda
1 teaspoon cinnamon
(½ cup nuts or raisins if desired)

Cream sugar and butter or margarine together. Add remaining ingredients and mix well. Drop by spoonfuls onto greased cookie sheets. Bake at 350° for 10–12 minutes.

*   *   *

The rising sun is obscured by a thick gray veil of cloud. Day grows lighter but casts no shadows. As I look out the window I have the feeling that there is one more fence post in the snow over by the hedgerow. Could that white form be a snowy owl? This is supposed to be a snowy owl year—one of the cyclic fluctuations, when snowy owls in unusual numbers come down from the Arctic following a crash in the lemming populations, on which they feed. Weekly the papers have been reporting sightings of these great white birds, but we have yet to see one.

I'm sure that is not a snowy fence post; I think I saw it turn its head. Ken disagrees. It doesn't move; it is just a post in the snow. I stare and stare and then give up. When we look again in the afternoon the post is gone! Very sheepishly we put on our snowshoes and pad over to the hedgerow. There are the giveaway four-toed tracks. We have "seen" a snowy owl. . . .

Later, just as I am about to go out and see what is keeping Ken so long in the barn, he comes back down the snow steps to the porch. We do not shovel a path to the driveway or barn; we merely trample one. When the snow gets deeper than the wooden back steps we cut snow steps up into the drift. We have passed the halfway mark of winter, so the steps go up instead of down from the back door.

Ken shakes the snow off his red-and-black plaid wool jacket.

"Oh, what a mess! What an awful mess," he moans. "All over my wallet, all over my jacket; how could I?"

"What's the matter?" I ask, startled.

Wiping his hands and shaking his jacket at the sink, he replies, "After I fed the ducks I heard the Couglers trying to get their car out of a drift. I went up and helped them push, but I forgot I had three duck eggs in my coat pocket.

"We will have to forgo the apple custard pie tonight," I laugh. We will miss the eggs but not the apples.

This time of the year is hard on Ken's Yankee conscience. Some of the fruits and vegetables stored so carefully in the cellar last fall are now inevitably beginning to spoil. The squash develop soft black spots and the apples melt brown from within. Since Ken can't bear to waste anything, he ends up picking more apples than we can possibly eat. "You can't just let them rot there in the grass. So many of them are even too good to feed to the pigs," he says. So into the cellar they go, by the boxful, by the bagful.

Months later when they start getting soft we are in trouble. We start having a surfeit of baked apples, apple cobbler, apple cake, and apple pie.

When revolt sets in, and no one in the family can bear another apple anything, Ken ruefully remarks, "I guess you have to waste something sometimes."

*   *   *

The weatherman says, "Variable cloudiness with a chance of snow flurries" for us. To the south of us snow is still falling. The winds off Lake Ontario are piling snow on Oswego. The meteorologists, hydrologists, and engineers from the eastern United States and Canada who have gathered there for a conference on snow are thoroughly snowed in. At least they have plenty to talk about.

Ken has been out in the garage fussing with the jeep; he is wearing his red-and-black plaid jacket, flapping blue overalls, big green gum boots, and a brown-and-black checked cap with the ear flaps pulled low over his collar.

In a few minutes the little red jeep chugs off down the road to Smiths' store.

As Ken steps back out the door of the little store carrying his purchases, a snowmobile roars up. By the looks of the driver he is a suburbanite out for an "expedition." He is duded up in "moon" boots, a one-piece zippered purple space suit with yellow stripes down the sides. With his padded gloves he pushes back the plastic visor on his astronaut-styled helmet, turns off his throbbing toy, and admiringly eyes the jeep.

"A jeep; now that is some vehicle," he breathes. "You can go anywhere with that baby." He inspects the plow. "That sure is a great rig. I bet you make a lot of money plowing out driveways out here with that!"

"Ayep," Ken drawls in his best hayseed manner. He fastens the jeep door shut with a makeshift strap and rattles off chuckling to himself.

* * *

The thermometer still reads below zero. I have a bad cold, so Ken and the boys have taken over running the house. They cook great meals in the fireplace. But this morning we had a plumbing mishap.

Just before going off to work Ken decided we had collected enough dirty clothes for a washer load. All went well until the machine began to drain the wash water. Gurgle, gurgle, down the drain; then, whoosh! A fountain of water drenched the kitchen. I beat my way through the flying water and turned off the washer. The sheet of water showed clearly how the kitchen floor slants.

Since the kitchen drains are in the unheated crawlspace under the ell, they freeze when the weather gets very cold. I'm sure the previous occupants simply opened the back door and threw out the dish water. We have wrapped electric heating tapes around the pipes under the kitchen floor. But they don't work if you don't remember to turn them on.

It is nearly lunch time when I decide to bundle up and go out into the breathless, clear cold noon for the mail. The sun beams through the screens, covered for the winter with heavy clear plastic, and warms the little porch. The gutter over it drips icicles across the mock orange bush in sheets and garlands. The sassy little chickadees have learned how to come in through the open panel in the porch door meant for Belle, our beagle. We keep sunflower seeds in a big drum on the sunny porch. Today for the first time this year I hear the sweet whistled "fee-bee" note of the chickadees' spring song. It is nearly St. Valentine's Day—about the time these little birds faithfully add a melodic courting song to their repertoire of pert scoldings. I may have a few complaints about the calendar in the North Country, but we've got Valentine's Day just right.

After getting the mail, I stand a minute in the warm sun at the back door. A dapper tree sparrow, dark stickpin spot on his soft gray breast, picks some small seeds off the snow inches from my boots. The small toboggan is standing upright in a drift nearby. Surely it wouldn't hurt if I take just one ride. There isn't a breath of wind. I take down the toboggan, bang the ice off with my mittened palm, seat myself, and push off. I sail off down the hill in a sweet rush! I rudder with my right mitten, slide silently to a stop.

I sit there—immobile in the sun—enjoying the sparkling world. Nirvana. But there's our car coming around the corner at the bottom of the hill! Ken will be most displeased if he has come home to take care of his sick wife and finds her out tobogganing!

My peaceful reverie shattered, I stumble back up the hill, tripping with haste, dragging the telltale toboggan behind me. My heart pounds, blood races, lungs sear. Carefully I stand the toboggan back in its slot in the snow and hurry in to tear off boots, hang up coat, brush snow off the cuffs, and especially off the seat of my slacks as Ken pulls into the driveway. He disappears briefly into the barn, then comes in. Lunch—gasp for breath—is on the table. The biscuits I made are still warm—I have not been out too long.

Ken says, "I'm sorry I'm so late. I meant to get home a half hour earlier." On the counter he puts three frozen duck eggs, shells neatly cracked lengthwise by their icy contents.

"That's all right, dear," I breathe.

We watch the birds at the feeder while we eat our lunch. Raspberry redpolls gleam in the sun on the bare maple branches against the blazing blue sky. Flower-yellow evening grosbeaks fend off intruding blue jays with rasping words. I hope Ken doesn't notice the fresh toboggan track on the hill.

HOMEMADE BISCUIT MIX

This mix is best kept in a screw-top glass gallon jar. It should be stored at room temperature and away from light. If instead of keeping it in the cupboard, you prefer to keep it on the counter where it is handier, paint the outside of the jar with enamel paint. Do not add wheat germ to the mix in the storage jar. Just shake some into the bowl when you mix up a recipe, to add its nutlike flavor and nutritious crunch.

The Mix

7 cups all-purpose flour
2 cups graham or whole wheat flour
1 tablespoon salt
⅓ cup double-acting baking powder
2 cups solid vegetable shortening

Sift flours, salt, and baking powder together. Mix well. Cut in shortening until the mixture has the consistency of bread crumbs. Store in a tightly covered container.

Depending on the size of your family, use 1 or 2 cups of mix, add just enough milk to form a soft dough for rolls, a little more to make a sticky dough for biscuits, even more milk and an egg or two to make a batter of the consistency of heavy cream for pancakes or waffles. Add sugar or spices; experiment! You can use it exactly as you would an expensive commercial mix with preservatives in it.

* * *

There's nothing like a little wine racking to make one's cold feel better. One of our winemaking books, the British one, says, "Pleasant job, this!" and indeed it is.

Here are sparkling jugs of amber mead and banana sherry, jewel-toned raspberry, blueberry, date, and mint wines. The brews that are still bubbling we rack into clean jugs and return to the cellar.

I insert a clear plastic tube down into a jug just above the ochre lees. A suck on the tube brings the wine arching up out of the jug and down the tube into my mouth. I sneak a taste of the fruity liquid before tucking the tube into the waiting clean jug. The raspberry and blueberry wines, which we have never tried before, are pleasantly surprising. I squirt a little of each of the berry wines into small glasses for Ken to taste.

The wines to be bottled have already been racked once or twice before. Fermentation must be complete before you bottle wine or the bottles will explode. The wine will age and mellow in bottles, but it must no longer ferment. The exception to this, of course, is if you are making a champagnelike effervescent wine. In that case you add sugar and a champagne yeast at this point, and hope you've chosen stout bottles.

While I wash wine bottles and old-fashioned pale blue-green soda bottles with wire bails holding small white porcelain caps, Ken racks the date wine. He puts in the siphon tube, sucks, and chokes, making a wry face. He is not as lucky as I was. Vinegar flies have spoiled the wine. We have a jug of acetic acid instead of alcohol—vinegar!

The banana sherry is ready to bottle. We fermented ripe banana pulp with a sherry yeast. This improbable combination has produced a rich, red-gold sherrylike wine, really marvelous. Ken draws the liquid down ever so close to the lees. He doesn't want to miss a drop, but yet it would be a shame to muddy a bottle of this sparkling wine with a cloud of dead yeast. He pours the last bit into a glass and puts it on the window sill to settle.

Now he starts racking the mead. We give it the taste test; visions of Vikings and Dionysian revels are called up. "Honeymoon" is supposedly derived from the month of celebrations traditional after old English weddings, marked by liberal consumption of fermented honey wines. Mead, the aphrodisiac! I'd better hurry up and get well!

*   *   *

Nick, in his blue station wagon with the "U.S. Mail" sign fastened car-rack fashion on the roof, usually delivers our mail about 10 A.M. All along the route Nick leans out his car window and stuffs the mailboxes lined up at the side of the road. North Country mailboxes are often hung on long poles cantilevered out a good distance from the base post. This allows the snowplow to push quite a drift under the box, and the mailman can still pull up along side and reach into the projecting box. Frequently the pole is made to pivot; if it is not frozen up, it will swing out of the way and save the mailbox when the passing plow cuts in too close.

In spite of an occasional cup of coffee and exchanges of particularly exciting news, Nick's arrival time schedule varies remarkably little. If we have out-going mail we put up the red metal flag on the side of the mailbox. When the flag is down again or fresh tire tracks arc out through the road snow to our box, I know it is time to go out and get the mail and make my weather observations for the day.

If it rains or snows when a package arrives for us, we usually find it on our back porch if we are not home to walk up in answer to Nick's friendly honk. If we are in the yard when Nick comes by, we exchange news, get our mail, and watch him drive up the hill to Couglers'. Should a neighbor's car meet Nick on the hill, both vehicles may halt where they are for the exchange ritual with no fear of holding up traffic.

Winter is certainly the challenge season for rural mail carriers. Many is the time I have watched with my heart in my mouth as that station wagon (or even worse, the big, silver milk-tank truck) slid, slithered, and fishtailed up the icy hill.

Bill, the milkman, shares the trials of rural deliveries. Of course, most of our neighbors never see Bill; their milk is delivered by their own cows. The milk we get from Bill still comes in bottles. If he forgets to flip the lid closed on the milk box and the day is cold, the milk may freeze and pop the caps off the bottles in white towers of "ice cream." Once in a great while we may be out all day when the chain of events causes the bottles to freeze and they all break. How we hate to lose all those bottles.

The snow drifts by the front fence have been rising steadily, threatening to engulf the milk box at the next high tide. I have noticed for some time now that Bill and Ken and I have each been using the same single footprint in the drift side to reach the milk box. Bill pulls his truck up close to the snow and steps out with one foot to lean over and deposit our milk. Ken manages all right, but for me that foothold is a bit too high!

*   *   *

The night has been a wild, stormy one; it is no deathly silent snowfall, but a shrieking blizzard. We had just managed to fall asleep despite the howling of the snowy wind, when the roaring, grinding noise of the town snow plow pulled us back to consciousness.

I remember that Ken has left the car on the road rather than try to make it up the slope of the driveway. I wait tensely for the plow to pass the house; I hope they will see the car through the swirling snow. The plow doesn't come. I wait. I hear the motor but the sound comes no closer. The yellow warning lights of the plow flash on the ceiling of the bedroom and its headlights illuminate the delicately scrolled frost leaves covering our window. But the plow does not appear. The plow, the mighty plow, is stuck! After a time its lights go out and its motor dies. I fall back to sleep.

Again the room is filled with golden flashes and the roar of a plow breaks the night, but it is a plow with a different voice. Another plow has come to free the trapped behemoth.

It passes our car and churns on up the road. We listen to it working out there in the howling dark. Pity the road crew on a night like this. Three A.M.! At last we hear a plow returning down the hill, one plow—the plow of the second voice.

Morning dawns bright and clear. The snow in the air is windborne, no longer falling from the heavens. Up the road beyond the barn we see the humbled turrets of the giant snow plow.

The snow has been spread into giant drifts. The once familiar scene is curiously empty; many landmarks are gone, others dwarfed. The rail fence is gone along with the tall bird feeder on its pole; one huge drift stretches across the barnyard and up to the roof of the stable.

After breakfast the Town Road Supervisor and several men with shovels appear up at the stranded plow. Ken bundles up and stumbles up the drifts to exchange greetings and commiserate with them. The crew digs and digs. Then a huge yellow grader comes from behind, a chain is hitched on, and the grader pulls; but the plow is held fast in the giant drift.

"We'll have to leave this road blocked. In a couple of days we can maybe bring in a scoop from the front and open 'er up."

Off they go to cope with the more tractable of Pierrepont's miles of snow-swept roads.

* * *

Today is David's birthday and the presents from his grandparents have not yet come in the mail. From the kitchen window I can see that traffic is moving pretty well on the Pierrepont road so Nick will probably try to deliver the mail. He will see at once that our road is impassable, but I have a plan.

I phone the Canton Post Office. "Will there be rural delivery today on Route Four?"

"Yes, Nick will give it a try."

I tell my plan to them, and they agree to pass it on to Nick. I put on my boots and the old long coat to which I have added a fur-framed parka hood, grab the shovel from the porch, and flounder up the driveway through waist-deep snow.

I excavate the mailbox without too much difficulty. It has been hit by the plow a few times this winter and lost its bottom in the fray, but it still functions as an enclosure, so I tuck it under my arm and make my way down to the corner walking on packed road-side drifts until I reach the part that was cleared by the "rescue" plow.

At the corner where our road meets the Pierrepont road I clamber up the tallest snow bank, plant our mailbox firmly in the snow, and draw from my coat pocket a bundle of outgoing letters which I have wrapped in a plastic bread bag. Here is an improvised mail box that Nick can reach.

I climb down and head for home well pleased. An hour later, working in the kitchen, I happen to look out the kitchen window, and see a shiny yellow bulldozer parked on the drift where our milk-box–mailbox had been!

I grab the shovel again and hurtle myself down to the corner. Wind whips the snow now, not nearly as pleasant a journey as the first. I can hear the putt-putt-putt of the 'dozer engine, but not a soul is in sight. I clamber up the big drift again and, sure enough, there in the snow is my mailbox, now a parallelogram, but salvage-able. I manage to extricate it, and look for another location. I plant the box again but am not satisfied. It looks small and vulnerable beside that chugging giant. If the man on the machine did not see the box when he pulled up on it, how can I expect he won't run over it when he backs down? Dilemma. Where is the driver? Who would leave a "loaded" bulldozer just sitting around?

I decide to wait for the driver to return. The wind rages and stings my eyes with blowing snow. I back up against the drift on the far side of the road and lean on my shovel. The Eskimo lies in wait for the polar bear. I pull my parka hood closer and shift my harpoon to the other hand. It is a long wait.

Eventually a highway truck pulls up and disgorges the master of the yellow giant. He is, to say the least, astonished to see me. I explain my plight. He backs his 'dozer off my drift, takes a few passes at it to sculpture it more effectively for my purpose, and chug-putts off into the whirling white. I trudge back up the hill to my igloo.

Not much later, again standing vigil at the window over the sink, I am rewarded by the sight of Nick's blue station wagon parked at the corner. He gets out, unwraps my mail, waves a couple of packages triumphantly toward our house, and packs them into my milk box. As he pulls out again I hear the faint "toot, toot" of his car horn. Happy Birthday, David!

*　　*　　*

The four families on our road are all prepared for the "Pierre-pont Pony Express" today. Elated by my albeit spotty success record of yesterday, we have arranged for Nick to put everybody's mail in my milk box this time.

I call Budge Cougler when I see Nick pull up, and together we walk down to the corner over the sparkling drifts. The sky is an intense blue. Snow lumps creak under our boots and our breath puffs in white wisps as we chat in the cold morning air.

Our box is as full as Christmas. Joe Moran called Roz Smith at the store and arranged for Nick to pick up a package of chewing tobacco for him. There it is, folded in his newspaper. Now Joe can enjoy being snowed in. Together we deliver the mail to Walter and Emma Bowers, who live at the corner. In front of their door is a huge pile of snow and the only way down to the porch and the door is to sit down and slide. Like two otters we do just that.

We visit and swap snow stories over a cup of coffee. The snow-mobile laws in the towns have been suspended, and snowmobiles are allowed on all the roads. Grocery stores are advertising on the radio for emergency delivery by snowmobile. St. Lawrence University has closed—most unusual for a residential college. And a woman stranded after she had started for the hospital to have a baby had to be taken there by snowmobile. The bulk milk trucks did finally get through, so none of the neighbors had to dump their milk.

The town must be a real mess. Even before the storm you couldn't see over the drifts at the corners—every intersection was blind, and people had to wait hours for Canton's single taxi cab.

We leave Bowers' and make our way back to our own hearths. The Pierreponters are content. We have battled the blizzard of the winter, in the winter of the century.

MARCH

THE SUN IS BLINDING; flying snowflakes sparkle in the air. The wind is blowing loose snow into windrows across the road and driveway that we shuffle through as we tramp up to get the mail. Yesterday they freed the plow; it makes the rounds once or twice a day now to push back the creeping drifts of windblown snow.

Newspapers have begun listing weight restrictions for the country roads in anticipation of the spring break-up period in what is surely a gem of journalistic optimism. The North Country harbingers of spring, the crows, are once again becoming conspicuous in the snowy fields. California asparagus is appearing in the supermarket; flies are appearing in the house. Spring is coming.

The cover of this month's farm magazine shows a man on a tractor plowing warm, bare ground, surrounded by green grass and leafy trees! Tractor season has begun here, too. Tom pushes his toy tractor in looping tracks over the snowy crust, punctuating them at intervals by flopping on his back and sweeping his arms at his sides to make snow "angels."

The boys have made an impressive twelve-foot slide down the big drift that reaches the stable roof. The steep face carved out by the wind at one corner reads like a cliff of sedimentary rock. Giant frosting cornices hang blue over the edge of the barn and garage roofs. Every lump of snow in the drive is blue-shadowed like an iceberg or glacier. The boys' ski pole harpoons make holes that glow blue. They have dug a spacious snow cave in the snow-plow wake at the edge of the driveway.

I call the boys to see if their ruddy cheeks are turning white—a sign of frostbite. They are oblivious to the wind, which is blowing about 15–20 m.p.h. Though I am comfortable reading the mail sitting in the shelter of the house wall in the sun, it is only 10°, which because of the wind-chill factor gives the effect of −30° out where the boys are playing. I lure them to the lee of the house, where we sit in snow chairs and lawn chairs in the drift several feet above the slumbering bulbs and mint patch of my dooryard garden. I bring out sandwiches and we picnic in the snow in the warmth reflected from the house wall.

Belle lets herself out her flap in the storm door and begins to dig furiously in the snow. Does she remember that she left a bone in that spot or does she smell one? Paws scrabbling wildly, nose snuffling in the snow, she soon disappears into a huge hole and only her wagging tail is seen sticking out. A good two feet down she finds that bone, and soon lies contentedly on the packed snow path at our feet, gnawing her prize. I hope it was worth it; bloody paw prints mark the side of the hole.

Tame chickadees flit around us. David has scattered some seeds on the snow at our feet and grins as tiny sharp black feet close on his bare fingers—a chickadee takes a sunflower seed from his cupped hand.

After lunch I remind the boys to go to the barn to feed the chickens. They head toward the barn on their snowshoe-packed trail, past exotic wind-sculptured snow shapes. They swing themselves down into the barn by gripping the rail on which the door hangs. If the snow gets much deeper, they won't be able to get into the barn.

* * *

Three pine grosbeaks have called me to the window by their distinctive "churring" finch note. They are immature birds, their drab plumage faded even further by the intensity of the sunlight, which jewels the snow and glows through the icicles along the roof edge. When one flies over to the bare maple by the window I can see that its gray head is tinged with ochre: a young female. Her father's feathers are a bright plum, and her mother's pumpkin colored. The bird before me wipes its dark stubby bill on the branch and flies over to land on the snow by the other birds in the bushes near the garage. With stately deliberateness they reach up to pluck red nightshade berries. Tiny pieces of scarlet peel and brown calyx cover the snow under the dry vines.

The pine grosbeaks sit nestled on the snow or hop low over it in a characteristic way. Actions identify bird species as surely as we recognize the gait of a loved one as far away as we can see him. I have little patience with bird watchers who lower their binoculars as soon as they have identified a bird, instead of watching to see what the bird is doing.

A sparrow hawk swooping in sends the grosbeaks flying off in undulating flight, their robinlike bodies and long tails silhouetted against the snow. The little kestrel bobs on the power pole. The dark pattern around its face makes the bird look as if it is wearing a falconer's hood. The little falcon bobs again, cries out, and flies off. Birds in spring have such an exuberant, joyous, erotic elasticity of step!

As the birds—and my spirits—respond to the lengthening spring hours of sun, so too does this old farmhouse. The door no longer stays latched because of the annual spring shifting of the foundation. I answer its invitation and collect my cross-country skis from the porch. Today is a waxer's dilemma. It must be nearly 40° in the sun; the base snow is surfaced with shining granules of "corn" snow, but in spots fresh powder snow is piled up. The wind has left other spots bare ice. I don't take my ski waxing very seriously. I don't need the fastest ride possible; I just want enough wax to let me slide on my way down and keep me from slipping backwards when I ski uphill. Cross-country skiing is as easy as walking and makes North Country winters not long enough.

I head out across our snowy meadows. The snow lies in great sheets cracked into huge tiles by "Y" shaped cracks, tessellated by the weight of a settling ice crust. My skis echo against this sub-surface frozen layer. The way out is mostly uphill; thunk, thunk, thunk—the wax is holding well.

I swish through shiny "corn" granules, the sun beats warm on my back. I slide across a dirty puddle where dark road sand has been blown on the snow, melting out a hollow. We are ready for spring when country snow starts looking like city snow!

From the Couglers' maples by the road comes a crazy cacophony of starling song. Over a hundred of these peculiarly shaped black nuisances are singing in the treetops. They run through their repertoire of imitations of song birds—whom they have left in the sunny south and whose nest sites here they are already claiming as their own—as well as the sounds of whistles, squeaking doors, and noises of their own creation, all in that slightly hysterical tone of voice peculiar to flocks of starlings.

I reach the blue shadows of a hedgerow and step in out of the glare among the rocks and bushes. Although the length of my skis is awkward, they are so light that I can easily maneuver among the fat budded bushes and the weasel tracks, perfect penny-sized "hands" in the snow. I see where the little ermine dived under the snow; the roofs of the tunnels have now melted away.

Down the wooded row a red squirrel scolds at me. I hear crows in the next hedgerow talking to one another as I stand in the shadows looking out through bare branches at the wide white fields. Suddenly a pair of coyotes trots into view over a rise. Lean, sandy-buff, doglike, yet distinctively coyote, the pair crosses the empty field at its lowest contour. They are close enough that I can see darker streaks down their backs and the fronts of their legs, and the silky black hairs that tip their bushy brown tails. They stop and listen, cocking their large ears. I suppose they know I'm here, although they do not turn their narrow muzzles toward me. They stop, and time stops. I breathe again when they break the spell and trot on, headed over to Jim Latimer's high back pasture, intending no doubt to feed on the carcass of a dead calf Jim says they have dug out of the snow.

Monty Latimer told us last week that he had seen a pair when he was out snowmobiling—wolves, he called them. Any statement to the effect that wolves have long since departed this area would have been very unpopular until last year—there was a bounty on wolves, not coyotes. The myth was carefully perpetuated until the state legislature in a gesture perhaps indicating increasing environmental sophistication finally repealed the archaic bounty laws. Monty said he was sitting in the sun, snowmobile turned off, when two coyotes came by with three dogs chasing them. The coyotes were in no hurry, sitting and looking back at the dogs, then moving on just fast enough to keep ahead of their pursuers. When Monty called the conservation officer he was told that there is a law against dogs chasing deer, but not against dogs chasing coyotes so the officer wasn't interested.

I wonder if this is the same pair. They disappear over the brow of the hill and I realize suddenly that I am cold. I pick a path out of the hedgerow into the sunlight and ski briskly back down the meadows toward home.

On the downhill run I lean forward and, driving my knees forward at each stroke, fall into a piston-like rhythm, trying now to get a good ride for each slide of my skis. I balance carefully as I clatter across a slanting ice sheet.

I check in at the woodchuck's stone pile. The snowy mound is thoroughly marked with tracks—he has been enjoying the sunshine. In his doorway I find a chewed burdock stem, a pile of brown crumbs sifted down into the entrance hole.

A line of pigeon-toed woodchuck tracks leads in the direction of my next destination, the beehives. A peppering of fine dark chaff under a dry Queen Anne's lace blossom along the way tells me what the woodchuck had for lunch. Beside it in the snow is a dead bee, and there another, and another. With growing dismay I follow a line of dead bees all the way to one of the hives. Dozens, hundreds, of bees lie dead or feebly crawling on the snow. Their dark bodies have already begun to melt little graves in the snow. At the hive entrance the snow is fouled with yellow blotches. What are all these bees doing out here in the cold? I resist the impulse to gather up those foolhardy bees that have not yet frozen to death and poke them back into the sheltering hive. I think I have spring fever!

I ski home, rush in to tell Ken about the errant bees, and he re-assures me that the winter flights are good for the hive. Bees infected with a dysentery-producing disease will be the first to leave the hive for relief, so fewer carriers of the infection remain in the hive.

I am impressed. He smiles and holds up the bee book he has been reading this afternoon. He listens with interest as I describe the coyote encounter. Coyotes seem to be extending their range in the East, benefitting perhaps from man's land-clearing practices and the retreat of the wolves. Although we have yet to hear them sing here, we are glad to know they are in the neighborhood. Besides being exciting to watch they are excellent rodent control agents, and perhaps one day they will make our rocky pastures ring with their wild evening song.

Wolves and mountain lions have retreated to Canada, but bears are still reported in the area. Some students of Ken's came across black bears just last week in the woods to the south of our place.

Denned up in a snow cave beneath a fallen log were a mother bear and her two new cubs—fortunately all asleep.

Snug in my rocker by the firelight after my exciting outing I read in the St. Lawrence County history a wild-animal tale of a century ago. At that time Jim Latimer's farm, where today the coyotes ran, was owned by Moses Leonard. Here is his story, which I found in the yellowed pages of that history:

> The son, Moses, the subject of this biography, at the early age of twenty years began the life of a hunter and trapper, and from that time to the present, excepting a few years when he was incapacitated by sickness, he has been engaged in hunting and trapping game, and is probably able to count up more scalps of wild animals as trophies than anyone now living in the state.
>
> Mr. Leonard has kept no record of the number of different wild animals he has shot or trapped, but from the most reliable data, thinks he has killed 300 wolves, over 100 bears, 44 panthers, from 1200 to 1500 deer, and of fur-bearing animals, like otter, foxes, martin, etc., a vast number.
>
> Mr. Leonard, now nearly seventy-two years old, still retains his passion for the wild woods, and has spent nearly two months of the present fall (1877) in the forest, hunting deer and catching small animals for their skins; but he claims that in his case the infirmities of age and the scarcity of game keep in exact ratio.
>
> Mr. Leonard was frequently engaged in exciting encounters with wild beasts. Notably [sic] among them was his encounter with a large bear. Going one day in the forest, armed only with a light axe and accompanied by his dog, he saw directly in his way a large black bear. He told his dog to "go" for him, expecting that when Bruin was attacked by the dog he would take a tree, when his brother, who would soon be within call, would come with his rifle and dispatch him. The dog attacked vigorously, and was soon seen in the huge jaws of the bear. Mr. Leonard, seeing his favorite dog being killed, ran to the rescue. On his approaching too near to his bearship, who had put the dog "hors du combat," he turned to attack the hunter, who met the attack with such well-directed blows upon his head with the axe, cutting off one of the bear's ears in so doing, the Bruin turned to escape, and was pursued for a long distance by the hunter with uplifted axe.
>
> Mr. Leonard, while relating this adventure to a gentleman residing in Lewis county, in this State, several months after the occurence, was told that a monster bear had lately been killed in that county having large scars upon the head made with an

axe, and one ear cut off. Mr. Leonard is satisfied that Bruin had *his* mark; he did not claim it, however.

* * *

Sugar snow is falling in those distinctive great feathery flakes that foretell the beginning of a maple sap run. We have work to do; jugs and pails stacked in the old milkhouse must be rinsed and set out by the trees, the special ⅝" tapping bit for the drill must be found, as well as a pocketful of nails and scraps of wire.

As we all garb up for tree tapping, Tom finds in David's old galoshes an unexpected treasure. He pours something out on the floor, and we count eight dried corn kernels, eleven pumpkin seeds, half an almond, one cashew nut, and a crumb of stale corn bread. A mouse's larder!

In the barnyard, in the falling snow, we all pause and hold out our arms to catch the flying flakes. They are perfect picture book crystals, the largest single flakes as big as garden peas. Groups of crystals are knitted together by their lacy edges to form mammoth flakes as large as quarters or even half dollars. In the breathless silence the giant flakes float slowly, slowly, straight down, like feathers enchanted.

The boys load the sap equipment onto the small toboggan and at last we are ready for our first rite of spring. We tramp up the driveway to the line of maples at the edge of the road. At the first tree Ken kneels down to drill an inch and a half hole in an upward slant, as low as he can comfortably reach. At the end of the sap run, when the last sap is being collected and the last of the snow is melting away, perhaps six weeks from now, these buckets will be hanging more than high enough on the trunk.

The bit screws into the lichen-coated tree trunk, sending out sweet, wet sawdust. The boys pass their father a yellow nylon spout, or spile, which he taps into the hole. Over the mouth of the spile Ken fits a length of plastic tubing and judges the spot to pound in a nail from which we will hang a gallon glass jug to catch the sap. A wire loop on the jug handle makes the highly unorthodox rig secure. Farther down the line of trees we will use the traditional metal spiles and sap buckets with tin covers, but here by the house we want the clear glass so we can watch the dripping sap shatter the watery surface in the jugs in diamond flash, flash, flash, flash in the afternoon sunlight.

Of course we cannot leave full glass jugs on the trees overnight or they would freeze and burst. The jugs hanging on the warm sunny south side of the trees are first to fill, and I can watch from my window to see when the jugs need emptying. I feel more in tune with the trees when I can look out and see at a glance if the sap is running. A warm day after a cold night gives the best sap flow. And most likely it will be a school day, leaving me to empty all those jugs by myself at least twice, and a third round will be waiting for my men.

These trees seem to give more syrup than the ones we tapped in Vermont. In all fairness I must point out that small-crowned woods trees comprised our Vermont sugar bush, while these full, round roadside trees benefit from much greater exposure to the sun. People here in New York are very sensitive about the maple rivalry between the two states. Together Vermont and New York produce two thirds of the nation's maple syrup and sugar crop. We actually turn out more syrup than our neighbor to the east, but as the local syrup producers say, "We send barrels of our syrup to Vermont and they get the name for it." It is true that much of the maple sugar candy sold in Vermont is made from good New York sap.

The Iroquois say they invented the ancient art of maple sugaring. They used to move their whole villages out to camp in the sugar bush for the moon of the maple. The trees were gashed and fitted with rude spiles to carry dripping sap into cleverly fashioned elm-bark vessels set on the snow below. They boiled it by throwing hot stones from a fire into the sap trough. Thus eventually they produced a sweetener that could be stored in elm-bark boxes and used to flavor their meats, their corn soups, and their succotash the whole year through.

The month when the maple sap ran was for the Iroquois a time of gaiety and conviviality as well as hard work. So it is today. The Indians reverently gave thanks for the gifts of the maple. And so do we.

* * *

At last, the first day of spring, ushered in with the welcome sound of gentle splashing rain; in the cellar the cistern bubbles and sings merrily. The cellar floor is flooded with water coursing across to the drain on the downhill side.

At breakfast we watch a pair of crows celebrating the season

with a ritual dance—they bow, fan their tails, and click their wings
smartly across their backs. The arc of the pond bank has melted out
from the cold white, a brown sickle reaping the winter snows.

Our rain-streaked kitchen window frames the rolling countryside spread in surrealistic bands: a row of red-topped, black-
stemmed maples wearing low-slung belts of dark sap pails, this
bucket baggage cutting strange shapes out of the meadow white,
a stripe of far-hill blue shading off to a spring gray sky.

The pies in the oven are ready so we can start for church. The
little white church in Crary Mills is enjoying a renascence. Largely
as a result of the Huntleys' efforts with our Ostrander and Latimer
neighbors, the little church has once again opened its doors and
assumed a place in the area's social life. The minister is shared with
another little country church, but we have our very own church,
and every so often our own church suppers held at noon, right
after the service, so everyone can be back in the barn for milking
come evening.

Our car is parked at the head of the driveway to be sure we
don't get mired in; and we make our way up to it through the
slush in the driveway like so many salmon hurling themselves upstream. The hot pies carefully balanced on the dashboard, lightly
held as the car bounces over frost heaves and pot holes in the
winter-worn roads, make circles of condensing fog on the inside
of the windshield.

We stop for the Sunday paper at Smiths' in anticipation of a
pleasant rainy afternoon by a cozy fire. Spring is really here;
Smiths' checkout counter is heaped with bags of marbles. We make
our purchases—including marbles—and speculate on the length of
the maple sugaring season.

All along the road wet maples are hung with sap containers. In
spite of the rain the sap is running. If you were to listen closely at
one of the trimly tapered buckets, you would hear the rain dripping
on the peaked tin cover over the bucket, and as if in echo, the
drip of the sap from the spile into the dark of the sap bucket.

Where the snow has settled enough farmers have already begun
spreading rich, black manure on the white fields. We pass Red
Ostrander, Court's brother, out on his tractor with a spreader of
steaming manure behind. Looks like he won't be in church this
morning. At the corner by the Huntleys' we find a flock of more
than a hundred crows working over the freshly spread fields. The

lookouts posted in the hedgerow trees give the alarm call when our car stops and many of the handsome black birds flap slowly off to the bushes in the back pasture.

We turn into a cut between the snow drifts to park by the church. In the little churchyard surrounded by spruce and cedars, behind the white clapboard church, the taste in monuments runs mainly to obelisks and urns, white marble spotted with orange lichen or somber gray granite. The lane across from the church bears a different kind of marker: a purple roadsign emblazoned with the white silhouette of a man on a snowmobile. This road is open to snowmobiles—those roaring snow machines that compete so well for the Sunday morning hours of Pierreponters.

The pies are carefully carried up the wooden steps of the traditional little New England village church, through the Gothic arch of its dark-green doors. The boys clatter down to the basement for Sunday school. On the wall of the vestibule, above the old melodeon gathering dust, a brightly crayoned drawing of a rainbow, youthfully lettered, tells us that God sent it to Noah as a promise that there would be no more great floods—a useful article of faith for spring run-off season in the North Country.

The minister, Mr. Milbrey, a school teacher from the 'Berg, (Ogdensburg), has arrived. He greets his little flock, settles his notes at the lectern in front, and walks back to the vestibule to hang up his overcoat and put on his black gown, which considerably subdues his yellow shirt and red tie.

When the babies are settled in the box pews and the men called in from their conversations in the hall, Mr. Milbrey nods to Rosalie at the organ and she begins to play. At the right moment, Mr. Milbrey walks once again up the aisle in proper processional fashion.

After the invocation and announcements the children come up the stairs from Sunday school, clutching their church comics and construction paper creations, and thread their way to seats beside their parents. Seven sweet, shining young girls take seats in front of the organ—the choir, resplendent in glistening clean hair, brightly colored barrettes, and 4-H project dresses, bright piqués and checked ginghams—another sure sign of spring.

Mr. Milbrey's deep voice blends with the light girlish ones in *I Love to Tell the Story,* and then he begins his children's sermon.

Red Ostrander and his wife slide into the pew in front of us as unobtrusively as possible.

"You missed something," loudly hisses the bouncy little three-year-old next to us.

"If your offering be small, let it be accompanied by much love; if it be large, let it be equaled by love," rumbles Mr. Milbrey, and smiling Court Ostrander and his red-haired brother walk up the aisle with the collection plates. Red, the late arrival, the quick-change artist whom we saw so recently in his fields, still has his galoshes flapping around his ankles. The two ruddy-faced, genial farmers lean their arms on the back pew as if it were a rail fence, while Rosie finishes her hymn. Doesn't one of them have a plug of chewing tobacco in his cheek that he's still working on? I wonder if so many farmers chew because it would be too dangerous to smoke in the barn. They carry the offering plates up to Mr. Milbrey, followed by a beaming toddler. The brothers return to their seats; the chortling little moppet is retrieved.

As Mr. Milbrey launches into his sermon, his parishioners inventory with merited satisfaction the rich new cocoa paint on the wide wooden floorboards, the freshly white embossed tin wall panels, and the brightly varnished wainscoting. I smile up at the old kerosene chandelier above us. Its ornate gold filigree saucers once held glowing oil lamps, and from around its central axis four chubby cupids—posing as cherubim—smile down on the pious below.

Children pass cobwebs to one another; the girls in the choir titter as one of them drops a chunky boy's ring; a plastic baby bottle smacks the floor. A miraculously silent moment occurs when Mr. Milbrey calls the small congregation to prayer. I confess to a feeling of relief as we stand for the final hymn and benediction. Watching all those squirming youngsters, especially my own, is exhausting, and judging from the spirited visiting in the aisles afterward, I suspect many of our neighbors feel the same.

Everyone heads downstairs. In no time at all, three long tables are set with "Drink Milk" place mats, vases with plastic flowers, and well-filled glass toothpick holders. All thirty-three of us are soon seated, two little ones in high chairs at the table ends. Baked beans, cole slaw with raisins, cold bean salad, meat loaf squares, macaroni and cheese, chicken shortcake, Spanish rice, potato salad, stuffed eggs, and fruit salads beckon from the tables' centers—and scalloped potatoes. Mrs. Red Ostrander explains that they were late because she dropped one pan of her scalloped potatoes in their driveway.

Mr. Milbrey says we are going to have a kind of reenactment of the Last Supper as a Lenten observance. He passes out paper cups and aluminum pitchers of Hawaiian Punch. "Parents, please pour," he says. The men uneasily and longingly eye the butter on the tables as loaves of sesame-seeded French bread are passed from hand to hand and each breaks off a piece. We partake.

"Mommy, I wanted chocolate milk!"

When the casseroles have all made the rounds several times and we have finished our cream pies, apple pies, cherry pies, chocolate marble cake, and coffee, the men group themselves at the edge of the room, ignoring the little ones running around the tables. Laughter rings in the kitchen, where a few of the wives are washing up the dishes. Paint cans still stacked up in the corner by the kitchen door attest to the recentness of the revival of this little church.

When Ann called us to see if we were interested in having the church reopened she never asked what, if any, our religious tenets were, and I forgot to ask what kind of church it was. The Crary Mills church is reopened for fellowship, and so the youngsters can sing in a choir; the circuit minister can worry about the theology end of it.

* * *

Yesterday we left behind us the white peaks of the Adirondacks to drive down the New York Thruway, which links New York City to the rest of the state in the same way that the Trans-Canada Highway holds together that farflung nation.

We have taken advantage of the boys' spring vacation to drive down from the attic of New York State to visit family, to go to the wonderful museums and the opera, to enable Ken to talk mice with a colleague at the American Museum of Natural History. We will partake of those aspects of civilization that great cities offer, but how ironic it is to find the cultural triumphs of mankind in a nest of knives, where fear and hatred stalk the streets.

While Tom and David play country mouse and city mouse with their New Jersey cousins, Ken and I thread our way through the

maze of bedroom communities on the bus to New York City. The
spacious mansions on the New Jersey ridges peer through dirty
air at the murky Manhattan skyline. Here live the men who fill
the top management positions of the very industrial giants that
affront our senses here with their pollution. These are well-edu-
cated, well-traveled men who in many ways enjoy the highest
standard of living in the world. But they seem not to see the bilious
air, the turgid waterways. Or they see but are mesmerized as one
after another the wooded hills are cleared in unplanned town
growth patterns, as the precious wetlands of the Jersey meadows
are swallowed up by nearly five tons of garbage a week.

Out the bus windows we watch the lunatic clog of single-pas-
senger cars and roaring, belching trucks. Then we are swallowed
up by the tunnel which empties us out into the great pulsating
city—New York.

Shop signs in a variety of languages and alphabets attest to the
polyglot nature of the city. The overwhelming sensory richness is
dazzling. It would be fabulous except for the blocks of megalithic
housing, the empty alleys blowing with dirty papers and forlorn
rags. What man can learn to tolerate! But how unnecessarily!

We shoulder our way through the hurrying crowds over to Fifth
Avenue, with its shiny limousines and flag-decked tall buildings.
Like that valley of tombs by the Nile, this is a Valley of the Kings
where wealthy mortals toil in vain laying up a store of riches they
cannot take with them into the spirit world. Ahead of us walks a
lady in a leopard coat.

"I want to see if that is real," hisses Ken between his teeth, so we
follow her into Tiffany's. I peer into the sparkling jewelry cases
while Ken stalks the cat coat.

He whispers at my side, laying his hand on my sleeve, "Isn't
that awful—it *is* real! That is just immoral; I'm going to get a
picture of it."

In another minute a plainclothes guard puts his hand on Ken's
sleeve and whispers, "No pictures in here, please." He thinks we
are planning a heist!

When we emerge again into the sunshine on the swarming side-
walk, Ken gets his picture. I am relieved when we board a bus and
head down Fifth Avenue, past throngs of people with turned-off
faces quickly passing each other, past a man kneeling out in the
street shouting to a policeman and a small circle of onlookers—

lurching buses, hordes of automobiles, weaving taxis, cacophony—a theater of the absurd!

We walk across Central Park. Frederick Law Olmstead's marvelously foresighted creation, before it gets a cosmetic cover of new leaves, is indeed a tattered remnant of the natural world, and yet how valuable the parks can be to the people who live here. Beyond question nearly all of us will be living in cities in the not too distant future. Reorganizing urban areas to an appropriately human scale is a mind-boggling task but an imperative one. Any pasture is worth greening.

When we reach the Natural History Museum Ken disappears in the direction of the research collections. I linger among the totem poles of the vast shadowy hall of the Northwest Coast Indians, and then make my way upstairs to the African exhibits. Another leopard skin catches my eye—the robe draped on a mannequin portraying a tribal chief.

It reminds me of the time a few years back when we were invited to New York City to attend a press luncheon at the national headquarters of the Audubon Society. Here in the fur fashion capital of the world Assemblyman Edwyn E. Mason, from Hobart, New York, was explaining his bill to prohibit the sale in this state of articles made from the skins of endangered animal species. Elimination of a major market for their hides might save from extinction such animals as the leopard, and the tiger, polar bear, vicuna, and the alligators of the world.

Over delicatessen sandwiches and New York State champagne the genial assemblyman and his staff of aides mingled with the ardent people from the Sierra Club, Friends of the Earth, and the bearded men of Science from this museum and the New York Zoological Society. Reporters sifted through the group collecting mimeographed press statements and scribbling on their pads as the bearded curators one-upped each other with "when I was in New Guinea," "on my last trip to Kenya," and "the other day in Ceylon."

The wife of the Indian Vice-Consul swirled in wearing a purple pants suit, trailing a blue silk stole, with a veritable breastplate of silver filigree encrusted with turquoise adorning her throat. Madame Vice-Consul read a statement pleading for our country's help to save India's tigers.

The reptile experts from the Bronx Zoo demonstrated with a pair of stiff sad hides that all import of crocodilians had to be banned because it is impossible to tell the endangered species from their more numerous relatives when all you have is a tanned piece of hide in a pocketbook. The director of the zoo gave the appalling figures of the number of leopard pelts exported annually—and legally—listing Switzerland as the country of origin, since it was no longer legal to export the furs from the African countries. Obviously, to be effective the ban had to be on import.

The bill, which was to serve as a prototype for others around the world, was passed. The lady we saw today did not buy this year in New York that immoral coat she, but not the cats, could live without.

*   *   *

Heading home! We leave behind us the blue knobs of the Catskill mountains. The road cuts through fossiliferous layers of sedimentary rock—we are driving on the ancient Ordovician sea bed laid down millions of years ago.

We parallel the Hudson River, flat and greasy below Albany. Undulating flocks of birds headed the same way we are dot the air in the grand valley at the confluence of the Mohawk and Hudson Rivers, once the homeland of the Mohawk Indians. In the geographical symbolism of the Iroquois the Mohawk River represented the hallway that ran down the center of the great longhouse that stretched from the Mohawks' door at the East to the western door of the Senecas.

We follow the broad Northway from Albany up to the Adirondacks. As wooded hills rise up around us a sign by the road bids us welcome to the Adirondack Park; a sign intruding incongruously on one of the hills invites us to eat at Howard Johnson's.

We travel a side road winding through the unlovely towns in the park and the grand blocks of "forever wild" lands belonging to all the people of the State of New York. Here and there private stands of forest are punctuated by signs offering despoilment in the name of "Scenic Realtors, Incorporated." The Adirondack Park is not exactly an entity; it is a checkerboard of public and private lands.

We meet again the Hudson, here tossing narrow and clean between great sagging blocks of snow hanging tilted over the rushing waters. On the banks fat, sleek white birches glisten in the pale sun like a line of white horses waiting to have their necks patted.

Here the cars we meet still carry skis in the racks on their roofs. Deer antlers sprout over the doorways of the small cafés and the hardware store windows sport the distinctive silhouettes of white ash splint Adirondack pack baskets. The men coming out of the little post offices wear big boots, red-and-black or green-and-black plaid wool shirts and matching peaked caps, and chew on pipes. The ladies carrying home their bags of groceries are snugly zippered up in snowmobile suits.

Spring is coming even to the heart of the Adirondacks, but the signs are subtle. Some of the lakes are only half covered with pock-marked frozen mantles of ice, although others are still held fast in white shrouds. In front of the sign at Blue Mountain Lake that marks the divide between the St. Lawrence and Hudson watersheds the first meadowlark of the year flies up into the thin sunlight. Wide brown shoulders have appeared all along the roadsides in the short time since we made the trip south.

We are engulfed in a sugar snow storm—it's like driving through a feather pillow. The tires on the wet pavement and the windshield wipers make companionable noises as we follow the winding road. The gusty wind that farther south would be tossing bright kites hurls smokes of fresh snow down on us from gray rock cliffs and makes snow-dust devils dance on the snow-covered lakes.

The clouds break again at Little Tupper Lake, where the whirling snow looks disarmingly like the rising mists of a summer morning. At Big Tupper the wind whips dark wavelets in a curving channel slashed across the frozen lake surface. Across the lake the sun highlights the snowy peak of Whiteface Mountain rearing up behind the tall smokestacks of the plywood veneer factory— like fabled Mt. Fuji viewed through the smoke stacks of the industrial suburbs of Tokyo.

Nearing home, in the woods the trees are "kettling out," the depressions in the snow around their bases as sure a sign of maple sap weather as the sugar snowflake feathers caught by the tall black spruce spires bordering the road in the fragile serenity of the end of the park where practically none of the land is owned by the state.

We pass the bog, deserted today, where on the way down a

yearling deer had stepped daintily across the road in front of us and bounded off, white pennant tail aloft. Just beyond Sunday Rock, the Adirondacks behind us, brown knolls begin to appear in white meadows. A gang of robins is working over the bare yard where a man is busy taking down his Christmas light strings. Sap buckets sway on trees in the capricious wind.

It is all a perfect welcome to mad April, the suicide month, when even the most faithful of us occasionally fear we may have been deserted by that fickle lover, spring.

APRIL

APRIL FIRST is officially the opening date for shipping in the St. Lawrence Seaway; trout fishing season begins soon. April Fool! The trout streams and the river are still frozen fast.

The snow has melted away from the back steps. The lawn looks terrible—bare and brown, flattened dead grass with patches of snow mold in the hollows and everywhere the bones Belle chewed on in the winter sun have melted out to the light of day. It looks like an elephant graveyard.

I'm glad to see that robins, song sparrows, redwing blackbirds, and killdeer have come back, but isn't it about time the redpolls and evening grosbeaks went away? I was not able to keep a very close count of the kinds of birds we saw on our trip back. Ken is ever ready to slam on the brakes for a better look at a bird, so I have learned not to crane my neck looking at birds out the window to a telltale degree until I have determined the position of following traffic.

Ken found out this afternoon why one of his students had failed to meet the rest of the group at the appointed place and hour for their morning field trip.

"I got out to the marsh early, Dr. Crowell," she said. "I got so excited watching a hawk that I drove my car right into a ditch. By the time the towtruck got me out, it was too late."

"That's too bad," said Ken sympathetically. "What kind of hawk was it?"

The girl gave him a funny look. "When I told my roommate,

she said, 'When you tell that to Dr. Crowell, the first thing he'll ask is what kind of a hawk it was.' " And they both laughed.

Birding season is beginning in earnest, and so I see by today's paper is auction season. On the advertising page of the *St. Lawrence Plaindealer* where Roger previews his auctions appears this message:

AUCTION

The undersigned will sell at Public Auction at Bugsville, one mile north of Wart Factory on the Bulltoad Road, East of Appendicitis Farm. Some Day, next week, beginning at 1 G.M. sharp, the following:

18 Head Horses, 1 Spavined mare, 39 years old, 1 Iron Gray Gelding Mare, with false teeth, always 5 years old. 1 man-eating jackass—shod with Giant Grip Horse shoes, some kicker! 1 running horse, runs at the nose, 1 pedigreed Holstein, sired by night and damed by everybody.

24 Head Cows, 12 cows, good kickers, 7 yearling Heifers, coming 4 years old, 2 brood sows with cream separator at side, 7 of condensed milch cows, 2 of which are bulls. Also 2 fell cows and 2 that never fell. 1 Plymouth Rock calf—will have pups by day of sale—weather permitting and 1 Bossy Cow—boss of the cows.

Sheep, Goats, Poultry & Hogs, Sheep—1 Hampshire Ram with detachable rims, 7 yous, 10 lambs, 7 Mary, 3 not. Goats—5 Billy goats with red whiskers—unexcelled for dairy work as each is a good butter. 3 Nanny goats—1 Goatee. Poultry—1 Republican Rooster—has pep. 1 Democratic Rooster—has pip. 1 single comb Jersey Red hired girl (some chicken!). Hogs—1 Hire man—coming 37 years old, 3 big bores coming 20, 7 Bowlegged spring pigs.

MACHINERY

9 Dung Forks—8 equipped with fly net attachments, 1 rolling pin, narrow-toed corn cultivator, 2 bull rakes, 1 cow rake, 1 sulky rake, 1 sulky wife, John Dear corn planter, crow corn separator, pint gasoline, 1 old fashion Buck Saw with full directions for use. 1 Holstein Frisian plow—will be fresh by day of sale. 1 Castor oil manure spreader—works while you sleep. 1 six-cylinder stone boat with automatic cut-off.

HOUSEHOLD GOODS

Talking machine, bad as new, Side Board—nothing on it, 6 kegs—empty. 18 pint bottles, almost empty. 1 Keepit Still, large capa-

city. Twin beds, one as good as new, baby carriage with balloon
tires. Also other articles too sad to mention.
Terms—Cash, Balance in County Jail.
Cold Lunch! Snow balls and picked frost, served at midnight.
Y. HOLLER, AUCTIONEER
I. HOLDEM, CLERK
APRIL FOOL! From Roger Huntley, Auctioneer

*   *   *

A starling whistling down our chimney calls us all out to play
in the sunshine. Weekend sunshine is always precious but today,
the last day of the boys' spring vacation, it seems doubly so. The
jugs on the trees tell us we may go for an outing before it's time to
collect the sap. We decide to go on a ski picnic, stopping off first
at the beehives to feed the bees.

The bees have cleaned all the extra combs we have given them;
their stores are very low—and flowers are still quite some time
away. To raise brood for the coming work season, the bees need
pollen. Ken consults the bee books and mixes a pollen substitute:
one part brewer's yeast, three parts soy flour, one part powdered
milk, one part water and two parts sugar syrup. It looks and smells
like some strange health food! It tastes as if it is probably a pretty
good imitation of pollen. We pat the pale yellow dough flat, divide
it into three cakes, wrap them and pack them with our lunch. Jars
of sugar syrup rattle against our thermos in the knapsack.

We carry our skis down the hill, away from the house, to get to
the snow. April snow comes and goes like waves of the sea, but
the tide is clearly on its way out. Our cross-country skiing might
be more accurately called snow island hopping. Today is probably
our last chance for spring skiing.

Our skis carry us down the hill through the grainy jewels of
"corn" snow. A song sparrow says it all for us in an exuberant
trill. We are all wearing ragged jeans and thick gray wool socks
that will soon grow hot around our ankles. Presently jackets get
opened, then peeled; mittens ride on the ski pole handles instead of
our hands.

Behind the pond we pause to marvel at a maple leaf that has
melted its way down through the snow—about four inches down—
leaving a hole of its shape, perfect in every detail. Our tracks

grow wet behind us as we make our way along the cold east sides of all the hillocks.

Red-and-black ladybugs join pale-beige moths and electric-blue spring tails—snow fleas—on the snow. Dried brown Queen Anne's lace stars look no less lovely swaying above the sparkling snow than when they nodded icy white above the warm, late summer meadow green.

As we near the beehives, we hear a brooklet gurgling under the snow beneath our feet, making bewitching music as it goes to join the waters of the pond. The air above snow has a most exquisite sweetness.

At the first hive we remove the roof and place one of the pseudopollen cakes over the frames. By the hive entrance Ken puts a small jar of sugar syrup that is fitted to a small metal and wood platform like a chicken waterer in miniature.

Now off across the meadow for our own meal; I think everyone in the family likes winter picnics even better than summer ones!

The sun is hanging in the maple treetops; it is time we were gathering sap. Ken builds a fire in the cookstove out in the garage, which is now our sugar house. He will be in charge of the boiling.

The boys and I slog up the driveway in our rubber boots to bring back pails of sap, two at a time. We have the old family shoulder yoke; someday we will have to try using it. It does not look very comfortable, but I suppose your arms would appreciate it if you had to carry larger buckets than we do. Nevertheless I'm sure Great-grandfather was glad to see the yoke moved to the necks of oxen to do the sap gathering. Nowadays some who sugar quite seriously—and whose sugar bush is on an appropriately tailored hill—employ a system of plastic tubes that carries the sap right from the spile at the tree to the sugar house. But I would not want to miss the damp smell of the melting, reawakening earth, the song of the roadside rill and the redwing blackbird high up in the dripping maples. Above my head in one of the grand old maples in our yard a starling calls, "Me towhee!" The liar!

We carry full-to-sloshing buckets past the sunny south side of the house, where the first yellow crocus is opening up. Ken helps us pour our heavy loads into waiting milk cans. He has flat pans—my baking pans, to be exact—arranged across the entire surface of the stove top. Sap bubbles vigorously giving off clouds of sweet-smelling steam.

How pleasant it is to sit in the sun at the doorway of the garage, enveloped in the rich fragrance of the steam, sipping cups of hot sap. We snack on donuts dipped into our enamel cups; the boys have brought out some eggs to boil in the sap. They are fully in favor of any of the old traditions that mean more eating in a day!

Listen to the crows spacing themselves out across the countryside! From up by the Couglers and back by the Lelands come barking caws in measured groups of four. They sound as if they are trying out the acoustics of an auditorium from the stage: can you hear me here? How about here? Now over here, can you hear me now? We hear, faintly, the greatest number over by the Ostranders' freshly manured fields. Three of the handsome black birds flap slowly by on their way to join the crowd.

One pan of sap is nearly ready to take off now. In it the dancing, rolling, evanescent bubbles have become a whiter, more substantial foam. The individual bubbles enlarge and burst with a clicking sound. Ken pulls that pan off the heat. As it cools a writhing, shrinking skin forms over the amber liquid, mare's tails of scummy white streak the surface. We pour it through a piece of flannel to strain out the scum and sugar sand—nitre, the mineral deposits in the syrup—and there it is, our first syrup of the year.

The first is always the lightest, most delicately flavored of the season. The first sugaring also marks my personal New Year. For others the midwinter renewing of the day length may signal the new year, but perhaps I am harder to convince. When the trees are sure that spring is coming again and the sap rises, then I am content. My new year has begun.

*　　*　　*

Back to school today. The school children of the country were not able to be much help with maple sugaring this vacation. For all but the last day of it, the weather was too cold for a sap run. (We had told Dick Briggs to take our sap while we were away but the trees did not cooperate.) Sugaring is generally a good extra occupation, since you can collect the sap and wait to boil it at your convenience as long as the weather is cold enough so that the sap doesn't ferment.

The boys waiting for the bus do a little sap collecting of their own. They suck on the plastic tubes from the glass jugs and tilt up the buckets like a pair of old tipplers. David stretches up for a frozen sap-sicle formed by sap oozing onto a cold scale of bark from a wound somewhere up on the moss-covered trunk.

Both boys take a run down the fence rail like a pair of red squirrels at play, not a daring feat—the wide snow bank is only an inch or two below the rail. Overhead a hairy woodpecker completely circles a horizontal tree limb. He performs the trick again like some clever little old-fashioned circus toy. Down, around, and up again!

Going out to the mailbox, I find there is still ice on all the puddles the boys didn't stomp while waiting for the bus. The soft, cool air is filled with melody; runoff from the meadow behind the mailbox bubbles by in the roadside ditch beneath a pane of ice. The mud deltas have already melted for the day. Backroads and driveways are much less navigable now in the mud season than they were in ice and snow.

Thus spring comes to the North Country. Every night the mud freezes but by noon the next day it has melted again to sticky ooze. There is reward for our patience with the halting progress of the northern spring: where spring rushes in you get no maple syrup. And I actually appreciate that it comes slowly enough that for quite a while I can keep track of each new bird arrival and savor each new inch of daffodil.

Morning is now a riot of bird song, but only a week or two ago there was just a tentative squeak or two to be heard. After the long winter silence the robins' song seems as melodic and passionate as a Brahms concerto.

At breakfast the redwing blackbird performs in the window maple, "Conk-a-ree!" he sings, fanning his jet-black tail and ruffling his gorgeous scarlet epaulets with the striking yellow borders. A rival walks the edge of the pond outlet where a stream meanders down across the meadow. Our bird flies down to the fence post at the edge of the toboggan run to assert his rights.

Pairs of house sparrows tumble through the bushes in copulation, but for the most part it is still a men's club world for the birds; the females have not yet returned from the sunny South. Brick-red breasted robin males square off to begin settling boundary disputes, bluffing, strutting, daring the intruder with ritual encounters rather than much actual bloodletting. Wherever the ground has melted out, the starlings and redwings enthusiastically search for something to eat on the soggy, winter-worn meadow. A robin proceeds in hop-run-listen rhythm across the pond bank, out over the frozen pond, hop-run-listen there too, and up the other melted bank.

The order of return of the various bird species is more set than the strictest observance of protocol by dignitaries of state. The birds slip away species by species in the fall, but that is so much harder to observe that we do not feel their loss as intensely as we feel the joy of their return.

As I look out my kitchen window, the window over the sink, I see the bare limbs of the little butternut tree where the phoebe likes to perch. All the years of our tenancy phoebes have nested in the cellar entranceway that forms a tunnel in the pink sandstone under the long screened porch. One year, when we had neglected to open the storm door that gives access to this tunnelway, I was severely twitted by phoebe as I walked inspection in the garden there. The minute I had pushed the heavy door ajar, the little bird darted in to inspect the cool dark recess, where the tiny half-cup nest of the previous year was plastered to an overhead beam. I remember how much snow I had to kick away from the door to get it open. We have just about that much snow now, but where are the phoebes? The empty butternut branch makes me anxious.

*   *   *

We have laid out cups of colored dyes on newspapers on the kitchen table to color Easter eggs for tomorrow. From the refrigerator I bring the crockery bowl filled with hard-boiled eggs of all sizes and shapes and colors even before we begin to decorate them.

The little bantam eggs are pale beige and nearly equally pointed at both ends. The large Rhode Island Red eggs are rich brown and often speckled. The duck eggs, largest of all, are alabaster white, and the shapely pointed guinea eggs are tan and blotched.

Tom dyes brown eggs a lovely robin's-egg blue in the blue dye cup.

We can tell which kind of bird in our little flock laid our breakfast egg by its taste. The bantam eggs are richest, then those of the Rhode Island Reds. The duck eggs take a little getting used to —the yolk bland, the white so shimmery watery clear, extraordinarily elastic; they are wonderful for baking but they make horribly rubbery scrambled eggs.

David is coloring a huge duck egg—probably a double yolker— a vibrant clear yellow. I dye the eggs with the darkest spots in rich orange and soft rose hues. They come out attractively mottled in warm earth tones. Ken specializes in dyeing what we call Peter Rabbit eggs: green, yellow, and red horizontally banded eggs.

Eggs' shapes are tailored to the nest site. Screech owls, flickers, and chickadees lay nearly spherical eggs that utilize the limited space in their tree nest holes most efficiently, while birds like the murre, whose eggs are laid on narrow sea cliff ledges lay nearly triangular, or pyriform, eggs that roll in tight circles like toy tops instead of over the edge of the cliff.

David likes to lay the curious pyriform guinea eggs lengthwise in the dye and turn them just often enough to get bands of color; purples, blues, lavender-pinks and misty sea green he manages by switching from cup to cup.

In Africa wild guineas live in large sociable, noisy flocks and roost in the thorn trees at night. They reputedly like to take their dust baths in potholes in the roads, enlarging them and exacerbating local road conditions. Perhaps this unfortunate habit is what brought our two guineas to grief last fall on the Lelands' road.

Wild guineas lay ten to twenty eggs in a scant depression in the dry, hot ground. Presumably their pointed shape keeps them from rolling away. What tough shells their eggs have! I have to give them a real whack against the iron frying pan in the morning. However, this tough shell makes them ideal for withstanding the rigors of the Easter morning egg hunt. The leathery shells of duck eggs are also ideal for this purpose.

The eggs we have dyed please us immensely—all bright, gay, some comic, others beautiful. The egg: the world's most perfectly designed container.

*   *   *

We have had a great spell of sap weather, cold nights and shirt-sleeve days. Today will be a big boiling day around here, and it is Easter. I'm afraid the Crary Mills church service will be lightly attended. We have invited out a bunch of Ken's students for a do-it-yourself pancake breakfast. For them it is breakfast; for us it is more like lunch. David and Tom have found all the Easter eggs that Ken and I hid last night, and they have hidden them again in the front rooms for the students to find. Ken has a group out in the garage getting the sap operation going out there.

Our big kitchen is buzzing. We already have a pot of syrup on the stove finishing up. By doing the bulk of the boiling outside we are less likely to cause the wallpaper—or the plaster—to fall off the walls in here. Usually the picture hangers fall out of the wall, dropping the pictures to the floor as an early warning. When the syrup gets close to thick enough, it burns all too easily, so we bring it in here to finish the boiling on the stove. Before the automatic partitioned evaporator was invented, most farmers had a separate fire and pan for sugaring off, or else they took it up to the kitchen for their wives to finish on the stove. Even this system isn't foolproof, though. I once burned the bottom right out of a pot on my fine modern, easily adjusted stove. I didn't think the sap was nearly ready and stepped out into the inviting spring sun for just a minute. When I returned I found the kitchen billowing with black smoke and I was sure the pot bottom was welded to the stove burner.

The bubbling kettle gives the house a wonderful smell. As a pretty blonde girl, bare feet peeking out beneath her jeans, sets the table with her friends, a smiling young man with a head of bushy brown curls takes over at the griddle. Pancakes are soon flipping through the air.

"How did you learn to do that, Pete?" I ask in astonishment.

Even his mustache grins as he acknowledges the compliment. "I was a chef last summer."

Syrup, pancakes, and young people go to the table in the dining room. I enjoy watching the subtle game of musical chairs as the boys and girls arrange themselves next to each other. It is always interesting to see who shows up in pairs when they come out here for visits or field trips. Ornithology field trips seem to have replaced proms. Ken pours out some syrup on his finger and licks it critically.

"Too good for pancakes," he announces. Later in the day he will have his share on vanilla ice cream, where, he says, you can really taste the maple. He always tries to size up the discrimination of our guests to determine what quality of syrup they should be offered. No use wasting good syrup on anybody who wants that dark artificial stuff from the grocery store, he says.

"How was your trip to Montezuma?" Ken asks the boys who had just been birding down at that wildlife refuge at the head of Lake Cayuga.

Two of the three boys nearly choke laughing.

Finally blond, genial Tim manages to say to his mystified audience, "We had quite a time." And his pals Roy and Rick grin in more than agreement.

"We got there pretty late in the afternoon," Tim says. "We decided we'd better wait till after dark to settle our bags and gear in case it was illegal to camp there, so we drove around the refuge on all the dirt roads we could find."

Roy turns to Ken and says, "We saw huge flocks of Canada geese coming in, wave after wave of them. It was fantastic!"

"In one field we saw at least three hundred geese all feeding, and then pairs of them would wrap their necks around each other," puts in Rick.

Tim continues, "When it got dark we decided to try to catch one to examine it more closely." Rick and Roy can hardly contain themselves. "Anyway, I was leading the group and I was determined to be the one to catch the goose. Rather suddenly at the edge of the field I caught up with this dark object which I thought was a goose. But this goose turned out to have a black furry tail pointing straight up and white stripes along its back. A skunk!" We all burst into laughter.

Roy takes over the narration. "Tim said a few choice words and then took out in the other direction but not in time. When he reached us, we almost died from the smell. He had white gook all over his coat and pants so we tied his clothes to the back bumper of the car and took off to find the ranger. When the ranger saw Tim, he laughed like hell and gave us directions to the nearest laundromat in Seneca Falls."

"Man, what a town that was," Tim says helping himself to more pancakes. "There were gangs of townies roaming up and down the street. The ranger told us to wash my clothes in gasoline so the guys took them into the laundromat and left me sitting in the car in my underwear—right under a street light. Pretty soon the smell of the skunk and the gas overpowered the laundromat crowd and they took to the street. Of course they came straight to me. Pretty soon I had a crowd of kids standing around the car making smart remarks. At first I pretended to ignore them, but they were pretty persistent bastards."

Roy adds, "We told the kids Tim was completely naked and not to worry about him chasing them!"

"I'll get even with you guys," Tim threatens, brandishing his fork.

"It's a wonder you guys didn't blow up the laundromat with the gasoline and the driers," says Ken, pushing a piece of scrap paper across the table to Tim. "You should read about Lorenz's experiment with the ducklings and the hawk silhouette. When he pulled a cardboard hawk cutout tail first, backwards, over the ducklings, they did not respond at all, but when he turned it around the right way, they were frightened by it."

On the paper Ken had drawn:

It would have been interesting to count the number of eggs that disappeared here this morning. All but one of the Easter eggs have been found, and the bowl of confetti-bright egg shells attests to the disappearance of quite a few of them at breakfast.

After breakfast, a bunch of us go off to see a real sugar house, leaving behind a few students to tend to the sap boiling.

Briggs's sugar house at Maple Knoll farm is set back from the road at the far edge of his sugar bush. We follow the deep ruts made by the collecting sledge to the classic wooden building with its peaked ventilator on top. Clouds of steam rising from it proclaim that they are boiling here today.

We walk around the huge holding tank (on the north side, so the sap will be less likely to spoil), which feeds the sap to the pans inside. One after another we step into the dark, hot, fragrant chamber. At first we cannot even make out who is here—half of Pierrepont it seems.

We greet our neighbors and Ken says, "Morning, Dick. **O.K.** to bring in some students?"

A voice through the sweet mist booms, "Sure, come on in. The more the merrier. How about some warm sap?" he asks walking around to the far end of the evaporator, where he fills a dipper from a pail and passes it around.

"Sap's been running pretty well lately," Ken offers.

Dick opens the grate at the end of the fire and tosses in some more wood. The fire roars. "Can't hardly keep up with it. We boiled 'till midnight last night."

Across the room Dick's father-in-law, who has been regarding our group with veiled amusement, scoops the white froth from one section of the evaporator. The sap flows automatically from one section of the evaporator to another, according to its density, by a system of float valves. The old man drops his skimmer into a pail and shakes a drop of cream from the broomstraw he took out of a cup on the window sill onto a section of boiling sap that seems about to foam over. Instantly the bubbling turmoil subsides.

He nods across the seething pan to Dick, who takes up another dipper and scoops it into the boiling sap on his side. Dick holds up the dripping implement so we can all see how the syrup aprons off the lip of the old scoop.

It is ready. Dick's conversation trails off as he carefully draws off the boiling syrup through a spigot at the side of the evaporator. Golden liquid streams into the waiting pail. He keeps his eye on the level of sap remaining in the pan—mustn't draw it down too far or the syrup might scorch.

From the bench behind him he takes a tall tin cylinder and fills it with the hot new syrup. Into it he drops a hydrotherm.

"It has to weigh eleven pounds per gallon, you know," he explains. "Too thin and it will spoil. You get it too thick and it will crystalize out in the bottom of the can."

"Making fancy syrup, I see," says Ken admiringly. Dick smiles as he pours the hot pail of syrup through thick white felt held over the mouth of a large pail by spring clothespins. He picks up a little rack of standard colored vials and holds it up to the window to show the students.

The Fancy grade bottle is a pale gold, Grade A is full gold, and Grade B is a dark amber. Boiling must be quick and clean to get the highest grade syrup. Toward the end of the season, when the tap holes and buckets get contaminated by bacteria and the maple buds show their first signs of swelling, the stronger flavored Grade B syrup is produced.

The syrup in the pail, now cooled a little, is ready to be put into cans. Dick opens the gate at the bottom of the pail and fills fancy cans with pictures of a sugar house on them, one after another.

"How much sap does it take to make a can of syrup?" asks a small dark girl in a wildly pink parka.

"Some trees are sweeter than others, but you figure it takes at least thirty to thirty-five gallons of sap to make a gallon of syrup," Dick explains.

"It's a lot of work," breathes one of the boys.

"Yes, but I like it," grins Dick. "This is my favorite time of year." The students can understand that. Many are seeking the communion of the craftsman with his work.

Over the years we have gathered a collection of maple sugar molds from auctions, junk shops, and antique shops. We have little stamped metal molds shaped like butterflies, hearts, scallop shells, leaves, and a variety of decorative shapes that defy description. With the students we have made batch after batch of maple sugar and filled the charming old molds. We heat the syrup to 240° and stir it vigorously in the pot when it has cooled some. Many types of sugar can be made, ranging from rock hard to creamy soft, with large sandy crystals or powder-fine grain, depending on the temperature to which you heat the sugar and how much you beat it while it cools.

When the table is practically covered with these decorative candies we decide to call it a day by making sugar-on-snow, or jackwax. For this remarkable treat we heat the syrup to 235° and take it outside when it takes on a waxy appearance. Ken has scraped a clean plateau in the snow drift at the edge of the driveway. We drizzle initials and swirls onto the snow. The warm maple wax melts into the snow just slightly and colors it faintly.

A jar of forks is passed around. Some of the students eye the plate of dill pickles also on the drift with skepticism. Everyone twists up the amber wax with their fork.

"Incredible!"

When the forks slow down—this is a very rich treat—the pickles are passed, greeted now with enthusiasm. They taste just right after the maple. After their astringency one yearns again for sweet.

A plate of plain donuts is handed around. The merry group leans over the snowbank again, alternating jack-wax, as it is called, with pickle and donut.

"Crazy!"

This strange combination is traditional. It never fails to remind me of the circumstances of our introduction to sugar-on-snow. At a church fund-raising supper we had feasted on ham, baked beans, potato salad, and cole slaw. Then pie plates of snow were handed out and pitchers of hot thick syrup were placed before us on the tables, flanked by platters of donuts and plates of pickles.

"Now you'll see why I chose this table," Ken whispered to me, referring to the sweet elderly ladies across from us, who he obviously expected would pour the syrup ever so sparingly, leaving plenty for him. Oh, the look on his face when he passed the pitcher politely, smugly, to them first, and then watched the old girls one after another cover their snow plates completely! Over the past seventy or eighty years they had developed a truly awesome capacity for what most people consider a potent sweet!

* * *

Pouring rain! The jugs on the maples are only a third full. I can see from the house that the top inch or so of sap is amber-hued: it will surely taste "buddy." Sap season has come to an end.

Confucius is said to have refused to eat anything out of its appropriate season. For the most part today I can agree with him; it makes you more conscious of the gifts of each season in its turn. I compromise a little—our freezer helps us through the long winter—but I concede that there are some of summer's choicest offerings I no longer freeze. Oh, they freeze perfectly well, but it just isn't the same. We enjoy the plethora of garden vegetables, then fresh corn on the cob, and in their turn apples and pumpkin pies, and the great Christmas cookie season.

Just now we are eating a lot of Easter-egg salad sandwiches. That means extra bread of course. I always enjoy the living elasticity of kneaded dough. At this time of the year it is a special pleasure to send the rich nutty fragrance of baking bread out to cheer every corner of the house on a cold gray day when we are all aching for the warmth of spring.

The crusty curve of the top of a loaf of still warm bread is to me one of the most beautiful lines in the world. As the image of Buddha mirrors in his shoulders the curve of the elephant's brow, and his ribs are of the lion and his eyes are leaves, so the new loaves share their curves with my children's laughing cheeks and their planes with the broad backs of my husband's hands.

I watch helplessly but happily as the better part of a fresh loaf disappears, slice after slice sawed off as soon as the bread has cooled enough to be touched. My father's mother always said fresh bread will give you a stomach ache. My father, and my husband, and my sons all say, "It never tastes as good as it does when it is still hot enough to melt the butter!" Perhaps Grandma's admonishment was a good way of saving some for the next meal.

NOUVEAU RURAL GRAHAM BREAD

2 packets (teaspoons) dry-active yeast
1¾ cups water
¼ cup molasses or white sugar
⅓ cup corn oil
½ cup powdered milk
2 teaspoons salt
2¾ cups graham flour
2¾ cups white flour

Dissolve yeast in warm water. Pour all the wet ingredients into a bread bucket, then add dry ingredients and crank away until the mixture leaves the sides of the pail and clings to the hook. (This is such a fascinating process to watch that it is worth getting a bread bucket even if you give the bread away.) If you are using a large mixing bowl, add the powdered milk and salt to the wet ingredients, then add the flours a little at a time, mixing well after each addition. Add more flour if necessary to make a soft but not sticky dough. You will probably prefer to use white flour for the additions. Strangely enough, when you first begin to eat homemade bread you may prefer a mixture that is mostly white flour, but as you get used to eating it, you will probably prefer it darker and darker.

Let the dough rise 1 hour, or until double in bulk, punch it down, knead it and shape it into loaves in 3 pans 7″×3″×3″ or 1 or 2 of the 5″×9″×3″ size, depending on the size of the loaf you prefer. Let rise again until double in bulk, then bake at 375° for 30 minutes for small pans, 45–50 minutes for larger loaves. Brush crusts with melted butter.

Homemade bread is cheaper and tastes better than that usually available in the stores. It is easy and fun to make your own bread. It does take time, but the yeast is doing the work, not you. While the dough rises, you are free to tend to other chores.

Dissolve the yeast in warm liquid a few minutes before you are ready to mix up the dough. Water makes a crustier loaf than milk. One of the secrets of making good bread is mixing it well. The old-fashioned bread buckets with a stirring hook did this especially well. (They are being made again—a hardware store can often order one for you.) The amount of flour needed will vary with the humidity of the day and the type of flour in your region. Too little flour makes a coarse bread that is likely to collapse. Too much flour makes heavy bread. Add just enough to make a soft dough that does not stick to your hands or the bowl.

Put the dough in a warm place to rise, such as the oven. Turn the oven on just long enough to make it warm, not hot. Turn the oven off, put in a small bowl of water, and you have a perfect place for bread rising. Put the dough in a large bowl, cover it with a clean linen towel, and put it in the oven to rise until double in bulk. The dent from your finger pressed on the top will remain when the dough is ready.

Take the dough out and punch it down. Give it a good slap to force out all the carbon dioxide the yeast has produced.

Knead it on a lightly floured board. Press down and away from you with the heels of your hands. Pull the dough back into a fold with the tips of your fingers. Give the dough a quarter turn and press down and out again. Repeat until you feel the dough become smooth and elastic. Eight to ten minutes is the standard time, but most flours don't seem to require that much working. You can knead the bread by leaving it in the bread bucket and cranking it. The stirring hook develops the gluten most efficiently.

Shape the loaves and grease their tops lightly by rubbing them against the bottom of the greased bread pans. Let the dough rise in the pans until double. Bake until the crust is browned, and the loaves sound hollow when tapped. Remove bread from the pans at once. For a soft crust, brush with melted butter or cover with a tea towel while the loaves are cooling. Cool before slicing.

*   *   *

"Come to the window and look in the butternut tree; phoebe has come back!"

How glad I am to see that friendly little wagtail. Just because phoebes have always nested on that side of the house, why must I be so especially anxious that a pair continues the tradition? How vainly we poor mortals do strive to render permanent the ephemeral! For we lose the essence of the flower in the everblooming plastic; we jade the palate with the ever-available, and we empty gestures of their meaning by ungenuine repetition.

*   *   *

Snowmobiles are parked now in front yards under bright, tailored vinyl slip covers, and beside them are accumulating piles of new cedar fence posts, sharpened and stacked like giant handfuls of new school pencils.

The pond water glows emerald in the late afternoon light. From the shallows the dark forms of two trout dart away at my approach. The circle of ice on the pond is waxy blue-white like chalcedony, fractured by great long cracks, punctuated by small clear blue mirrors of the sky, and it floats iceberg fashion to the far edge of the pond under the gentle nudging of the wind. Snow still lies on the pond banks, but the brown meadows beyond are already tinted by the new shoots of grass, an iridescent sari woven of emerald and ochre silk.

I climb the hill to the garden, marveling at the thatch under my feet, bored through with tiny tunnels. I examine new shoots of greening grass neatly clipped off, and the stalks of inch-long hay in the hollowed chambers—the work of the meadow vole who chews tender blades and then meticulously, compulsively, neatly, piles up the tougher lengths of rejected stems. Almost brushing my shoulder swoops a graceful marsh hawk, its long legs, sharp talons dangling down—ready to pinion such a creature.

My flower garden is strewn with grim, charred bits of the Cougler's barn, and I still find artifacts from the wing of the house that used to be there—innumerable shards of white ironstone dishes, blue onion pattern china, curved fragments of oil lamp chimneys iridescent with age, chocolate brown pottery, fragments beyond number of bubbly blue-green bottle glass, not to mention a china doll's leg, old marbles and various mysterious items of hand-forged iron hardware.

Today I want to lift off some of the smothering mat of maple leaves by the wall. I peel up layer after frozen layer—they even come up in blocks—and already here and there new shoots pale with a promise of green are boring their way upward: daylilies, daffodils, a thistle rosette, and some eager burdock.

I break off and bundle up armloads of last summer's phlox and goldenrod. Many of the goldenrod stems are swollen with ball galls. How many times the boys and I have cut these open to look for the fat little fly larvae curled up in the center! Then we can find the escape tunnel made by the young maggot before his long sleep. When his metamorphosis to mature fly is complete, he would not have the chewing equipment to eat his way out of house and home. The scientist won't let you call this foresight, just a beautifully programmed set of behavioral adaptations that spells survival for the goldenrod gall fly! The downy woodpecker is said to be able to locate the hatch cover to this tunnel and probe into it to get the juicy maggot morsel. That's a pretty good trick—the pinhead-sized spot is often invisible to our eyes.

I pause in my gathering to notice how bare but beautiful the countryside looks now with neither its snow blanket covering it nor its leaves. The hills are lovely soft shades of gray and mauve and earth tones. The sky, so long empty, is now crisscrossed by the distant undulating of flocks of birds making their way north.

The Canada geese are returning in long, dark distant lines; the female redwings are back; and barn swallows once again shortcut through the narrow corridors between our buildings at breakneck speed. The color of the male birds in nuptial plumage is stunning. The first myrtle warbler of the season stopped by the mock orange bushes under our breakfast window this morning; lemon-yellow, black and white, and its tiny head so vividly gray it looked blue.

From the rail fence a song sparrow sings. His head thrown back, beak wide open, he seems joyously, confidently, to pour forth his song, but it is a monotone—cheep cheep, cheep cheereee! Terrible! A song sparrow with a tin ear. Thoreau aptly rendered the rhythm of their melodic mature song, "Maids! Maids! Hang on to the teakettle, teakettle,—ettle—ettle." It seems that birds have to get back into practice each spring, a maturational process somewhat similar to the way the juvenile first learns its song.

Another softer melody comes to me. My winter-tattered bundles of last year's flower stalks lie untouched as I watch a pair of bluebirds, the epitome of spring freshness. By the wall of the house where the sun has warmed the insects to activity, the bluebirds are picking them out of the air. The azure male flashes brilliantly in the sun and whirls away to the maples by the road. He is promptly followed by his more subtly colored mate. They seem interested in the bird house the boys put up on one of the trees. One and then the other slips in through the tiny hole and reappears. The male sits on the perch at the entrance. Suddenly the dark spindle shape of a starling dives down at the bluebird. Again and again it swoops at the bluebird with its dagger bill. The pretty sky-colored pair flies off.

A second starling carrying a piece of straw in its bill lands on the entrance perch. It drops the straw and puts its head tentatively into the hole. Its head, not its shoulders. The hole is too small; it does not quite dare squeeze in. I could have told you so, you pest.

With a vengeance I gather up old leaves. But I cannot long remain angry with nature—the first sky-blue hepatica blossom is smiling up at me from the frozen leaves under the butternut tree. Long spoon-shaped anthers of pale gold surround the pale-green female pistils in the center of five exquisite blue moons of pale-edged petals. Equally lovely are the score or so of silver-haired buds nodding beside it.

From down by the first hedgerow comes the familiar cry of a, of a . . . ? It takes me a minute to place this year's first call of the flicker. I count ten robins down by the pond spillway. Even though there are not many birds here at this time of the year, seeing them all together gives the impression of a crowd; they are not spaced out in their own territories as they will be later.

A pair of robins comes whirling by in tandem flight, a female ardently pursued by a male. They maneuver so adroitly, so identically, that it looks as if they are separated by some fixed invisible distance. But as surely as there will be empty blue egg-shells scattered on our lawn in another month, and naked little robin babies gaping in the nest, that surely I know he will eventually gain on her; the satyr will overtake the nymph.

* * *

The ice on the pond has been thinning rapidly; there are now great moth holes in it, and the ragged edges refreeze at night but only to a wrinkled film that disappears at a gentle smile from the sun. The berg has melted away to a mere shred at the back of the pond so today Ken and the boys are letting the ducks out of the barn and herding them down to the water.

The ducks seem glad to be back. They make such a fuss of bathing, dipping, preening, and bathing again. They swim, float-ing so low that, loon-like, only the tips of their tails and their necks are sticking out.

They are a handsome picture in the golden light of the late after-noon, floating on the dark water. And for the first time in nearly half a year the pond again has a reflection.

* * *

The wind sends cold gray April clouds scudding low over the hills, but a dark V of Canada geese winging north reassures us that April is only showing her fickle nature today. Ken and I are headed to our little woods, and I hope to gather pussy willows from the soggy field that bounds it on one side.

Our timing is perfect: the marsh bushes are covered with gray pussies popping out high and low. At no other time of the year is the difference between swamp willows so apparent. Many species of miniature gray pussies bloom on tall trees; fat, dark, giant ones line short, stout orange stems; velvety deep-pile ones bloom on long slender rods. We seem to have no common names for all these different kinds, just as the Eskimos are said to have more than twenty words to describe snow in different states but only a single word for all the tiny brief-blooming Arctic flowers.

To step into the woods is to step back a few weeks in time—there is still half a foot of snow under the trees. Green needles carpet the snow in the dark under the hemlocks; the work of porcupines? Apparently not, for everywhere the dark green litter is strewn across the snowy floor. The ice conditions of the winter must be responsible for this pruning.

Above our heads disembodied bird voices whisper, sifting through the treetops. Kinglets? We peer intently but see no flash of feather. Only the faint, sibilant calling, moving nearer perhaps, then receding.

We push deeper into the quiet woods. We can see far down the dark corridors between the ancient shaggy hemlocks and silvery beeches because the understory leaves are not yet out. In spite of the deed filed at the county office, I always have the profound sense of being a visitor here, a very privileged visitor, but nevertheless a bit of an intruder.

Plump cushions of mosses and sprays of polypody ferns look optimistically green on the cold, dripping, granite sides of Fox Rock. I point out a pile of cigarette-stublike droppings left by a ruffed grouse on the snow in the cleft of the great gray boulder. Ken leans his head in, and then stepping into the narrow passageway, he gives a whistle and exclamation of surprise.

"Come in here!"

I ease my way sideways between the towering rock halves and peer around my husband's shoulder. At the back end of the little cave on a neat tower of plump cigar-shaped porcupine droppings lies a disarray of gray fur and black-and-white porcupine quills.

We follow blurred tracks out the other end of the tiny canyon and find first the bloody lower jaw of the hapless porcupine, then the stained, crushed, chewed skull. Those long chisel-like incisor teeth with their extra hard, tobacco-yellow outer layer of enamel will girdle our hemlocks no more. The molars are as white as ours, with pretty undulating wave patterns on them. One tooth appears only partially erupted through the jaw bone—a young animal?

Stretched across the snow like a macabre chain of sausage lies the still dark-filled intestine, the tip of the tail, and the dark, long-needled pelt. Nothing remains but the prickly hide from the back, as neatly scraped of flesh as if done by the flensing knife of a taxidermist.

It looks like the work of a fisher. Not many animals can take on an ambulatory, armored, pincushion of a porcupine and win, no matter how hungry they are. A pile of fresh feces and clear tracks pins the blame on the fisher. I thrill with excitement; the fisher is a rare animal but the signs are clear, and the fisher is known to be holding his own in the Adirondacks.

The scene is as clear to us as if we had witnessed it ourselves: the clumsy, waddling porcupine attacked by the agile fisher, his raised quills and beating tail no help to him as the needle teeth of his hungry enemy kill him. Porky had evidently come down from his feeding tree, and believing himself well nigh invulnerable in his prickly armor, had settled himself in cozy retreat in the rock cleft—and let down his guard. In the shadowy sadness under the old hemlocks I half expect to hear a bloody scream. Eat! Eat! Eat! The life of a predator must be a hard one, as hard as the death of the prey.

From a grove of white birches comes the ghost song again, but this time we have no trouble finding the kinglets, tiny, greenish, toylike birds whose eye rings give them a baby innocent expression. We call to them with swish-wishing noises. One little bird lowers his head so we can clearly see his ruby crown patch of red feathers. A chickadee buzzes over to see what the fuss is all about. It wears a yellow band on its left leg—it is one we had banded up at the house at our feeder.

"What are you doing down here?" I laugh.

He scolds us from a pussy-willow bush as if to say, "What are you doing here yourself?"

*　　*　　*

The moon is nearly full tonight. The first of the spring peepers send their silvery trills over the dark meadows. Honking geese travel across the face of the moon. From the lower pasture comes the sweet sound of a snipe winnowing the air with his tail feathers. It is an enchanting evening.

It is also the night we must remember to turn our clocks forward. For a week now I have been thinking that Daylight Saving will be the saving of me if only it would come soon enough. This bunch of roosters I live with has been getting up at 4:30 A.M.! Even with the most efficient room-darkening shades that we could find and even on dark rainy mornings, Ken and the boys still know exactly when the sun is going to edge up over the distant hills. The first footfall on the floor by the bed, no matter how hushed, immediately galvanizes all three into action. The day has irrevocably begun. They can't seem to set their biological time clocks any differently. Oysters flown to the west coast that open their shells in anticipation of east coast tides on Eastern Standard Time have nothing on them. With Ken's personal biological time clock set the way it is—the cause or the result?—it is fortunate that he studies birds instead of stars! Of course, he thinks it's the rest of the world that has its watch set wrong, and the birds at least are on his side.

MAY

WE HAD a much-needed gentle rain last night. The last clouds are just now scurrying away over the horizon; it is going to be a beautiful day. There were over seventy grass fires reported in the area over the weekend. You may be sure the volunteer firemen heard the rain on their roofs last night with great relief, for they knew it was also falling on acres and acres of tinder-dry grass thatch.

The meadows seem to be greening up right before our eyes. We have finally gathered up most of the pieces of the Couglers' barn from our lawn and gardens. We feel a little sheepish because we have saved the most impressive of the charred bits in a shoebox, just like people who save their gallstones after an operation.

The blue stars of chionadoxa and the first daffodils are nodding in the garden by the kitchen door step. The sun that makes me linger lazily over my morning cup of tea has brought out energetic bees to visit the flowers. The bantam rooster now in full flower of manhood has taken matters into his own hands and has just led his ladies out of their winter quarters in the barn to the sunny pleasures of the hen yard.

The first white-throated sparrows stopping by on their way to the spruce forests are incredibly dapper with their black and white head stripes and spring-new blue-gray setting off their startlingly white throat jabots.

When I was a girl I would have made a paper May basket and decimated the woods and gardens—ours, or the neighbors' with equal enthusiasm—for blooms to hang on my parents' bedroom doorknob. I have not heard of this custom recently but otherwise the first of May has not changed a whit over the years!

* * *

From the swamp at the edge of the woods comes the song of the spring peepers and the wood frogs. I am headed down the sunny slope where the apples grow to record this song with my cassette recorder. Later this enchanting song will be heard mostly at dusk, but for the next few days these little amphibians who have come for miles around to this particular spot for their socializing will sing all day if they are not silenced by an intruder.

As a precaution I stop for a while to sit on top of a knoll commanding a splendid view of the rocky hillside, the spreading pastures, the pockets of silvery pussy willow and garnet-spangled red maples just coming into bloom. This knoll is one of my favorite spots for surveying the scene. I am not alone in that judgment; I see a pile of fox scats by my rock in the middle of a well-trodden trail. Members of the dog family—wolves, coyotes, foxes —leave their calling cards at points of interest along the trails they use. This rock is a scent post and many a canine leg has been lifted here!

The batrachian chorus from the swamp has grown louder as I have been sitting here. That "batrachean chorus" phrase much beloved of hard-core nature writers has always seemed to me an erudite, unnecessarily Greek, circumlocution for frog song, but as I sit here on this lichen-covered boulder by the swamp it seems an entirely appropriate description. They are certainly speaking a foreign tongue and what they are saying, sounding to me crazy, is exciting. The frog chorus in Aristophanes' comedy, *The Frogs*, written some 2,400 years ago, sings again and again: "Brekekekex ko-ax ko-ax." How much that sounds like the chorus here in my northern New York amphitheater! I can only speculate as to whether that tells students of biogeography anything about Greek and American frogs or tells us anything about the rate of evolution of frog song. It does, I think, tell us something about the timelessness of Aristophanes.

I move silently, slowly into the swamp. The sunlight filtering through the tangled bower of alders turns my tiny northern swamp momentarily into a southern cypress swamp or a primeval Mesozoic swamp. The alligators here seem to have double vision: the long dark forms in my swamp have four eyes. They are the large female wood frogs with the smaller males clasped on their backs in copulation. In the dark pool a male flips up his swim-fin feet in an audible splash, dives under the water, and comes up behind a female. He mounts her back, clasps her around the middle under her arms and the pair, like the hundred others, sit motionless in the clear cold water amid the fallen but undecayed leaves of last autumn. Eventually she will lay eggs and he will shed sperm on them in the water. Then they will return each to their own special woods until the next great vernal rendezvous. How precious are these lowly wetlands—insignificant pockets of swamp and yet the traditional gathering places of the amphibians—to the song of spring!

Yet-unmated females float languidly in the water, legs stretched out in what must be an alluring pose. Male after male puffs out his vocal sacs in mating song, a sac on each side on his back, about where his shoulders ought to be. They give their ducklike quack, literally flip, and head off in amatory pursuit.

The peepers I cannot see—they are no bigger than my thumbnail, change color like chameleons, and have disks on their toes that hold them onto the stems of the alder tangle a foot or so above the water. But I know they are there. I record and I record.

The frog song is orchestral, but what directs the pattern of crescendo and diminuendo? It has no melodic line, no direction, and yet I feel it is a lush fabric of music. When I get back to the house and play it Ken will ask, "How can you listen to that for a whole tape?" But then I can also listen endlessly to Baroque polyphony, which others may find tiring. Messiaen says Nature is the source of all music, and I am inclined to agree with him. How I love the thrush song I have that has been slowed down and transcribed for a recorder!

One pair of wood frogs near me seems not the slightest bit interested in me. Waving one hand to distract them, which is probably not necessary, I pounce on the pair with my other hand. I wrap them, still coupled, in wet leaves and hurry home with them to watch them more closely in a jar. In the eyes of Science is nothing private?

*   *   *

The general topic of conversation in Pierrepont these days centers on the question of whether or not spring is late this year. The opinions seem to depend on whether you are talking to an optimist or a pessimist. My dearest pessimist friend gaily assures me that many is the year that she has had snow in her front yard clear into June. The optimists note uneasily that the evening grosbeaks have not moved back up north yet, but my, don't these big yellow birds look handsome with the bright daffodils and all the new greenness?

As I make my rounds of inspection in the gardens, my arms folded behind my back in a gesture I seem to have inherited from my father, who also goes out just to watch his garden grow, I discover perfectly formed rosettes of heart-shaped violet leaves on the exact spot where two days ago the cold soil was barren.

The trillium have poked up their shoots of tightly furled leaves, which will open like a beach umbrella in a few days. Crumpled fists of rhubarb are beginning to show over at the edge of the vegetable garden.

The black-and-white warblers have come back, and the yellow warblers, so insect life must once again be stirring. But up at the beehives things are ominously silent. I see on the ground dead bees with their leg hairs packed with pollen—they were evidently caught by a temperature drop.

In every direction from our hill top I hear tractors humming in the fields as farmers hurry to get the last of the winter manure spread before the spring plowing and planting chores begin.

The marshes ring with blackbirds: a flock of hundreds moves up the hedgerow by me. I see by their distinctive wedge-shaped tails that many are grackles, those handsome, cross-looking, golden-eyed buccaneers who will soon be stalking across our lawns. And as I end my rounds at the kitchen door, I see a handsome male white-crowned sparrow, as dapper in his stripes and blue-gray as his white-throated cousin. The two species look very similar and their songs somewhat resemble each other's, but it is as though they had the same music teacher but the white-crowned sparrow has forgotten quite how the tune should go. The white-crowned sparrow customarily arrives a few days later than his cousin, and in just a few more days he too will move on to colder woods. Is he early; is he late? Spring is a march that sometimes rushes, sometimes falters, but it cannot be stopped and it keeps its own calendar. This year is on time.

*   *   *

You learn to know your pastures more intimately when you go

often to gather greens. The earliest mustards grow best up by the barn; the long ruffled tongues of dock are poking most luxuriantly up through the dry thatch on the edge of the pond.

We walk down the nearest hedgerow where a ripe pussy willow shedding soft yellow pollen greets us. We play our favorite guessing game—what flowers will those inch-high shoots turn out to be? We recognize the wild ginger and false Solomon's seal, but will need more clues to identify the red-purple shoots spread out in such profusion that you'd think we would surely remember what blooms there.

At the end of the hedgerow a clump of dainty, sparkling white bloodroot nods to us. On the bank by the fence are hundreds of spotted leaves of trout lily, also known as fawn lily, adder's-tongue, and dogtooth violet. The yellow, fully recurved petals of the flowers gleam splendidly in the full sun. Farther along are myriads of the speckled leaves with no sign of bloom. For years I've watched this patch without a single bloom reward. Trout lilies are reputed to require seven years for maturity. Any year now they will surely spangle this hill with gold if they can count at all!

We rattle through a stand of graceful dry milkweed pods—still no trace of milkweed shoots—and head up the hedgerow that leads back up toward the pond, past a red maple in bloom, past elder bushes with purple bud clusters and twisted new dark leaves, which will be fanning out before many days pass. We count four robins taunting and diving at one another, the boundaries of their territories evidently not yet settled. A redwing blackbird clucks at us from a pendent elm branch. Sharp-eyed Tom stoops to pick up half of a lovely eggshell, turquoise with dark blotches on it. Could it be a crow's egg? This is where we found their courting tracks in the snow—so long ago it seems, the snow, yet also only yesterday.

When we reach the pond we find all four ducks preening themselves on the bank. Biggy leads his harem down to the water with much muttering of disapproval at this interruption.

Then, stepping around the ancient hay rake rusting in the grip of years of summer grass, we spot three hastily covered nests all in a row underneath the tines. We count eight or ten eggs in each by carefully lifting back the roofs of dry grass and feathers pulled protectively over each one. So that is why we have not been able to find any eggs down around the pond!

Between the nests and the pond we gather the shiny green rosettes of winter cress, or yellow rocket, leaves. This weed of the meadows is considered by most the pesty relative of mustard and broccoli. We harvest a few rosettes of dandelion greens as we make our way back up to the house, gathering up the dark ragged leaves with one hand and slicing off the whole top with our knife in the other hand. From the other side of the pond a toad calls, sounding like a clock being wound, then warming up to more melodious trills. This is a fine way to gather sustenance!

Most of our neighbors eat cowslip greens, some eat dandelion greens. For many it is a spring ritual nearly forgotten from their grandfather's day. For a whole other set of people the wild harvest of spring is something they have just discovered. The books on eating wildlings are all out of the libraries and freshly sprouted botanists stalk the land.

The menu of the fields is not merely a healthy eating adventure left over from the days of my grandmother and her mother. Cowslips, dandelion greens, yellow dock and yellow rocket, the mustards and the milkweeds, the fern fiddleheads—the Iroquois knew them all.

On to the sink with our potherbs. The greens are carefully washed—dandelions are sandier than spinach would ever dare to be —and the animal life is picked out. I see by the holes in the cresslike rocket leaves that we are not the first to partake of this feast.

I pour boiling water over the large kettle of greens and add a pinch of baking soda. After this has again come to a full boil I pour off the water, refill, and boil some more. Ours is not a particularly sensuous language—we do not have a word to describe the particular shade of spring gold-green of the liquid I pour off. The greens themselves have turned a brilliant emerald—but again, not quite, not quite as bright a hue as emerald.

Even more inadequate is our language to describe the aroma of the steam that comes from spring's first kettle of greens! I taste to see that no trace of bitterness remains and that the greens are tender. Then I drain and butter them.

The family sits down to a peasant's dinner of hash, soft-boiled eggs—today's crop—and the greens. With golden-brown homemade bread and strong fruity raspberry wine we have a feast fit for a king. The star of it all is a "mess" of greens. The various kinds form a sort of taste spectrum between artichokes and asparagus on the one hand, and kale and spinach on the other.

"Please pass the weeds."

While we dine we watch the ducks exploring the spillway of the pond for their dinners. At least the ladies are looking for something to eat; Biggy walks behind, nervously whispering to them, head held very high, ever on the alert for danger. Poor dear doesn't dare lower his head for a single bite of whatever it is they are finding. He thinks they have gone too far and he anxiously calls them back. Reluctantly the three ducks follow their lord a little nearer to the pond.

A pigeon from the barn roof flaps down over their heads to settle down beyond them for a drink. This intrusion cannot be tolerated. Biggy waddles firmly and fiercely toward the pigeon. The interloper flies up only to land again a few yards away. In his best Churchillian manner Biggy demonstrates that this is not sufficient. The pigeon retreats and Biggy triumphantly rejoins his harem, who have at least had the grace to stop eating and watch the gallant display.

The evening light turns the thatch at the pond's edge to a circlet of pale gold. At the spillway the first daffodils toss in the breeze. They bloom later than the ones warmed by the house, which are now at their prime and already being joined by the first tulips. The inky black pond waters are ruffled by the playful breezes that sweep along the purple cumulus clouds, tree swallows skim over the water, the sun flashing now on their white bellies, now on their iridescent blue backs.

The sugar maples along the road have blossomed in a barely discernible golden haze, but the outstanding color is the May-green of the meadows. The dark-blue hills glower in the distance but all the middle ground and all the foreground gleams in a lively shade of plush new green.

The rolling meadow contours are beautifully emphasized by the green velvet. Only in May, for soon the pasture grass will grow lush and tall grasses will ripple in a darker, less vibrant green.

But tonight, our pastures, our world May green!

*   *   *

The air is still and hot and heavy with the perfume of the line of blue hyacinths in my kitchen door garden. Black wasps and heavy buzzing bumblebees visit the yellow trumpets of the daffodils. Barn swallows twitter on the wires and drop down to the driveway for a warm dust bath. They swoop in and out of the barn, which is really one colossal bird house—there are so many nests plastered to the rafters and sitting on beams in its vast recesses.

Out in the henyard the big Rhode Island Red hen squawks and scurries away from the little bantam rooster chasing after her, but, undaunted, the little cock takes off again after the big blonde. They disappear through the open milk house door. In a few minutes he reappears at this end of the barn through the little hen yard door. He struts over to one of the black Cochin hens.

"Cock a doodle doo!" Bragger!

For what seems like the tenth time today the guinea hens have let themselves out of the hen yard. All day long I have heard the rackety cry as the wanderers found themselves confronted by some strange threatening object such as a bicycle or they failed to recognize the other side of their barn. More than once I have had to go out and chase them back from the field across the road. Guineas have a peculiar trait that makes herding them exceptionally challenging. Although ungainly looking, they are so fast on their feet that if you lunge in any direction to head them off they take that as a challenge and run faster than ever in exactly that direction, and more often than not they easily outdistance you and you find yourself farther than ever from your goal.

When I have succeeded in maneuvering the guineas back to the relative security of the front yard I hear yet another cry. From the field beyond the pond comes a loud, "Cut! Dawk! Cut-Dawk!" I suppose it's the rooster and now I'll have to go get him. It's a cock pheasant! He calls again and struts regally across the foot of our meadow, tail dragging like a peacock, face a gleaming scarlet in the warm sun. How elegant! From the safety of our hedgerow a hen pheasant is no doubt observing this performance with as much interest as I. I certainly do not have to shoo him home.

*   *   *

When the afternoon rain seems to have let up a little I take a burlap sack of dahlia bulbs to the Latimers.

"Well, Ruby, do you think the ground has warmed up enough to put these dahlias in yet?" I ask, putting down the sack.

"Ought to be about time to get the peas in," says Jim, passing his empty plate to Ruby and rocking back in his chair.

"Now Jim, you know they all rotted last year because we put them in too early," protests Ruby from the sink.

Jim points a toothpick at his daughter. "Patricia, if you get the pole for the purple martin house painted, I'll put it up this evening." Turning to me he says, "Marnie, what do you know about this Horizon Corporation that plans to sell lots for a big vacation home city over the other side of Sunday Rock?"

"I haven't heard a thing about it," I answer in astonishment, "What's it all about?"

"Don't know yet, just heard on the radio this morning that this outfit was going to put ten thousand houses on a big tract they just bought from a paper company."

"Inside the Blue Line?" I ask incredulously, thinking of the Adirondack Park boundaries.

"Yup."

A thousand questions came rushing into my mind but then the kitchen door opens, and in walks Jim's brother, Bud, who lives in a nearby town.

"Got any woodchucks yet?" Bud asks his brother.

"Not yet, but I'll get one propped up pretty soon," Jim promises. The whole family laughs.

"Oh, Jim, tell Marnie that story," Ruby says.

More than glad to oblige, Jim relates it. "One year we propped a dead woodchuck up on that rock pile across the road. We just set in here and watched out the window as Bud here came driving by. He stopped his truck and got out and shot that thing, and then he shot it again. We nearly busted our sides laughing when he came in all disgusted and threw down his gun on the couch, muttering about how somebody had tricked him." Jim grins even wider. "We fooled a couple of carloads of college kids too!"

Bud laughs. "Well, you're not going to get me again on that."

As I drive back up the hill to our house between the long row of maples still leafless but at least now bucketless, I smile to myself, figuring that about now Jim is probably explaining to his brother about our peculiarity. We have tacked up hand-painted signs saying NO CHUCK HUNTING PLEASE on several of our fence posts between their house and ours. We sympathize completely with the farmer who doesn't care to have one of his prize cows break a leg or to be thrown from his tractor by meeting up unexpectedly with one of their damned holes in his own meadow. But we finally got fed up with having so many carloads of weekend nimrods stop, jump out, and take pot shots at the woodchucks in the rock wall fringing our meadow while we sat eating dinner at the kitchen picture window enjoying the pastoral serenity of the scene before us.

The boys were always afraid someone might get "Hereford," our favorite chuck, up by the house. I have no idea of the actual number of red-brown woodchucks who have assumed this identity over the years. He, or she, always lived in the stone wall above the pond and could be counted on to appear regularly in the evening sun to nibble his dinner of grass and stand tall like a dignified little man if we so much as laughed too loudly at our table.

I worried about the ability of this particular brand of hunter to distinguish between dogs, kids, and chucks since it never seemed to make any difference to the gunners whether we were sitting out on the hill at the time or not. Also I find extremely repugnant the sight of a woodchuck carcass draped over a barbed wire fence, even the food value of its body denied to the web of life, especially when woodchucks capably regulate their population density without—and in spite of—our help.

*   *   *

Our house sits just below the crest of the hill, to miss the full brunt of blasting storm winds, I suppose, but it is high enough so that we can see the apple trees and sunsets and cows looking down into our living room windows.

From the gently rising curve of meadow that we see from our front door comes the sweet melody of a bobolink just back from Venezuela. No one can put his song into words; it sounds as if he has taken all the notes he likes from all the other birds' songs—and he sings all those notes together in one tuneful cascade. When the bobolink appears on the hill it's time to gather cowslip greens. We intend to invade the marsh between us and the old red brick schoolhouse, the marsh where we now have reason to believe at least one muskrat lives, the marsh from which lately we have heard the pumping, booming call of the bittern.

Our band of cowslip gatherers slogs down across the meadows. We are all wearing boots, but the talling grasses soon wet us to the knees. Everywhere lies spring's wetness, that only fountain of eternal youth. The redwings scold us as we pass too close to their nests hidden away in the cattail clumps.

At the sunny fringe of the marsh the cowslips are in full bloom, bright coins flashing in the sun, earning their other name, marsh-marigold. We gather the tender young leaves to cook like other spring greens. From each plant we take just our share, being careful not to bruise the flower buds, the cowslips' second dividend. In no time we all have a green bouquet of the round leaves in each hand, so we start back through the swampy hillocks of sedge and cedar to the road.

We have been preceded. There in the middle of the road stands a bittern, that usually shy, usually invisible bird, so perfect is his brown streaked camouflage. We have disturbed him. He stalks like a barnyard fowl but stops, uneasy at our approach.

Down the road comes a car; now what will he do? He does just what bitterns have done from time immemorial when they're in danger: he freezes, with his head up, long bill pointed skyward, counting on the streaks on his breast to hide him in the grasses and the shadows.

Only he is standing now in the middle of a black paved road, a car is coming, and he should *move!* But statue-still, staring at the sky, he stands. The car slows, stops, the driver watches as incredulously as we. The bittern watches the sky. After a long time, perhaps when the hard highway feels wrong and the car has had time to become merely a rock, the bittern crouches and, stepping ever so slowly, finishes crossing the road and melts into the marsh on the other side.

The instincts that have served the bittern so well for so long may now betray him. Bitterns won't last very long if the whole species insists on walking the highways and then "freezing" in the middle of them.

Evolution allows the survival of only those organisms programmed with the proper responses to their environment. When the environment changes, if the organism cannot adapt its responses suitably to the new conditions it becomes extinct.

I often wonder who has the improper responses to our times. Is it Horizon Corporation, the second-home building company that wants to create a glamorous ghetto in the Adirondack Park, and the superhighway and dam builders, who cannot resist moving in because the acres are there, or is it the conservationists, who demand that the wild areas that remain must be saved now, to preserve from man's mistakes at least a part of the intricate, delicately balanced, ecological systems which have developed over many millennia?

Obviously we are each trying to develop a very different man, a very different environment, for tomorrow.

Nature never has room for the organisms that make mistakes.

*   *   *

What a glorious day! The morning sun shines on the breast of a red-tailed hawk surveying his domain from an apple tree. The starry white blossoms of the shadbush shine in the hedgerows.

At the onset of cold weather we put the glass panel in the storm door and caulked it shut with weatherstripping. Another layer of soft-gray weatherstripping was worked around the edges of the front door and both doors were locked against the wintry blasts for the duration. Now in celebration we unlock the door, peel off its bondage with a flourish, pull out the storm door and replace its center panel with a screen, and unlock it. Once again we have an entrance. David gives the old windup doorbell a good twist to welcome in the warm weather with proper ceremony.

I spend the morning in a desultory beginning at spring cleaning, punctuated by many interruptions. I rush outside, thinking I hear the year's first towhee, but it's that starling again. I inventory the white trillium we planted by our doorstep in the rescue operation when they widened and paved our roads. (How we worried that our beautiful maples would fall to the ax of bureaucracy, but the good and aesthetic sense of our local road commissioner prevailed and our beloved maples still stand.) Even my garden seduces me from cleaning—once I have stepped out the front door I count the last of the blue hepaticas, the first of the tulips, the garnet-colored ginger blossoms hidden away under their leaf canopy, and the pale-gold merrybells nodding in the shade of the garden wall.

Even emptying the garbage takes twice as long today. As I take our scraps to the compost heap behind the little stable I find a black Cochin hen enjoying her freedom from the chicken yard. She has settled into the cold frame built against the sun-warmed stable side. She ruffles up her feathers and drops live ants into them. I don't believe behaviorists have quite figured out the full significance of this not uncommon ritual. Watching her thoroughly ruffle up our cold frame relieves my conscience—I never got around to planting any seeds in it this year!

Next I am waylaid by the pond, a phoebe is bathing there. Like everything else a phoebe does, it takes its baths in swoops—a quick arc out to water's edge, and then circle completed, it returns to a willow branch to flit its tail and call its name in its soft burry voice.

From where I sit in the alluring sun I can see that the three ducks have pushed their nests at the top of the wall together into a large circle upon which all three try to sit with their heads stretched out flat on the ground, their long necks limp—a startling, worrisome sight at first glance.

A bobolink who has been preening in the box elder after a dip in the pond is suddenly flushed by a war whoop from the roof of the chicken coop. The boys are up there, gleefully flinging half-baked mud pies out in every direction. Their fort is under siege, but I hear also laughing references to "super cow" interspersed with their battle cries.

The slender spear of a metal post for the electrified fencing sails through the air; I am glad to see that all the hens seem to be in the barn at the moment. I ask the boys if they want to get some fish for dinner.

Although not one single trout has yet been taken from our pond —those trout Ken has been wasting pity on for being such innocents led to the hook—the boys scramble down at once with the confidence of youth. We get part of one garden patch forked over as they gather a can of worms.

As we walk around to the deep side of the pond we count twenty-six large toads staring at us with inscrutable Mandarin smiles.

A spotted sandpiper whirls overhead, landing gear lowered, wingtips curved down in a graceful arc, and settles on the beach opposite us, entertaining us with his rhumba bob, up and down he jerks in his own distinctive rhythm, his hallmark.

The boys begin casting. A trout is sighted. There are a few nibbles to keep things interesting. Ken comes to join us with his fly rod. He is careful not to disparage the boys' use of worms but he feels using flies is more sporting, which so far has meant he hasn't caught one of these trout either. "Just think," he mutters, "there is one fish in there for every ten feet of bank and we still haven't caught a one. I should have known trout weren't born innocent!" I too cast with my fly rod, but I am using a bit of worm. One of my favorite photographs of my grandmother shows her standing in a long skirt, starched white "waist" with leg o' mutton sleeves, long rod arching gently out before her, one hand on her hip. I feel close to her when I catch myself in that position.

I cast mainly to try to master that beautiful motion Ken does so gracefully, which sends the line out in a smooth curve that drops first the fly on the water's surface, then the invisible leader, and then the belly of the line. The best I can do so far is produce some satisfying swishes of the line as it whips past me before it splashes on the water.

"Just your wrist—don't throw it! Let the line straighten behind you," shouts Ken.

But I have a bite! The hook is set and the lovely silver form of the trout's underside appears as it turns. I play it a little and then tell Tom to take the rod. He too plays it up and down the shore before he lands it.

"Mommy caught a fish!" the boys cheer. It is nearly ten inches long. How did it ever grow that much over the winter? It is beautifully streamlined, an iridescent bronze, marked with six ruby spots, and flecked all over with gold.

That is, I feel, my quota for the day so I leave my men and go up to the far garden for some dandelion greens. I look back at the old white farmhouse, the tall pine, Ken kneeling by his sons, teaching them the fine art of the perfect cast. Did I encroach on Ken's rights by catching our first fish? His mother did not fish; she stoically read or knitted hour after hour as her men fished, occasionally observing dryly that the weather that day must be too warm or the water too high for the fish.

The dandelions grow most luxuriantly up in our garden. As yet there is no sign of the kale, but the dark flat circles of dandelion weeds will do quite well for now. In no time my bag is full. The greens cook down so much that I have to be sure to get enough—it is such easy work and the supply is so generous that I would have no excuse for not providing my diners with a lavish supply—especially now, while the nights are still frosty so the greens are not bitter.

When I return to the fishermen David has caught another, even larger, trout. I slip my hand into Ken's as we watch the boys fish.

"Is it okay that I caught the first fish?" I ask softly.

The answer comes without hesitation and with enthusiasm unalloyed: "Yes, of course. It was great for their morale!"

As I stand in the deepening twilight thinking how fortunate I am to be married to a man to whom "the battle of the sexes" does not always occur, I hear a woodcock "peenting" over on apple tree hill. The toads around the pond are tuning up their sweet alto voices. Jupiter twinkles just above the barn.

My younger son with his rod in hand comes walking up the path from the pond, not seeing me in the dusk, whispering, "Star light, star bright, wish I may, wish I might, have the wish I wish tonight. I wish I had a rubber worm."

* * *

"Let's go hunt wild trout today," Ken suggests.

We gather our gear and head for *the* trout stream. For years Ken has watched enviously as Gary and Monty bicycled back from somewhere with beautiful trout hanging from their handlebars. A scant hill away we finally located the tiny brook, which makes its way by many a neighbor's woodlot, meanders out through wide pastures, and shelters there in the pools fine native brook trout. Its secret is guarded by an alder thicket where the stream crosses under the road. We skirt the tangle and meet the stream where it leaves the dark of the hemlocks to come sparkling out into the sunny meadow.

Everywhere our world is bathed in the green mist of new leaves unfurling. The hillside under the sugar maple at the edge of the pasture is carpeted with peppermint-candy striped spring beauty; glistening white Dutchman's breeches dance in the light breeze by the remains of a split rail fence. The birches are in tasseled bloom and the first black flies are out. This is also the time of the great wave of warblers that sweeps through every mid-May, filling our thickets, treetops, and even the house shrubbery with their dazzling flashes of beauty and hauntingly sweet songs. Every spring I must learn over again which tiny warbler produces each familiar song. It is like standing helplessly embarrassed at the side of a friend whose name I cannot call up at just the moment I am halfway through an introduction. I once tried to repair such a gaffe by explaining that there was no insult involved: I have the same trouble with warblers. Of course the words were just out of my mouth when I realized that wasn't going to help any.

Leaning against sun-warmed boulders, we assemble our rods and Ken unfolds his old leather fly book to dole out to each of us our flies for the morning. For all the talk of matching the hatch—picking the artificial fly that most resembles the stoneflies or May flies or whatever insect is hatching at that particular moment—I have long ago learned that Ken may do that for himself, but I get the ones he is most willing to have lost in the alders behind me, or snagged on a root in the bottom of a beaver pond.

The black flies have found us now that we are sitting still. We all smell to high heaven with Ken's special fly dope mixture: one part Woodsman's, one part olive oil, one part pine oil. A liberal application of this keeps the black flies from settling on us to bite, but it does not keep them from getting in our eyes, in our ears, sneaking up our pants' legs or down our shirt collars if they can, and choking us when we inhale one.

We think different people smell different to the black flies. Unfortunately for him, David in our family smells the most delicious. Certainly if you pay any attention to them or should be so indiscreet as to become annoyed by them you instantly become twice as tasty to twice as many bloodthirsty black flies. However, a world with no black flies would probably also be a world with no warblers and no trout.

Ken gives the signal for the boys to advance. "Now keep back, don't let them see your shadow, or feel you clumping along the bank," admonishes Ken as they start to thread their way with their long rods through the alders.

"Teacher, teacher, teacher!" calls an ovenbird from the dark shadows under the hemlocks on the hill.

Ken finds a good clearing for each son and moves off down the stream. Now he is happy; for him the stocked pond does not have the allure of the wild stream, where the angler pits himself against the unknown. Which pool at the end of a riffle will harbor the wise old giant trout? If you send your fly floating down the dancing waters in just the right way, will he rise for it? And if you hook him, can you keep him from running away with your line to snare it around the sunken snag he knows of but you don't?

The boys too are enjoying themselves. Mostly they catch trees and minnows, but they are happy.

I catch my limit of alders and swap my rod for a plastic bag from my pocket to gather an easier harvest—cinnamon fern fiddleheads—beautiful delicate green crosiers lightly dusted with cinnamon fuzz

—tussock after tussock of them to choose from. I will cook them just like asparagus and serve them buttered. They taste like a cross between asparagus and artichoke if you can imagine that.

On the opposite bank I can see Ken. Too hemmed in by alders for a proper cast, he snaps his fly out over a riffle and lets it ride down with the current.

"Witchety, witchety, witchety!"

We both turn our heads, charmed by the little yellow-throat warbler.

Strike! Ken sets the hook, the fly disappears, and the battle is on. The trout runs; Ken stops it just short of what even I can see would be a defeating tangle of roots. He plays the fish, bringing it in and letting it run, until he finally eases it to the shore at his feet. He drops to his knees, and holding his rod tip high, rinses his free hand and slips his fingers under its gills to lift the fish.

With the care of a surgeon he removes the fly from its lip and slips the fish back into the stream.

When I step out on the opposite bank he smiles across at me. "That's a real fish. Who would have guessed! Twelve inches, maybe a little more—in a little brook like this. I'll bet there are more up in the woods there," he nods back toward the hemlocks.

Jewel-toned, the embodiment of grace, the tired trout Ken has been gently holding in the current revives and, flipping its tail, dashes back to freedom. I knew he would put it back when I saw him rinse his hand so his fingers wouldn't damage the protective coat of slime on the fish that protects it from fungus infection.

Ken grins almost apologetically, "I'll leave it for some boy to catch," and with a note of pride and satisfaction in his voice adds, "if he can!"

Together we walk back to the boys.

"Hi, Mom; Hi, Dad. Look at all the neat chub we've caught!"

*   *   *

This noon Ruby Latimer called and said Jim wanted to show us where a majestic pileated woodpecker has its nest in the trunk of an old beech tree down the road; soon the leaves will be so thick we won't be able to find it.

It is just a short ride to the fine grove of mature beech and maple trees. A lone silvery bole, topless, branchless, stands very near the center of the grove. It is in this old dead beech that the pile-ated woodpecker has excavated his nest hole—it is oblong, nearly a rectangle, and almost a foot long.

The ground around is littered with nickle-sized wood chips from the operation, some of which I pocket to impress Ken and the boys when they come home. Deep burgundy red-trillium and bright-yellow violets bloom in the leafy carpet around the old tree.

I make a mental note of the tree's location and we head back to the car. One last look over my shoulder as we are about to drive away and there is the bird itself, flaming red crest and heavy black bill, peering at us from its hole!

We make a quick stop on the way home to pick up a painted tur-tle intent on crossing the road. On my lap it scarcely slows its de-termined crawl. I will take it down to our pond, although I don't feel very sure it will stay there. Perhaps some other instinct will drive it on, relentlessly, restlessly, springtime on.

It has been a quick jaunt—Jim has to get back to discing his fields—so I am soon beside our pond. Long, clear strings of toad eggs float in the grass at the pond's edge filled with the dark pearls that are life.

I detour on my way back from the pond to the garden. At the bird bath I find a June bug—the early brown kind known as the May beetle—struggling on the surface of the water. I nudge it to the safety of the rim of the bird bath and wonder if it is any the wiser for the experience.

Coming the longest way round to the kitchen door—by way of the front yard—I pass between several small caterpillars ballooning around on threads, trapeze artists of the maples until a bird inter-rupts their act.

Down the driveway flutters a white cabbage butterfly, and almost following the leader come two Spring Azures, the thumbnail-sized common blue butterflies. An emerald-green tiger beetle is sunning himself—no, probably hunting—on the concrete at the back steps. It is a deep green iridescent marvel with golden flecks decorating the back edges of its wings.

How can I go into the house? The swallows are playing tag around the thin slice of the moon that hangs pale in the blue sky above the pond. There must be a "hatch" of something down there —the trout are jumping.

Thunderclouds are gathering on the horizon, as if the skies are uneasy in the unaccustomed heat, spring too rich a diet. Tom and David and Ken are down at the pond to see if the trout are still rising.

I stand upstairs in the open doorway to the vanished piazza and drink in the soft early-leaf colors of the hills; already the trees are garbing themselves in differing colors. Some are bronze, silver, or pale gold, and they range through the complete palette of greens according to species, to proportion of bud, of blossom, to leaf, and leaf maturity. From the pond comes the chime song of toads, joined occasionally by the melodious tinkling of a cow bell, and woven through the melody are the twitterings of the tree swallows who seem to be moving into the house that the bluebirds did not stay to use and the starlings could not use.

Leaving the door propped wide open so the golden light floods our bedroom, I sit at the desk to write some letters. Out the window I see a parent robin settle down on the nest in the pine tree to brood their eggs for the night.

A May beetle interrupts my solitude, buzzing in like a miniature helicopter. When I go to the door with him to send him back out where he belongs, I hear the splat, splat, of scores of others bumping into the house wall. From a pasture somewhere comes an even stranger sound, a sharp rap-rapping, like a giant woodpecker. A neighbor somewhere must be pounding his sledge on cedar stakes, mending fence. The grass is ready to be grazed.

Settled once more at my writing I can't help but notice that the pink honeysuckle at the window is just coming into bloom. A yellow warbler, bright as a tiny sun, with a necklace of faint rusty streaks on his breast, makes his way up the honeysuckle. The sleek little thing, bright black eyes peering intently into the leaf rosettes, sings a cheery, loud song. But I can also hear a softer, sweeter, private melody that he seems to be humming to himself.

Slowly, like a spiral of golden ribbon, he winds up through the honeysuckle and then on up to the pine tree; he ties up this precious day in gift wrap for me.

*   *   *

The Ostranders' big stock truck clatters into our yard.

David whispers something to Tom and Tom asks with perhaps

just a shade more apprehension than curiosity in his voice, "Have you got a bull in there?"

"No," laughs Court heartily.

"I've been hearing one," Tom adds, "and it sounds like it's over at your place."

Court grins. "I reckon you do hear my bull. He sure does bellow. He sticks out his whole long tongue when he does it too. 'Ahoooh!'" Court demonstrates in a most convincing manner and we all laugh. "His mother is one of the best cows in the whole county," and Court reels off statistics of pounds of milk, butterfat content, etc.

Al Ostrander and their hired man appear at the pasture's edge with a tractor and trailer full of fence posts. Both wear blue carpenters' aprons bulging with pliers, hammers, insulators, nails, and small jars of aluminum paint and brushes to paint the connections where one wire is twisted onto the next length of wire so that they conduct the electricity in the fence effectively.

We all walk down to join Al, who grins, wipes his forehead on his arm, and greets us: "Kind of warm, isn't it? Seems like we aren't going to get spring this year, just winter and summer."

"Have you got any seeds planted yet?" I ask.

Al replies, "Nope, not a thing. One year I had everything in about now, and along come June second and we had a frost. Froze every dang thing right off to the ground."

As we walk the fence line he continues: "Going to bring over a springing heifer. She's going to freshen pretty soon. And two Jersey cows we've got over at our place making bag now. They ought to freshen the middle of June. We figure over here we can keep a better eye on them. Nearly lost a cow the other night. She was out in the pasture with the others when she freshened. When we got to her she couldn't get up. Had milk fever. Lost the calf."

As we walk through the simmering sunshine I admire the skill with which the team trues up the fence line and builds the corners strong. I also admire the reflection in the pond of the elm leaf haze. The men look as if they are enjoying themselves; I suspect the beauty of the elm reflection is not lost on them.

I also chuckle to myself at farm jargon and how revealing it sometimes is. A cow due to freshen is about to give birth, whereupon she will also get back into milk production. How clearly the emphasis is on that milk rather than on the new calf! I also suspect there is some perfectly logical reason why heifers about to give birth are called "springing heifers" or simply "springers," but most expectant human mothers would not find the term very applicable to the way they feel at the time!

I understand that the "we" who are going to keep a closer eye on these mothers definitely includes me so I venture to ask Al how I will know when one of them is about to have her calf.

"Oh, she'll probably lie down. Might see a foot sticking out. By the way, how are your ducks doing?"

Now that sounds to me like a safer line of conversation. I reply, "All three hen ducks are setting on a nest up under an old hay rake in the grass by the stone wall. When we first discovered the nests they were neatly covered with a lid of feathers and grass and two of the nests each had ten eggs in them and the third had one. Next time we looked there, there was a nest of twenty and one with a single egg."

Al laughed. "Well, one of your ducks got back to the nests first and stole all the others. When ours do that we pen up all but one. If they all try to set on the same nest the eggs don't fare so well."

"Tom thought he saw a weasel the other day. I wish they wouldn't all sit together—I'd feel safer if they'd each chose their own hiding places. One of our guineas disappeared the day after we clipped their wings, so we just might be in for real weasel trouble."

Al assures me, "You'd find the guinea if it was a weasel. Wouldn't carry it off—just suck the blood out from under its wing. Working on without pause, he continues, "I've had a lot of trouble with skunks. Duck sets three weeks and then one of them skunks comes in one night and cleans out all the eggs. Right close to the house, too."

The Ostranders move on down the fence, and we head for our upper garden beyond the barn, years ago the site of the winter manure pile. The Ostranders routinely make a pass over it with their plow when they go by it on their way to plow the corn field they rent from us, so it is not a hard job to pound out and rake out the rich clods of good earth.

As every year, we plant the garden Iroquois style: corn, beans, and squash together. With the handle of my rake I poke the holes into which David and Tom drop the seed of their choice. The leaves of the dogwood are the size of a squirrel's ear. Although we honor the rule, like all my predecessors I worry whether the tender shoots of life from these dry seeds will receive, when they emerge, a warm reception or the breath of one last frost.

A flock of redwings comes screaming up the hedgerow. "Watch here! Watch here!" they seem to shout. They are driving ahead of them the huge, graceful, white-rumped form of a marsh hawk.

"Watch here!" calls the hedgerow. I decide that we have put in enough seeds for today and that the hedgerow needs checking.

Here are dainty yellow violets, and the huge blue meadow violets on stems a foot long. Here a great line of nearly unfurled croziers of hay-scented fern, and in the shade behind the ferns is a lovely carpet of foamflower, their scientific name, *Tiarella,* almost as pretty as their bloom.

The black cherry is in blossom and buzzing with bees. Its fragrance is almost overpowering. At the foot of the hedgerow red trillium and three-foot-high great merrybells bloom side by side.

Out in the grass is perhaps the best find of all: the wild strawberries are in bloom! Yes, I was right—there are all sorts of things in bloom here that we might have missed for the year had we not come over to this hedgerow today.

*   *   *

This morning practically dawned sultry. It will be a long hot day in school for the boys so we hurry breakfast to give ourselves time for a good walk together before the bus comes.

In the meadow the male bobolinks are courting. One of them flies up in the air and circles like a paper glider floating back to earth, melody bubbling forth all the while. Every little rise of ground or tall clump of weeds has a male bobolink on it, ready to take off again to repeat the performance for the female audience hidden in the grass.

A pair of goldfinches outshine the sun with their own effulgence as they fly past us, twittering to each other. Welcome back!

A half a dozen crows are making a terrible fuss in the elm trees. I wonder what is bothering them. I like the clannishness of crows —they come at once when any one bird gives the distress call. We do not see what the problem is this morning, although I'm sure the boys would gladly lie here for hours to solve the mystery while the school bus passes them by. I shepherd them on up the hill.

At last we reach the road, where the boys find two gossamer bags of tent caterpillars in a pair of wild cherry trees. A few early-riser caterpillars are making their way up the slender branches to continue their defoliation project, but most are still in the bag. We touch it; I recoil involuntarily—it is warm!

David runs to the barn and returns with a pail into which we drop the occupied tents. We hope to save the little trees by picking off all the caterpillars we can. We work quickly—the school bus is due any minute now.

The next sound we hear, however, is not the bus grinding up the hill but a starling screaming and fluttering at a hole in the maple tree across the road. Its foot seems to be caught. The dangling bird flutters and screeches again. Suddenly it flies free and the face of a flicker appears at the hole! That hole-stealing starling finally seems to have met its due!

The tan flicker face peering out of the hole looks nearly as pleased with his performance as I. That of course is an illusion—it is the dark feather mustaches which give him that look. Those mustaches are very important to a flicker: Paint a pair on the female and her deluded mate will fight her away from their connubial home, allowing her to return only when the mustaches have been removed.

The bus at last. The boys have already had a full morning out, and tomorrow begins the long holiday, so I do not feel too sorry for them.

Having given my own indoor chores as little time as possible, I am soon out in the sun again, this time with paper work to do, out on the slightly ramshackle unroofed porch off the back door of the ell, which my friends call "Marnie's balcony."

It is only 9:00 A.M. but already it is humming hot. What is that humming sound? I abandon my paper work as readily as I did my housework and investigate. It seems to come from the electric fence down by the pond. But when I put my ear as close as I dare to the electrified strand of barbed wire, it does not sound as if the hum is coming from the fence. The sound is definitely louder down by the pond.

Then I see it—a column of insects towers some thirty feet up into the air above the pond bank! After a few leaps I manage to bring down a few of the dark diptera: they are midges. They look like mosquitoes except that they lack that pesty biting probe.

The water at the edge of the pond is black with empty larval cases. I scoop up a handful. They would fit, the mystery is solved: a midge hatch in a humming holding pattern, in their social ritual of adulthood. What a fascinating sound, this part of the song of the universe!

The bus returns. Almost before it is out of sight the boys are swimming in the pond for the first time this year.

The grasses at the pond's edge catch a lace of maple flowers, the long, pale-green pendants that have delicately perfumed the front yard for the past week. The long strings of toad eggs lie empty now, like limp, transparent soda straws. The tubes seem to be intact. Do the little polliwogs line up and wriggle out single file? There are hundreds and hundreds of pea-sized polliwogs resting in parallel rows on the submerged rocks.

The leaves on the maples have opened out like tiny fans, each still no bigger than a butterfly, but the hour glass has been turned over, and the sands of time flow in a new direction now. The long days of anticipation and promise have given way to the season of fulfillment.

In the distance I hear the droning hum of Ruby Latimer "tractoring." She says it is her favorite day of the year when she can put sunburn cream on her nose and spend the afternoon out in the fields doing the spring harrowing.

When I first discovered David had brought the pail full of two bags of tent caterpillars into the kitchen, I would have protested emphatically to him had he been there. I immediately envisioned the horde creeping out to take over every nook and cranny in the kitchen.

Since I had not the slightest idea where in the wide meadows he was, I had a second look and second thoughts about the caterpillars. They are a lovely dove gray, with tawny bristles in slender ribbons all the way up to their black velvet heads.

Furthermore, they are not invading—not here at least. All they are doing is going around the rim of the bucket, bumper to bumper, exactly as the traffic is this very moment on the Connecticut Turnpike and countless freeways all across our land on this eve of Memorial Day weekend. Around and around they go, all in the same direction, all at the same speed, but every so often an individual heads off against the traffic. Invariably it is not long before it too is turned around and headed in the direction of the overwhelming majority. I see no conflict between individuals. I wonder how they communicate, or how do they orient with respect to each other, or why?

It is certainly Memorial Day weekend here: the mint is ready for iced tea; all afternoon lines of campers and pickup trucks bearing canoes on top have headed out the Pierrepont road to the Adirondacks. This is the noisiest evening of the season. The green frog is calling, two or three kinds of toads are trilling, the midges are humming, the May beetles are buzzing and banging about, the snipe is winnowing in his usual spot at the foot of the pasture, and the first whippoorwill back is calling from the hedgerow.

JUNE

IT IS a lovely wet morning—spring rain. An oriole scolds from a bush in his buzzy blackbird voice, bright against the soft gray background. It is not raining hard enough to deter the tiny ruby-throated hummingbird from visiting the ivory trumpets of the honeysuckle blossoms one by one by one. The whole valley has a dreamlike quality; graceful elms are veiled in blue mists like a painting of the Hudson River School.

All of Canton and Pierrepont, too, go about their chores at a slower pace today, blessing the sweet, refreshing rain. We are exhausted from a community-wide four-day orgy—bright, sunny 80° weather for four days in a row over the Memorial holiday weekend.

On Memorial Day we went into town and watched the small parade march the few blocks down Main Street for the brief ceremonies at the Civil War statue in the village green: the fire trucks, the veterans, a cub pack, and a brownie troop or two, the junior band and the high school band—all followed by the huge gleaming silver bulk of the milk tank truck, and the half dozen cars that constituted the total of the traffic tie-up.

Our pond rippled from one end to the other all day long as families came out to swim. The little ones played in the sand and waded after polliwogs. The teen-agers paddled and tipped the canoe, making it echo with their voices as they giggled to each other in the air space in the overturned hull.

An endless parade of hamburgers sizzled on the grill; we were teased about our "weed feed" as our friends helped themselves to seconds and thirds of buttered milkweed greens. We had picked the new shoots,* up to six inches long, brought them to a boil in water with a pinch of baking soda. That was poured off, and the greens cooked just until tender in another water. And the bottles of rhubarb mead turned out to be sparkling!

Maple flower strings are everywhere, lacing the grass, fringing the pond, clinging to the screens. The maple leaves are already the size of a child's hand. The hedgerows have turned into green jungle walls. As the fragrance of the lilacs and lily of the valley fades, the smell of new mown grass takes its place. Lawn mowers buzz and clatter across the yards; giant mowing machines hum in the hay fields. Bees hum in the flowers, and screen doors bang, resounding, shut.

Pickup trucks wear campers on their backs, and the campers wear canoes on their roofs. Motorcycles and bicycles join the traffic on the Pierrepont road—out to the country, out to the Adirondacks. Out into June! Out!

Four days of such weather we had to make the most of. It happens only once every how many years that we get a Memorial Day weekend like that?

But today everyone is inside, sunburned, behind in their work, and gloriously tired, while the sweet rain falls gently on the tulips and an oriole sings.

I go to the porch to stir the crock of dandelion wine. It will be a fine wine! Many hands made quick work of gathering the full tufted blossoms—the dandelions were just at their peak this weekend. St. George's Day, April 23, is the traditional day to gather dandelions for wine in Merrie, warmer, England.

Our pasture blooms are nearly two inches across, glowing on foot-long stems. Of course the very best blossoms grow on the other side of the electric fence, in with the big cows, which just made gathering more fun for those of the daring age.

While mothers picked off every bit of the bitter, white, oozing stem from the flower heads in the pails, daughters made crowns of blooms and chains of loops by tucking one hollow end of the supple green stem into another. Fathers garlanded with dandelion chains sneaked away and stretched out in the deep grass on the sunny hill like sated Polynesian kings. Sons made horns out of

---

* Note: Several species in the southeastern United States are toxic.

blades of grass stretched between their thumb knuckles—strident noisemakers which brought their fathers back into the games with a most satisfyingly awful "blaaat."

Before the blossoms had wilted, I put two or three quarts of them in the crock, poured on a gallon of boiling water, and left it, covered, out here on the porch to steep for two days.

Today I bring it in and boil the whole infusion with the grated peel of two lemons and an orange for ten minutes. I strain the hot mixture through several layers of cheesecloth and stir in two and a half pounds of white sugar (for a light, dry wine—add another half pound of sugar if you want a sweet dessert wine).

When it has cooled I will add the juice from the fruit and a handful of raisins, and finally, the yeast. The pale green-gold liquid will bubble merrily on my counter in its jug with the fermentation trap on it until the end of the week. When the bubbling has slowed the jug will go down to the cellar to await racking and bottling when it has cleared and the fermentation has stopped.

You are supposed to wait until Christmas to drink it, but ours always tastes delicious by autumn. Furthermore, it is said to improve with aging, but to me it always seems greedy to wait for it to get even better.

The telephone rings. A man with a pleasant voice tells me his name, but it does not ring a bell.

"I work for Agway. I installed your freezer in your cellar a few years back. I noticed that you make wine. I was wondering if you saw the recipes for dandelion wine in the newspaper last night and how they compared with yours. I think I'll try it."

* * *

"Honk, honk!" Tom calls as he comes in the door grinning. He holds out a hat in which three downy balls of fluff are huddling. "Look at the baby geese we got from the Latimers. Honk, honk! They think I'm their father."

He puts the hat down and takes out three little goslings, which teeter somewhat uncertainly on their dark webbed feet. They are covered with yellow down, mottled with dark markings. Their foreheads slope abruptly down to their black leathery bills.

They take a few steps; their feet slide out from under them, sending them sprawling. They stand up tall and try again, cheeping in a strident tone.

Sitting on the kitchen floor, David, Tom, and I each soon have a gosling nestling in our lap. Tom is nearly correct: they do think we are their mother. Konrad Lorenz, the great student of animal behavior, had greylag geese that would follow him all around his estate outside of Vienna. He found that the newly hatched goslings would accept forever after as their mother whatever they first saw, a process that came to be called imprinting. Researchers have even successfully imprinted ducklings so that they will obediently follow anywhere a box with an alarm clock in it!

These babies cuddle down in our laps, and squeal whenever we put them on the floor. We dip our fingers in water and then in corn meal, and call them to us. They come running and before long they are nibbling food off our fingers. They tire easily, so spend most of the time nestling up against us.

"Mom, guess what?" says David as he babysits. "We watched a heifer practicing getting milked while we were at Latimer's."

"What do you mean?" I ask, offering my gosling another finger full of food.

"You know how the cows come into the milking parlor by themselves?" David says.

I nod, picturing the white-tiled herringbone milking parlor. Jim stands in the middle at a lower level and pulls a rope that opens the door, allowing a cow to enter. She walks to one of the four stanchions arranged in herringbone alternating fashion around him. Jim fastens her, washes her udder, disinfects the teats, and puts on the milking machine. Then he lets in another cow, then another, and another. When the cows are milked dry, one after another, he unhooks the milking machines and they walk around the edge of the parlor to wait in front of the exit door until Jim operates it, and the cows amble out to a feeding barn.

"Well, the cows don't just know how to do that," David explains. "They have to be taught. We watched them putting a heifer through it to get her used to it."

"Umm" I nod. I am getting tired of sitting on the floor. It is also time for the boys to go to bed—tomorrow is a school day.

We fix a box for the goslings and put them into it. They begin crying immediately.

"Off to bed now, boys." I insist.

Everyone else is safely off in dreamland, but the keening of the three goslings is keeping me awake. Are they warm enough in their little box under the lightbulb? Perhaps I had better go check.

The moment I appear in the kitchen, illuminated by the light-bulb, the baby geese cry even louder. They are going to waken the whole house at this rate. Everything looks all right in their box. They stretch their little necks toward me and call imploringly.

I gather some stationery and a towel, and settle myself on the floor. I wrap the babies in the towel and put it in my lap. At once they cuddle up against my arm. In no time they are nodding off to sleep, their little black bills tucked under my arm. They are certainly imprinted on us. Here I am, Mother Goose.

I write a few letters balancing the paper on one knee. The floor is getting hard and I am getting very sleepy. I move the goslings off my lap and stand up. They begin crying again in unison and scurry desperately across the floor after me, sprawling and tumbling, flapping their tiny wings.

I am not going to sit up with these goslings any longer, and I am not going to take them to bed with us either. Help, Dr. Lorenz! Such demanding little babies! Help, Dr. Spock!

*   *   *

The box of geese is sitting on the washing machine so that the cord from their warming light will reach the plug behind the machine. David and Tom think it great fun to peer in at the downy babies nestled together asleep under the lightbulb. The three goslings peep softly from time to time as if to ascertain even in their sleep that the others are still there.

As soon as they sense that the boys are there they awake and stretch their heads out between the slats of the box. They nibble the boys' noses, sending Tom and David into peals of satisfied laughter.

The boys head out the door to meet the school bus and I am left to cope with their squealing babies. They scramble over one another and stretch out their slender little necks to look at me imploringly. I put them on the floor, lift out their watering dish, and put it where they can reach it. Exploring seems to make them thirsty.

Belle seems to know that the goslings are out and she trots into the kitchen. She follows them as closely as she dares. One gosling becomes separated from the others. All three set up an intense squealing. Belle looks up at me with a wrinkled brow, her silky beagle ears hanging way down. She walks slowly, egg-footed, past the lone gosling to take her place, trembling, on the floor on the other side of my feet, her paws tucked under her chin, her gaze riveted on the three little geese. Such self-control!

The three goslings patter across the kitchen floor, casting aspersions on my housekeeping, inspecting every nook and cranny for crumbs like so many fussy old maids.

While they are on their expedition I take the opportunity to clean their box and tend to another new member of our household—a deer mouse, on his way to or from the laboratory for some experiment when he was spotted and claimed by the boys.

He had been asleep in his cage, curled up in a nest of shavings, on his brown back with tiny pink paws tucked in close against his soft white tummy. When my goose-maintenance chores disturb him, he rouses himself, and stretching up full length, he pokes his pink, almost prehensile nose out between the cage bars begging me for a treat.

I produce, as he knows I will, a chunk of apple, which I hold for him while he grasps the other end of it with his paws and quickly gnaws it down to size so he can pull it in between the bars to work on at his leisure.

Then I hear loud crying from the porch. And there on the lowest step is a baby crow! Quickly I rout Ken out of his study and send him out the front door with a shirt in hand to circle around the house and toss the shirt over the foundling while I go over and sit quietly by Belle so she won't get into the act. As if we needed more baby pets right now! But crows make such splendid pets, and it is surely not every day that you find one crying on your doorstep.

Ken comes in grinning, with his shirt-wrapped bundle, and I dash up to the attic for the old canary cage. We slide open the bottom of the cage, gently unwrap the crow, and ease it up into the cage, a perfect fit! A canary he certainly is not, but because he has only a mere stub of a tail he can stand up straight on the perch placed at its lowest position, and glare at us.

His eyes are a beautiful pearl-gray blue. Some of his back feathers and most of his wing feathers are still encased in white sheaths. He opens his beak, revealing a scarlet, gaping, hungry maw. That signals even to his untutored new foster parents that he is hungry.

Under Ken's direction I mix up dry dog food, egg, milk, and chopped worm. Then Ken departs for work and mine begins.

Clumsily I reach my hand in through the door of the canary cage and try to aim the gluey morsel down the crow's throat. He clamps his beak shut on my fingers but the food goes down, accompanied by surprising gulping vocalizations.

Every half hour I repeat the process. That is what you must be willing to accept when you adopt a wild animal baby. Wherever you go, they must go—for days and days, until they are grown enough that the parental tasks become lighter. Most wild animals are protected against the loving administrations of naïve humans by a system requiring a permit from the state conservation department. Crows, however, are protected only by their wits.

By evening, some twenty feedings later, my aim has improved: most of the food mixture goes into rather than onto the crow. He has even learned to stoop down a little to give me a better shot at the red maw. I realize that those first noises he made were hostile; feeding is now accompanied by incredibly sweet chucklings, and he uses the strap of his warm tongue to clean off my fingers.

At suppertime he calls me from the stove by a caw and a gape and a flutter of wings. I push the food into him until he no longer opens his beak, approximately the same system his parents use. We have passed what is for me the most trying time in acquiring a pet—he no longer hates me!

Ken discovered a pair of crows fussing over another fledgling out at the hedgerow so we have no qualms about keeping this one. They will have their hands full rearing just one. Of course, we will too.

This has been quite a day, but the kitchen is now quiet and smells sweetly of the cedar shavings in the line of animal cages on the washing machine. The geese are dozing. Crow is napping beside the mouse, an incongruous juxtaposition. When he is fully grown, that crow would eat that mouse, but at the moment the pair slumbers innocently side by side.

The telephone rings. As I hurry to answer it the geese awake, and seeing me pass begin their keening. The crow, startled, caws angrily, and Belle comes barking out to see what the excitement is.

This place sounds like a zoo. Maybe I shouldn't answer the phone; how am I going to explain it to the caller?

I don't have to explain. It's Jim Latimer calling. Have those geese laid any eggs yet, he wants to know. . . .

*   *   *

Hot and sweaty, we return from the garden, where we have been putting in some more seeds, doing some hoeing, and piling up layers and layers of mulch around every little seedling that has sprouted so far—a protective armor to hold at bay the armies of weeds poised to invade.

We head down to the pond with our new friend, Crow, Croaky, or Crowkie. He teeters uncertainly on my shoulder, digging his claws in further to secure his perch. He makes a much more demanding posture exercise than balancing books on your head.

The boys dash into the water while Crowkie and I watch from the beach. He has shown no sign that he recognizes water. I dip my hand into the water and sprinkle a few drops on Crowkie's head. To my surprise he opens his bill and gapes for more. I oblige; he obviously relishes his first drink. How do you suppose parent crows get their nestlings a drink? I sprinkle on more drops.

Together we watch the boys swimming. I become aware that Crowkie's long-legged stalking and hide-and-seek games in the grass have been replaced by another set of movements. He is bathing! On dry land, to be sure, but nevertheless he ruffles up his feathers and shakes imaginary water off them. Now what, Mother Crow?

I decide that the ducks' food pan will make a safer first bathtub than the pond. I fill the pan and put it down beside me. Curious, Crowkie comes over to investigate. I put my arm in front of his breast so that he steps up onto my wrist, then I coax him onto my hand and lower it into the water.

Crowkie looks down at his wet feet in astonishment. He has to learn to take a bath—his feathers are a mess from our clumsy feeding attempts. I have never seen him even try to preen himself. I flip water droplets onto his back. Suddenly he squats down and repeats those bathing movements that have been programmed into the recesses of his young brain. Bathing!

He is soon a very soaked, bedraggled young crow. I rub some of his feathers clean. He shivers and stands tall, as if awaiting another inspiration. He continues to shiver. I can't stand it—I wrap him, protesting vigorously, in a towel to dry him a bit and leave him standing alone on the beach, indignant, possessed of an amazing amount of dignity for such a wet, forlorn-looking young crow.

When I return from my swim, Crowkie is over in some tall grasses. He is rubbing his head through them, ruffling his feathers as if he were using a towel. He reaches around and makes a few preening motions over the feathers on his back. Lesson number two seems to be occurring to him.

* * *

The mountains have taken on their summer blue. Hills and hedgerows are clothed in a heavy plush muffling green, with a light gauze of apple or hawthorn in blossom here and there.

The winter cress has bloomed mustard yellow. The morning sunlight dances with a yellow swallowtail butterfly.

David and Tom are playing marble polo on the kitchen floor with Crowkie, who has moved his residence to a large pen by the stove. He spends most of the day perched on it, not in it. The boys shout and roll the marble. Crowkie grabs it from them with his powerful beak. In a surprise maneuver he sends it behind him, rolling it through his legs. Tom grabs the marble just before it disappears under the refrigerator. He fires it over to David. Crowkie intercepts. He swallows the marble.

That ends the game. The boys look at each other in horror— is that also the end of Crowkie? How can he handle such a large, indigestible object? The kitchen is suddenly, ominously, silent. The boys decide that it is time for them to go out and wait for the bus.

Oh, crow, why did you have to do that? What can we do for you? I consider calling the vet as I rinse the dishes in the sink.

Crowkie, object of such concern, appears on the counter. He deliberately overturns a tea cup and watches fascinated as the liquid drizzles down into the sink. As I continue rinsing the dishes he looks longingly at the stream of water. He wishes he had enough nerve to jump into it, but he doesn't quite.

He leans out for a few drops of water. I drip a few drops down that gullet which now contains a marble. I cup my hand, fill it with water, and hold it out for him. He drinks, raising his head feathers in what I believe can be accurately interpreted as pleasure.

He looks longingly again into the sink. I suppose I have to let him try it; like the boys, I have to let him get himself into almost anything that he can reasonably be expected to get himself out of so he learns how to take care of himself. He jumps into the sink, stands like a bather who hates that first shock of getting his stomach wet. Finally he decides it is worth it. He splashes and frolics and then steps out.

I know what comes next, but there is nothing I can do about it. My crow friend is sitting on my shoulder, cooing and babbling in my ear. Then he shakes like a dog. Wet crow smell is not unlike wet dog smell. Crow, you dear, funny nuisance!

Suddenly chaos erupts in the living room. I rush in to find ashes all over the rug and a vase that once held flowers lying on its side on a table, dripping water onto the scattered flowers below.

Bang! A starling that came through the fireplace chimney crashes against the window pane. I lunge for him to pin him in behind the drapes. Crash! There goes the lamp. The starling takes off again, crash, into another window. Crowkie caws; this is a grand fracas.

A shirt—finally I remember that I need a shirt to catch the bird with. I grab a light jacket out of the closet and in no time I have captured the errant starling. I survey the wreckage. I could wring its neck.

But I do not; I go to the door and throw it none too gently out.

That settles it. Now, I'll have to spend this lovely morning cleaning. Crowkie is shut grumbling in his pen and I set to work rehabilitating the front rooms.

Even though we still use a fire in the fireplace to take off the morning chill, I feel I should at least put away for the summer the wool afghan on the couch. An inspiration comes to me—instead of taking it upstairs to an attic trunk I could put it in the sea chest over in the corner. Much more efficient; I even begin to feel virtuous about cleaning and organizing.

As I raise the lid to the sea chest I discover one red, yellow, and green striped Easter egg. Smiling to myself that there *was* one more to be found, I reach for it. Pow! It explodes at my touch. My ears ring. Shards fill the chest; an overpowering sulfurous gas fills the room. I run out onto the front porch. I think I am going to be sick.

I escape to the fresh air of the meadows. When I find things slipping out of control I feel the need to run away and yet I feel compelled to stay and persevere constructively. My meadow outings allow me to do both: I'll gather some milkweeds for supper.

The grass reaches up to my knees. The willow that leads the hedgerow is covered with downy cotton catkins. At its base is a

carpet of delicate hay-scented fern, edged with a ring of huge dark
striped jack-in-the-pulpit. The wild strawberries here have set tiny
green berries.

My spirits soar with the sparrow hawk that circles high up from
a dead elm.

"Killee, killee, killee!" it calls.

It floats on outstretched wings, banded tail fanned out, a checkered
lace against the sun. At the foot of the pasture a snipe winnows on
in his sweet note unconcerned, but all about me robins "chert,
chert" in anxiety.

Their uneasiness is mirrored in the sky. The western horizon
is rumbling in turbulence. I can see gray ribbons of rain already
over the St. Lawrence river valley.

I quicken my step and gather my greens, pausing only long
enough to pick carefully a few branches of hawthorn blossoms,
sprays of five perfect creamy white cups around gold saucers,
slender thorns two inches long hiding behind the beauty.

I hurry home across the bottom of the field. Here the grass
grows breast high; even dandelions reach above my knees. I gratefully use the paths trodden down by the woodchuck as far as his
rock.

Reaching the crest of the hill, I pause to admire the bright new
leaves of the butternut tree gleaming against the dark of the distant
hills. The butternut is shaped almost like a pagoda. My hawthorn
branches look exquisitely Oriental. I mentally design my *ikebana*
as I pass the barn and turn down the driveway.

My flower arranging is interrupted by the diving thrust of a
starling at a bird on the wire. The fast disappearing platinum sunlight glints on the old-rose breast of the fleeing bird. The sweet
burring note from the dead snag at the top of the pine confirms
my guess—the bluebird. I should have rung that starling's neck.

In spite of the pouring rain we have to go out. The boys got
off the bus over at the Ostranders' to play with Cheryl, but the
storm is developing into a cracking thunderer so we drive over to
pick them up. The Ostranders will be hurrying to get their milking done in case the storm knocks out the power.

We pull into their driveway and find the children but no cows
in the barn. Al stands at the back door calling. "Coe o, coe o!" out
into the driving rain. I know what he says ("Come, boss") because

I've asked him, but I'd never have found out just by listening, since he omits all the consonants for shouting purposes. The cows know very well what it means, but they refuse to leave the shelter of the trees on the hill and come down through the rain to the barn.

Court enters fuming, soaking wet from a futile attempt to round up the cows by tractor. Old Rex, the collie, slinks wet and whining into the barn.

"Bad dog" both men mutter at him. He won't go out and bring the cows in.

Lightning cracks uncomfortably near. Gerry rubs her hands anxiously on her apron and suggests that we might as well wait until it lets up a little before we dash for our car. We make a little small talk to help dispel the tension, but give it up to stare silently out into the torrent. Sheets of hail come pounding down, making white exclamation points in the puddles.

"There goes our hay, beat right down to the ground," groans Court. I picture acres of devastated meadows, shredded seedlings of corn and tomatoes, pockmarked flowers, and those poor three ducks of ours huddled together on their one nest. For once I hope their ducklings have not hatched yet.

The wind picks up. Everyone looks at one another in frustration and despair. Those cows are certainly not about to come down now. Ken reaches out to pull shut the door of the milkhouse, but it anticipates him, crashing shut, shattering its pane of glass on us.

Instinctively I turn away. With a mother's subconscious ever on duty I know that my children are safe behind me, but a stabbing pain clear to the bone in my leg tells me I have been hit. I can feel the blood trickling down into my boot, and when I saw Ken he was right in front of that murderous blast.

"Ken, are you all right?" I gasp weakly.

"I'm fine," comes the reply from behind the milk cooling tank. By a miracle he too had stepped back.

We sweep up the glass from the wet floor, and Gerry fits a new strainer into the milking apparatus.

"I hope we get to milk tonight," she laughs ruefully.

I turn so that she can't see my leg; the Ostranders have enough worries this evening. The hail has stopped, the rain seems to have slackened. The first few cows step in through the back door of the barn. We head home.

At home we find the Couglers' eighty head of young stock

swarming over our hill—black-and-white Holsteins, red-and-white Ayershires, white-faced Hereford crosses, a few Charolais, almost every sort I can imagine. The electric fencer had been hit by lightning, and the cattle had stampeded over here.

The buried telephone cable was put out of commission by lightning, how I cannot imagine. The men who came to check it unhooked the electric fences all along our meadow. They walked right past the cattle and left the fences unhooked! What a mess—home on the open range tonight.

* * *

Instead of finding Crowkie on the floor of his pen as we expected, this morning we found the marble. By which end of the crow it made its egress I couldn't say.

The sun shone splendidly on our meadows, and on the hummingbirds in the honeysuckle; the four little robin heads waved in their nest, and once again we found ourselves believing in gentle June. Yesterday already seems long ago.

Ken and I have been asked by one of the county offices to do a bird census on the land being purchased by Horizon Corporation for their proposed development.

We turn in at their gate; a broad-winged hawk circles above us. Though not uncommon in this area, they are becoming rare. We drive by an old logging road into the area designated to become the center of the development. There, if Horizon has its way, will be golf courses, a ski slope, a complex of manmade lakes, and the community service center—a euphemism that does not begin to imply the staggering number of restaurants, gas stations, motels, liquor stores, hairdressers, laundries, sport shops, and so on that normally provide services to a community of twenty thousand people, the number they have indicated that they eventually intend to have tucked away in these woods in secluded second homes on one-acre lots.

A log bridge spans the narrow run of the wild Grasse River at this point; a small waterfall fills the air with water music. Warblers are darting out from the trees to snatch insects above the river. This part of the Grasse is a geologically young river, very close to its source, so the banks rise steeply. The walls of the ravine are covered with painted trillium, spring beauty, chaste white violets, and pink ladyslipper orchids. Along the narrow flat edge of the stream grow marsh marigolds, and alders shelter the rare alder flycatcher.

We make our way upstream along a heavily used deer trail, past a few massive white pines that the paper company loggers had not been able to reach because they were too far down the ravine. The deer signs are incredibly abundant: droppings every few yards, bushes sheared off by their browsing—it must be an area where the deer yard up in the winter.

A trout leaps for a fly above the amber waters of the stream. These cold waters, flowing out of a true northern bog, are said to be among the few that still harbor native strains of trout.

We were almost overwhelmed by the sense of being the last visitors into Glen Canyon before it was flooded, or the last to view the temples of ancient Egypt before they were covered by the rising waters of the Aswan Dam.

A blackburnian warbler, nicknamed little flame throat, flashes out from the dark spruces. How I long to linger in the sun on the bank and watch the orange-throated jewel of a bird for as long as I can. But not today. We are supposed to be inventorying species. Mark him present and move on. We check off warbler after warbler: the black-throated green, the yellow-throat in the alders, the thin, high voice of the black-and-white warbler, the myrtle warbler, a Nashville warbler, the buzzing call of the black-throated blue warbler.

It occurs to me that birding is not unlike stamp or china collecting. Both the beauty and the rarity combined tempt us to assign a factor of value. How often I have laughed when I've heard someone say he saw a "good" bird, meaning a rare one. As an artist I love the birds for their beauty, as a student of behavior I love to watch what they are doing. This census is the most frustrating thing I have ever done because I cannot watch the birds at my leisure, and because I am haunted by the threat of losing them.

We slather on more bug dope. Will Horizon's customers tolerate clouds of blackflies for a couple of months each year? I shudder to think what pest control schemes they might try.

At the edge of a bog we watch in awe as one of the most seldom seen of all the warblers, a mourning warbler, silently works over the spruces, his dark blue-gray head shining in the sun. Wild calla lilies gleam at the water's edge, where a mink frog rests in the shallows, another gem of a creature that is found here and no farther south in our state.

The bog is a floating sea of sedge and sphagnum moss, an exotic world that quivers at our every step. We find insect-eating pitcher plants, and the delicate rose or white blooms of miniature laurels and several other tiny heaths that grow only in the bogs.

Add a little sewage from surrounding cottages, raise the water level, and it all becomes a water skier's recreational paradise like any number of other pseudo-lakes across the country—an Adirondack treasure no more.

Losing a piece of wilderness is like losing a dear one, far away. As long as you know they are there, safe and well, the separation is bearable. But let death take that loved one—when you learn that you can never touch again in awe that centuries-old redwood because it's been cut into picnic tables and flower tubs, that you can never lie again on the mossy bank of the bubbling spring of your childhood because it is in a concrete conduit running under a subdivision—then you know what loss means. And if you loved it, you mourn its passing until your own.

The lands we walk today have been cut over, and they are private lands that lie within the boundaries of the Adirondack Park. They epitomize precisely the dilemmas facing the whole of the Adirondacks.

Logging provides year-round employment for many of the Park residents, and wildlife has probably benefitted from the cutting. Many foresters argue that they must be allowed to manage the state lands too or all the forests will deteriorate like so much overripe fruit, but many others are afraid to let any man begin tampering with the "forever wild" lands of the park.

These lands were set aside in 1894 by a constitutional amendment known as Article XIV: "The lands of the state, now owned or hereafter acquired, constituting the forest preserve as fixed by law shall be forever kept as wild forest lands. They shall not be leased, sold, or exchanged, or be taken by any corporation, public or private, nor shall the timber thereupon be sold or removed or destroyed." This policy may be changed only by putting it to a vote before all the peoples of the State of New York, so the public lands are safe. But the park is now threatened by the mosaic of private holdings that could be developed unwisely. Such states as Maine, Vermont, and Colorado have been ahead of us in zoning regulations, so there is much pressure on the Adirondack Park Agency by enterpreneurs who would exploit the private lands for their own gain, without regard for the integrity of the park as a whole. Only a few miles from here the town of Altamont, with its permanent population of some 6,700, had zoned itself for a projected population of 640,000—a Connecticut developer owns 18,500 acres there. Sunday Rock is about all that stands between our farm and the Adirondacks. Will I see the day when it marks the boundary between us and the largest city in St. Lawrence County?

This is, of course, only the latest round in a very long battle. The Adirondacks have had to weather the assaults of man from the time the first virgin pines were marked for masts for the royal navies of France and England. Lumber barons, industrial tycoons, and power companies have clashed time and again with forever-wilders. A new wave of campers demands elaborate hookups for their luxury vehicles and marinas for their power boats. Too many people looking to get away from it all can now afford second homes in the woods. Even the trails on the mountain peaks are eroding under the endless tramp of lug-soled, well-meaning feet, carrying us in a self-defeating search for serenity.

How will the legislature and the Park Agency respond to these pressures? What new threats will develop? Where will it end? That depends on how we use planning and zoning. Conflicts will remain as long as there is a single tree to shade a man sitting under it for the peace of his soul, and another man to come along with a plan for chopping down that tree to make something of it or put something "better" in its place.

*   *   *

The boys are down at the pond fishing. They cast long shadows on the green meadows in the late afternoon sun. Across the way Alan Ostrander on his pony is sending his cows home with the help of his dog.

The radio has just announced that they have found the Horizon Corporation surveyor who had gotten lost out there in their woods. I wish Horizon Corporation would get lost!

I am proud of the North Country people up here in the forgotten corner of the state. They are not the hicks in the sticks they were thought to be. They are not so sure they like the idea of Horizon in their midst. They are not even taken in by that once magic word "job"—they sense that the pockets filled will not be their own. They are beginning to resist unplanned growth: it sounds too much like cancer.

Like their Yankee neighbors they do not really relish zoning, but they are coming to recognize the cause of the blight that mars the Thousand Islands and scars the Adirondacks. The ecologists— and the astronauts—have taught them that there is no such place as away, either to throw our trash or to which we can escape without bringing our problems with us. We are going to have to trade the right to exploitation for the right of stewardship.

* * *

There is snow on the mountain tops in the Adirondacks this morning. The only snow we have here is white flying dandelion seeds, although the temperature did drop to the forties and there were frost warnings last night. However, it is not cold enough to convince the boys that it's not warm enough for bare feet.

As I scramble eggs for breakfast I talk to Crowkie as he sits preening himself on the edge of his pen. He can come and go as he pleases now, indoors or out. It is very heartwarming that he seems to enjoy our company and follows us everywhere like a dog.

Crowkie loves scrambled eggs. We have been having them rather frequently lately on that account.

"Come, Crowkie," I call, holding out my arm.

His mouth opens wide. It is less brightly colored now than when we first got him. He also has picked most of the white sheathing off his feathers. He is a very handsome young bird.

"Come, Crowkie," I insist, showing him a pinch of scrambled egg. He gapes wider and quivers his outstretched wings, begging like a baby.

"No, Crowkie, you have to come to me. Come, Crowkie," I repeat. I move my arm closer and we compromise. He jumps onto it and I reward him with his breakfast.

While we eat ours, Crowkie hops down and takes a bath in Belle's water dish on the kitchen floor. Belle walks out to the kitchen. Crowkie adds an insult to his performance; he reaches into her dish and picks out a morsel of dog food. Belle looks at him and then at us.

"Come here, Belle." Ken calls comfortingly.

She walks slowly over to the breakfast table. "Good dog!"

As she passes by the pirate crow in haughty silence, the black-guard reaches out to tweak her tail with his powerful bill. He misses, fortunately for both. I decide it's time to intervene but Crowkie refuses to retreat.

He whirls into a wild fluttering dance, accompanied by a special set of vocalizations we've never heard before. Belle darts at him a few times like a playful puppy, but her heart is not in it. She turns to us with her wrinkled brow look.

I don't know either, Belle. How *do* you go about playing with a crow?

When the boys are safely on the school bus, Crowkie and I go out to sit in the sun on the back steps and finish our breakfast. I give him the last of the egg, checking to see that his rear is appropriately positioned for the jettisoning that invariably follows feeding. He is very good about that; he stands up tall, lifts up his rear, and ejects well clear of me.

Then I have to be on guard lest he decide to use my hair for a napkin on which to wipe his beak. He is most fastidious. His powerful beak clacks shut disconcertingly close to my ear—he has just saved me from a mosquito.

He chuckles in my ear, begs for a sip of tea, and probes delicately around my collar. The fine end of his tongue is hard and stiff; he uses it with remarkable finesse to pick up ants, or simply to feel things experimentally.

His personality is so different from that of the geese. He is a most independent soul. When he walks the kitchen floor he is looking for adventure, not going crumbing like the geese.

He is an artist. He is willing to appropriate almost anything, take it apart, tear it up, rearrange it, fully exploring its creative potential.

He is usually a good sport. He loves to play tug-of-war with a shoelace or piece of string—he always has a good supply tucked away—but you must win at least half the time. He pulls it away, but then brings it back and waves it at you until you take hold and try again. The only real lapse in his sense of fair play is his delight in the ungentle art of ambush. He stoops to nipping ankles from behind, and revels in the challenge of latching onto a tender young boy's calf muscle and hanging on there until beaten off.

In spite of his few bad habits I wonder why crows aren't more popular than parrots for pets.

Crowkie and I gather some meadow roses, daisies, and buttercups to dress up the tea party I am having this afternoon. The air is sweet and cool and fresh.

We detour through the meadow to our garden and find enough lettuce for a first salad. The young beans and corn are nearly six inches high. Crowkie catches a tiny grasshopper. There are quite a few of them in the grass—miniatures, less than a half inch long but formed exactly like the adults of last September. They have a lot of growing ahead of them this season.

We skirt along the stone wall behind the barn. The mother ducks are not on their nest. The eggs are gone! There are no ducklings toddling after the three ducks. What happened? I search the grass and find one broken egg, a clue, but I do not know how to read it. Too bad—we would have enjoyed watching a flotilla of downy ducklings on our pond. The would-be mothers were so patient.

I see in the pine that the baby robins have left their nest. This empty nest is a more auspicious sign than the duck nest, I trust. I will miss watching the babies from our bedroom window, but it does mean that the mother robin will no longer remove their excreta in jellylike packages and deposit them on our front fence. She chose just one rail for her sewage treatment center, and made it white from end to end.

I am making slow progress this morning. My rhubarb coffee cake is done, but Crowkie has shredded my flowers to bits! Back out I go, this time to my garden. I will solace myself by making a real floral extravaganza: magenta and pink peonies, lemon-yellow day-lilies, graceful spires of blue lupine, and a few deep blue iris.

One of the Jersey cows is lying down in the grass—yes, there is a little calf beside her. What a beautiful day on which to be born! The brown-eyed mother licks and licks her wet baby. It must have just arrived. I'll have to call the Ostranders.

The Ostranders are pleased with the good news and will be over before long to bring the pair back to their barn. I unload my armful of flowers into the sink and prepare to lure Crowkie into his pen. I'll take no chances with this bouquet.

My rhubarb cake has fallen! It looks pitiful.

"Crowkie, what is that white mess all over your stomach and on your legs? Oh, you bad crow, that cake didn't fall, it was pushed!"

I slam the lid of his pen down on him and he turns his back on me. I wonder if I have a box of cookies in the pantry somewhere.

In walk David and Tom. I forgot that they had only a half day of school today. They are just in time—the Ostranders have come to get the calf and its mother.

We all go out to the pasture. But where is the calf? We walk up and down, scanning the meadows in vain. It is nestled down in grass somewhere, completely hidden from sight. Mama knows where but she isn't telling.

The boys spot the calf curled up like a fawn. The Ostranders' new hired man, a boy just out of school, is elected to bring the calf while Al leads the mother to the waiting truck. The boy is not quite sure how to pick the calf up.

"Put your head under it and carry it around your shoulders," Court instructs.

The boy complies, and in one easy motion gets the calf over his shoulders like a scarf around his neck. He holds a pair of slender legs in either hand. Times have not changed as much as we think; I recognize immediately the pose of an Archaic Greek marble statue called "the calf bearer." It was carved twenty-five centuries ago, and that's still how you carry a calf today in Pierrepont.

Over peanut butter and honey sandwiches David and Tom agree to babysit for the kitchen menagerie out of doors during my tea party. The wife of the University president is bringing their daughter, Nancy, out to discuss a bird behavior study Nancy hopes to begin. If they come in the front door they will never know that my kitchen is a zoo.

Out the window I can see the boys rolling down the hill, flattening great swathes of tall grass as they go, three little goslings padding frantically after them with tiny wings outstretched, their down glowing almost green in the grass and the sunlight. Peeping plaintively they pad furiously to keep up. They have chosen most unmaternal surrogate mothers!

I change my clothes, lay out the tea tray with tea pot, sugar bowl, cookies, napkins, and spoons, then sit down on the couch to await my guests. A gleam behind a cushion catches my eye. I pull out the cushion and find two pencils, a half dozen paper clips, some strips of paper, an assortment of screws and tacks, a dime, and some red yarn. It's Crowkie's secret hoard! I scoop up his treasures and take them out to the kitchen to deal with later.

When I return to the living room, Crowkie greets me—standing big, handsome, black, and delighted with himself, on top of the

plate of cookies, triumphantly waving a tea napkin like a captured
banner to all four corners of the compass.

"Crowkie, out you go!" I slam the door after him, but it was
funny. I remove the sampled cookies just in time to answer the door
and greet my guests.

The president's wife is charming. We talk, have tea, and I give
Nancy a list of references for her project. I feel quite civilized in
spite of my day.

Into the room on very long legs stalks the crow.

"Come here, Crowkie," I call hopefully, thinking of stockings
and ankle ambushes. He marches right over and very obligingly
steps onto my wrist. Nancy and her mother are delighted. The
intruder is on his best behavior.

He has his trying moments, but he really is as good as a parrot—
once in a while.

*   *   *

Our bedroom is the only room in the house absolutely forbidden
to Crowkie. There we keep everything he really must not steal. He
knows that he has never been in that room and has tried to slip by
me on more than one occasion. So strong is his fascination with it
that he has taken to sleeping at night outside our bedroom door. We
put down a piece of newspaper in his favorite place and we can
plainly see that he does not desert his post the whole night through.

Today while I was making the bed I let him in, only after I had
done some crow-proofing, and I stood watching him like a hawk. He
stalked in, circled the room, and curiosity satisfied, he marched contentedly out and back down the hall.

This morning he ate only half his scrambled egg. He begged for
the rest but held it in the elastic pouch of skin on the under side of
his bill. He then proceeded to deposit the mouthful in the darkest
corner of the kitchen. Yesterday we caught him tucking peas away
in the bookcase!

Our crow is growing up. Tonight we will not answer his begging
call at the porch window and let him in. He will have to begin
spending more of his life outdoors whether he likes it or not. When
he is fully grown he will one day want to rejoin his fellow crows.
We must be sure that he has the independence to do it.

I watch out my window in the twilight as Crowkie hops up the ladder the boys have left leaning up against the pine tree from some game. Count on Crowkie to do things in his own style! His dark form disappears into the shadows at the top of the tree. The coarse note of the tree toad joins the deep voice of the bull frog from the neighborhood of the pond. Crowkie begins his first night out. . . .

*　　*　　*

The local power company gives away free targets shaped like the silhouette of a crow. Shoot this instead of our insulators, they urge. To me this seems too close to condoning thoughtless killing. The public doesn't care enough about crows to have any laws to protect them, but can you imagine their reaction if the power company gave out targets shaped like a man?

I lay awake for hours before dawn this morning, worrying about our innocent crow. I saw him safely off to high perch last night but did he come down too low during the night? A raccoon could have grabbed him. Would he fly off into the face of someone's gun this morning? Was it really a good idea to make him move out?

He is not on the lower branches of the pine. I scan the tops of the maples. I hear the welcome begging cry from the very top of the old pine. Good morning, Crowkie!

He takes off in a diagonal flight over to the maples, managing to lose a little altitude. He begs again and I call again. He zigzags down once more to land at my feet.

Crow-child, how like boy-child! You must be free to go, and go you must, but how glad I am that you want to come back too.

*　　*　　*

The hills are beautiful with hay: golden bands of hay curing in windrows, fields of tall dark-green grasses topped by a red haze of ripe seed heads, waiting to be cut.

The wild strawberries are ripe! The rocky field is starry with the blossoms of a most delicate species of chickweed. We fan out across the sunny hill to gather in the berries and the sunshine each alone and yet together.

I have extra company; Crowkie sits on top of my sun hat. I can feel him diligently preening as I pick the tiny berries around me. I stretch for a particularly beautiful clump of berries and my bird friend loses his balance.

I feel devilish and dash away from him to hide in the tall grass behind a juniper bush.

He does not call me. From where I lie I can see him walking, head held high, stepping purposefully around rocks, through the grass. Some crows are calling off in the distance. He gives no sign that he hears them; he keeps on walking. He rounds the bush and, seeing me, erupts into such a sweet babble of sounds that I feel positively mean.

I lie there in the sunlight. Crowkie hops up on my ankle. His legs are cool and scaled like alligator hide, but the cushions of his feet are warm and soft. The sun gleams on his feathers, all one color black, but marvelously arranged. There are long bristles at the base of his beak, short snowflake-like feathers on his cheeks and over the rimless openings to his ears. How he loves to have his ears rubbed! The feathers form glossy scallops across his back and shoulders. He stretches a wing out into a fan of two lengths of long feathers. He is a very handsome creature.

He hops off to play tug-of-war with the grass, and I doze in the sun.

I dream back through centuries. It is the time of the berry moon. They are gathered in the elmbark longhouse as all the people of the Iroquois do at the time of the Strawberry Festival, and they give thanks.

"Hail, hail, hail, Our Creator," chants a Keeper of the Faith.

"We give thanks that you have let us live to see another season. We offer up our thanks that you have spared us for another year's planting. We pray that we may see the harvest. We are grateful to be, to be together. We are thankful for having each other.

"We give our thanks to our mother, the earth. We thank you, Our Creator, for causing her to yield so plentifully of her fruits. May she not withhold her fruits in the season coming.

"We give our thanks to all the plants, which all have their own names, for the medicines they give to heal us. When we see the fruits hanging on the strawberry we give thanks. Grant that we may see them ripen.

"We offer thanks for our Three Sisters, the Sustainers of our Life: Corn, Squash, and Bean. May they never fail us, or our children, or our children's children.

"We are grateful for the forests of our earth, for the trees that bear us fruit and give us medicines and heat us in the time of the cold winds. When we see the sweet sap dripping from the maple, let us return thanks to Our Creator. May the maple never withhold from us its sugar.

"We offer thanks for the animals, who give us food, and for the birds, each with names according to their kind.

"We give our thanks to the winds, which carry away disease, and to our grandfathers, the Thunderers, who live in the West and bring us the rains to water our crops and fill our streams and ponds.

"And to our elder brother the sun, who gives us the day and the seasons, we send our thanks. May the sun never hide his face from us in shame and leave us in the darkness.

"We return our thanks to our grandmother the moon, the night helper in the sky, whose phases are a measure for us, and to all the stars in the sky, which also all have their own names, the stars that guide the traveler home. May they always bring us the dew for the growing things.

"We give thanks to Our Creator, who has provided us with so many agencies for our good and happiness. We will be thankful in our hearts and send our thanks up in the smoke of our fires, O Creator of all."

*   *   *

There is a beguiling, contradictory sweetness about the last June days—the nearly unbearable strength of the sun's rays burning so directly upon us and the fresh northern coolness of the breeze that stirs across us.

The school picnic is over; bathing suits have joined the wind chimes hanging on the porch. Filamentous algae like mermaids' tresses grow once again in the pond water; blue darners and transparent-winged dragonflies hover over it.

Spring's first flowers have disappeared, leaf and all, from the forest floor. The rushing brooks are once again a trickle. Demure pink meadow roses bloom by the gate and quaint yellow roses bloom up by the barnyard. The raspberry petals have fallen, and little green grapes have set, as well as the apples, pears, cherries, and crab apples. The plants in the fields now grow by a time too subtle to be measured by the coarse clocks of men.

Low cotton puffs of clouds skid southward down the sky while high gauze wisps work their way east. A speck of a hawk turns gliding circles high above us.

I am again a child lying on my stomach on a pier out over the waters of the lake, smelling the heat of the sun on the planks below me and the cool of morning's breath above me, teasing yellow perch with my worm-baited hook, leading them up and down through water as clear and still as emptiness, in a time when summer was forever.

Swallows wheel up and around our pond in tall spirals that are my symbol of life and reality. The wheeling of the stars, the passing of the seasons endlessly repeating themselves: these are not closed circles. Perhaps we wish that it were so, but the spiral nearly, not quite, meets itself as it bores ever on into time.

I am both mother and child. My companions here are my own children. Although the ends of my own circles no longer meet at a year's turning, for them I now throw away the calendar. We will keep our days unstructured for as long as we can, and we will joyously lose ourselves in summer of the endless days.

INDEX